READERS' GUIDES

CONSULTANT EDITOR: NICOLAS TREDELL

Published

Lucie Armitt	George Eliot: Adam Bede – *The Mill on the Floss* – *Middlemarch*
Simon Avery	Thomas Hardy: *The Mayor of Casterbridge* – *Jude the Obscure*
Paul Baines	Daniel Defoe: *Robinson Crusoe* – *Moll Flanders*
Annika Bautz	Jane Austen: *Sense and Sensibility* – *Pride and Prejudice* – *Emma*
Matthew Beedham	The Novels of Kazuo Ishiguro
Richard Beynon	D. H. Lawrence: *The Rainbow* – *Women in Love*
Peter Boxall	Samuel Beckett: *Waiting for Godot* – *Endgame*
Claire Brennan	The Poetry of Sylvia Plath
Susan Bruce	Shakespeare: *King Lear*
Sandie Byrne	Jane Austen: *Mansfield Park*
Alison Chapman	Elizabeth Gaskell: *Mary Barton* – *North and South*
Peter Childs	The Fiction of Ian McEwan
Christine Clegg	Vladimir Nabokov: *Lolita*
John Coyle	James Joyce: *Ulysses* – *A Portrait of the Artist as a Young Man*
Martin Coyle	Shakespeare: *Richard II*
Justin D. Edwards	Postcolonial Literatrure
Michael Faherty	The Poetry of W. B. Yeats
Sarah Gamble	The Fiction of Angela Carter
Jodi–Anne George	Chaucer: The General Prologue to *The Canterbury Tales*
Jodi–Anne George	*Beowulf*
Jane Goldman	Virginia Woolf: *To the Lighthouse* – *The Waves*
Huw Griffiths	Shakespeare: *Hamlet*
Vanessa Guignery	The Fiction of Julian Barnes
Louisa Hadley	The Fiction of A. S. Byatt
Geoffrey Harvey	Thomas Hardy: *Tess of the d'Urbervilles*
Paul Hendon	The Poetry of W. H. Auden
Terry Hodgson	The Plays of Tom Stoppard for Stage, Radio, TV and Film
William Hughes	Bram Stoker: *Dracula*
Stuart Hutchinson	Mark Twain: *Tom Sawyer* – *Huckleberry Finn*
Stuart Hutchinson	Edith Wharton: *The House of Mirth* – *The Custom of the Country*
Betty Jay	E. M. Forster: *A Passage to India*
Aaron Kelly	Twentieth-Century Irish Literature
Elmer Kennedy–Andrews	The Poetry of Seamus Heaney
Elmer Kennedy–Andrews	Nathaniel Hawthorne: *The Scarlet Letter*
Daniel Lea	George Orwell: *Animal Farm* – *Nineteen Eighty-Four*
Sara Lodge	Charlotte Brontë: *Jane Eyre*
Philippa Lyon	Twentieth-Century War Poetry

Merja Makinen	The Novels of Jeanette Winterson
Matt McGuire	Contemporary Scottish Literature
Timothy Milnes	Wordsworth: *The Prelude*
Jago Morrison	The Fiction of Chinua Achebe
Carl Plasa	Tony Morrison: *Beloved*
Carl Plasa	Jean Rhys: *Wide Sargasso Sea*
Nicholas Potter	Shakespeare: *Antony and Cleopatra*
Nicholas Potter	Shakespeare: *Othello*
Nicholas Potter	Shakespeare's Late Plays: *Pericles, Cymbeline, The Winter's Tale, The Tempest*
Steven Price	The Plays, Screenplays and Films of David Mamet
Andrew Radford	Victorian Sensation Fiction
Berthold Schoene–Harwood	Mary Shelley: *Frankenstein*
Nick Selby	T. S. Eliot: *The Waste Land*
Nick Selby	Herman Melville: *Moby Dick*
Nick Selby	The Poetry of Walt Whitman
David Smale	Salman Rushdie: *Midnight's Children – The Satanic Verses*
Patsy Stoneman	Emily Brontë: *Wuthering Heights*
Susie Thomas	Hanif Kureishi
Nicolas Tredell	F. Scott Fitzgerald: *The Great Gatsby*
Nicolas Tredell	Joseph Conrad: *Heart of Darkness*
Nicolas Tredell	Charles Dickens: *Great Expectations*
Nicolas Tredell	William Faulkner: *The Sound and the Fury – As I Lay Dying*
Nicolas Tredell	Shakespeare: *Macbeth*
Nicolas Tredell	The Fiction of Martin Amis
Matthew Woodcock	Shakespeare: *Henry V*
Angela Wright	Gothic Fiction

Forthcoming

Thomas P. Adler	Tennessee Williams: *A Streetcar Named Desire – Cat on a Hot Tin Roof*
Pascale Aebischer	Jacobean Drama
Brian Baker	Science Fiction
Stephen J. Burn	Postmodern American Fiction
Sarah Haggarty and Jon Mee	William Blake: *Songs of Innocence and Experience*
Mardi Stewart	Victorian Women's Poetry
Nicolas Tredell	Shakespeare: *A Midsummer Night's Dream*
Michael Whitworth	Virginia Woolf: *Mrs Dalloway*
Gina Wisker	The Fiction of Margaret Atwood
Gillian Woods	Shakespeare: *Romeo and Juliet*

Readers' Guides to Essential Criticism

Series Standing Order ISBN 1–4039–0108–2
(*outside North America only*)

You can receive future titles in this series as they are published by placing a standing order. Please contact your bookseller or, in the case of difficulty, write to us at the address below with your name and address, the title of the series and the ISBN quoted above.

Customer Services Department, Palgrave Macmillan Ltd
Houndmills, Basingstoke, Hampshire RG21 6XS, England

Jane Austen

Sense and Sensibility

Pride and Prejudice

Emma

ANNIKA BAUTZ

Consultant Editor: Nicolas Tredell

First published 2010 by
PALGRAVE MACMILLAN

Palgrave Macmillan in the UK is an imprint of Macmillan Publishers Limited,
registered in England, company number 785998, of Houndmills, Basingstoke,
Hampshire RG21 6XS.

Palgrave Macmillan in the US is a division of St Martin's Press LLC,
175 Fifth Avenue, New York, NY 10010.

Palgrave Macmillan is the global academic imprint of the above companies
and has companies and representatives throughout the world.

Palgrave® and Macmillan® are registered trademarks in the United States,
the United Kingdom, Europe and other countries.

ISBN-13: 978–0–230–51712–7 hardback
ISBN-13: 978–0–230–51713–4 paperback

This book is printed on paper suitable for recycling and made from fully
managed and sustained forest sources. Logging, pulping and manufacturing
processes are expected to conform to the environmental regulations of the
country of origin.

A catalogue record for this book is available from the British Library.

A catalog record for this book is available from the Library of Congress.

10 9 8 7 6 5 4 3 2 1
19 18 17 16 15 14 13 12 11 10

Printed and bound in China

Contents

Acknowledgements   vii

Abbreviations and a Note on the Text   viii

Introduction   1

The introduction outlines the publication history of *Sense and Sensibility, Pride and Prejudice*, and *Emma*; and gives a summary of this Guide.

CHAPTER ONE   6

Contemporary Reviews

Chapter One looks at the critical responses of Austen's immediate contemporaries, for example at their insistence on the novels' unexceptional moral message. The chapter also discusses Sir Walter Scott's essay on *Emma*, in which he draws attention to her 'dexterity of execution'.

CHAPTER TWO   22

Victorian Reviews, ca. 1865–80

Chapter Two discusses the late Victorian view of *Sense and Sensibility, Pride and Prejudice*, and *Emma*. Critics such as Anne I. Thackeray, Leslie Stephen, Richard Simpson see the novels as reflecting Austen's benevolent and lady-like character.

CHAPTER THREE   42

Early to Mid-Twentieth Century Critical Responses

Chapter Three looks at the emergence of Janeites and Anti-Janeites; at the shift from a view held by critics such as Henry James, who saw Austen as a praiseworthy but unconscious artist, to the beginnings of serious Austen criticism in the works of A. C. Bradley, R. Farrer, Mary Lascelles, D. W. Harding, F. R. Leavis and Lionel Trilling.

CHAPTER FOUR   62

Later Twentieth-Century Critical Responses: Feminism

This chapter looks at the influence of the rise of feminism on Austen criticism, which becomes obvious when comparing the approach of critics writing before the 1970s, such as Tony Tanner, with that of critics writing post 1980, such as S. Gilbert and S. Gubar.

CHAPETR FIVE   76

Later Twentieth-Century Critical Responses: Literary, Cultural, and
Historical Context

Chapter Five considers how, following Marilyn Butler's seminal study, critics such
as Mary Waldron, Isobel Armstrong, Claudia Johnson, all see Austen as being
involved in her historical, cultural and literary context and her novels as expressing
this consciousness.

CHAPTER SIX   96

The First Decade of the Twenty-First Century

Chapter Six shows how alongside the continuation and variation of historicist
approaches, for example applied by Kathryn Sutherland, a New Aestheticism
emerges that goes back to focusing on the text, notably used by David Miller. The
majority of studies combine close reading with a contextual approach.

CHAPTER SEVEN   124

Film and Television Adaptations

This Chapter discusses studies of the film and television adaptations of *Sense and
Sensibility, Pride and Prejudice,* and *Emma.* Critics such as Kathryn Sutherland,
L. Troost and S. Greenfield investigate issues such as which elements have been
changed and how; for example the portrayal of women.

Conclusion   134

Summary of the Guide; the influence of gender on criticism of *Sense and Sensibility,
Pride and Prejudice,* and *Emma* over the centuries; critical trends in each period.

Notes   140

Bibliography   151

Index   165

Acknowledgements

Among the many people without whom it would not have been possible for me to write and revise this book, I should like to record my particular gratitude to Arne Bautz, Thomas Rischbeck, Eva Gabriele Bautz, Thomas Wendt.

I am very grateful for ideas, encouragement and patience to colleagues at Palgrave Macmillan: Sonya Barker, Nicolas Tredell, and Felicity Noble.

Abbreviations and a Note on the Text

AugR	The Augustan Review
BC	The British Critic
BEM	Blackwood's Edinburgh Magazine
BLM	The British Lady's Magazine
Champ	The Champion
CH	The Critical Heritage
Cornhill	Cornhill Magazine
CR	The Critical Review
E	Emma
EWDM	The Englishwoman's Domestic Magazine
GM	The Gentleman's Magazine
MR	The Monthly Review
NBR	North British Review
NR	The New Review
PP	Pride and Prejudice
QR	The Quarterly Review
SS	Sense and Sensibility
St Paul's	St Paul's Magazine

All page references to Austen's novels in this Guide, including those within critical extracts, refer to the Penguin Classics edition of 2003:

Sense and Sensibility, ed. and notes by Ros Ballaster (London: Penguin, 2003)

Pride and Prejudice, ed. and notes by Vivien Jones (London: Penguin, 2003)

Emma, ed. and notes by Fiona Stafford (London: Penguin, 2003)

Introduction

For almost 200 years, readers at various times and in diverse places and circumstances have interpreted Jane Austen's novels – readers reading with different attitudes and differing widely in what they find appealing. Austen's works have continuously risen in popularity: from holding a position of relative obscurity in the Romantic period, they have come to achieve extraordinary critical and popular acclaim in the early twenty-first century. This Guide illustrates key examples of the many different responses to three of Austen's novels: *Sense and Sensibility*, *Pride and Prejudice*, and *Emma*.

Sense and Sensibility was Jane Austen's first published novel, appearing in October 1811. The title page read 'SENSE AND SENSIBILITY: | A NOVEL. | IN THREE VOLUMES. | BY A LADY.' LONDON: | PRINTED FOR THE AUTHOR, | By C. Roworth, Bell-yard, Temple-bar, | AND PUBLISHED BY T. EGERTON, WHITEHALL'. As was to be the case with all her novels that appeared during her lifetime, *Sense and Sensibility* was thus already classified as a novel on the title page, in spite of the widespread practice among contemporary novelists, including popular and successful writers such as Sir Walter Scott (1771–1832) or Maria Edgeworth (1767–1849),[1] of calling their works romances or tales, thus avoiding the negative connotations, at that time, of the term novel.[2] *Sense and Sensibility* was published by Thomas Egerton, on commission, which meant that both the risk and the profits were the author's. She covered her costs and made about £140 out of the first edition of about 750 to 1,000 copies, which cost fifteen shillings per three-volume set.[3] An average first edition of a novel consisted of 500 to 750 copies, so Austen's first novel was already more successful than that of an average novelist.[4] The edition was sold out by July 1813.[5] During her lifetime the novel went through a second edition, which appeared in October 1813.

Pride and Prejudice was even more successful. It was again published by Egerton, at the end of January 1813. Its title page read 'PRIDE AND PREJUDICE': | A NOVEL. | IN THREE VOLUMES. | BY THE| AUTHOR OF 'SENSE AND SENSIBILITY.' | LONDON: | PRINTED FOR T. EGERTON, | Military Library, WHITEHALL'. | 1813. Again, it was thus classified as a novel on the title page, and was published anonymously. This time Egerton had bought the copyright, for £110, and as *Pride and Prejudice* went through three editions during Austen's lifetime he profited by it. The first edition consisted of about 1,250 to 1,500 copies,[6] which must have been disposed of fairly quickly, as the second edition was issued in October 1813, at a price of eighteen shillings.[7] *Pride and Prejudice* was noticed by three contemporary Reviews, *The British Critic* in February 1813, *The Critical Review* in March 1813, and *The New Review* in April 1813. In terms of numbers of contemporary editions, then, *Pride and Prejudice* was Austen's most successful novel.

Although both *Sense and Sensibility* and *Pride and Prejudice* were not published until the 1810s, Austen had written earlier versions of both these novels in the 1790s. That of *Pride and Prejudice*, then called 'First Impressions', had even been offered to the publisher Thomas Cadell the younger (1773–1836), who refused even to look at the manuscript.[8] She revised both manuscripts considerably before she offered them again for publication.

Emma belongs in its entirety to this later period of Austen's life as a novelist. It was published by John Murray (1778–1843), who was also the publisher of the celebrated poet Lord Byron (1788–1824), and whose imprint was more prestigious than that of Egerton. *Emma* was again published on a commission of ten per cent, in December 1815. It was again published anonymously and dedicated by permission to the Prince Regent (George Augustus Frederick (1762–1830), Prince Regent 1811–20, reigned as King George IV 1820–30). The title read 'EMMA': | A NOVEL. | IN THREE VOLUMES. | BY THE| AUTHOR OF 'PRIDE AND PREJUDICE', | &c.&c. | LONDON: | PRINTED FOR JOHN MURRAY | 1816. Of the first edition of 2,000 copies, 1,250 had been sold by October 1816, at twenty-one shillings (one guinea). The first edition of *Emma* brought Austen £221, but, as the second edition of *Mansfield Park* had involved a loss, Austen only received £38 and eighteen shillings for it.[9] *Emma* was reviewed in more contemporary Reviews than any other of her novels: in eight British periodicals and at least three foreign ones.[10]

The numbers of editions and reviews indicate that Austen was more successful with her contemporaries than most novelists were, but also that she was not in any way to be compared to the two literary giants of her day: Walter Scott, both as a poet and as a novelist, and Lord Byron as a poet. However, her popularity with both critics and the public was to increase steadily to make her one of the most celebrated authors of the twentieth and twenty-first centuries.

This Guide traces the most important criticisms that these three novels have inspired over the last 200 years. The first chapter begins by looking at the reviewing culture in the early nineteenth century, when reviewing periodicals were numerous and of unprecedented influence, and when to get discussed at all in a periodical was already an achievement. The chapter proceeds to consider contemporary reviews of Austen's novels, which emerge as superior to most novels, amusing and morally unexceptional, but not works of innovation or genius Chapter 2 looks at Victorian Reviews, in the years between 1865 and 1870. Austen's works became increasingly popular in the course of the nineteenth century, and especially in the second half of the century. This chapter draws on articles in reviewing periodicals to analyse critical responses of readers such as the historian and essayist Thomas Babington Macaulay (1809–59), the critic Richard H. Hutton (1826–97), the novelist Julia Kavanagh (1824–77), the novelist and biographer Margaret Oliphant (1828–97), the critic and scholar Sir Leslie Stephen (1832–1904), the writer and scholar Richard Simpson (1820–76), the journalist, philosopher, scientist and critic G.H. Lewes (1817–78), and the writer Anne I. Thackeray (1837–1919). While individual articles on Austen's works had appeared in the preceding decades, more reviews were published now, largely in connection with the publication of the first biography of Austen: *A Memoir of Jane Austen* (1870), by her nephew James Edward Austen-Leigh (1798–1874). In early-nineteenth-century reviews, Austen's life and person had not played a part, since she published all three novels anonymously. However, her name was known to Victorians, and her character is emphasised by reviewers, most of whom take up the image of Austen that the *Memoir* gives, of a dutiful, kind, and domestic woman, who saw herself first and foremost as a daughter, aunt and sister rather than an author. Reviewers portray her novels as reflecting her sweet and essentially feminine character.

Chapter 3 discusses the emergence of 'Janeism' as well as the critical counter-reactions this phenomenon provoked. The term itself was coined by the literary scholar George Saintsbury (1845–1933), a great admirer of Austen's. The prevalent critical and public attitude to Austen in the early twentieth century was one of holding her in esteem and affection, and seeing in her the benevolent maiden aunt who regarded writing as a leisure pursuit. Foremost literati such as Henry James (1843–1916) praised her, but insisted that she had written without an artistic or technical consciousness – a natural genius and literary amateur. The American novelist, short-story writer and humorist Mark Twain (pseudonym of Samuel Longhome Clement, 1835–1910) famously deprecated her, while the English poet, novelist and short-story writer Rudyard Kipling (1865–1936) wrote a short story about 'Janeites'. The early twentieth century also saw the beginnings of a serious critical approach to Austen's texts in the appreciations of critics such as A.C. Bradley (1851–1935), and Reginald Farrer, a view which was confirmed by R.W. Chapman's scholarly edition of Austen's texts (1923). The novelists E.M. Forster (1879–1970) and Virginia Woolf (1882–1941) also admired Austen, as well as taking her seriously as a writer of literature. Arguably the most significant part in dispelling the notion of Austen as an inartistic and amateurish writer was played by Mary Lascelles' 1939 study *Jane Austen and her Art*. A devout Janeite, Lascelles analysed the structure of the novels and showed their artistic complexities. The chapter goes on to discuss the views of critics such as D.W. Harding and Marvin Mudrick (1921–86) who insisted on Austen as an ungentle writer, critical of her society and readership. The studies of Q.D. Leavis (1906–81), F.R. Leavis (1895–1978), Lionel Trilling (1905–75) and his view of Austen as inherently moral, are also looked at. In spite of all the differences between the critics writing in the first half of the twentieth century, they all applied an a–historical approach. Also, they all contributed to Austen's place in the literary canon as a serious author no longer being disputed by the middle of the century.

Chapters 4 and 5 look at the second half of the twentieth century, when *SS, PP,* and *E* provoked more criticism than ever before. The chapter traces the developments of Austen criticism in the context of larger critical movements: from New Criticism, Formalism and Structuralism to New Historicism, Feminism and postcolonial readings. While critics in the 1960s and 1970s mostly focus on style and form, looking at a text as an aesthetic object, more recent discussions see the text within the political and social context of its genesis, and connect the text to the author's biography. Arguably the most influential study in the second half of the twentieth century was *Jane Austen and the War of Ideas* (1975) by Marilyn Butler (born 1937). She applied a textual approach in combination with an awareness of the author and her context: closely analysing the texts, Butler showed that, far from being ahistorical and apolitical, Austen's writings are full of signs that convey political opinion. While critics after Butler might disagree with her view of Austen as espousing Tory politics, the majority of them agree with Butler in seeing Austen as a writer deeply conscious of her political and social context, and the novels as reflecting this consciousness. While New Historicism and its concern with a text's historical, cultural, social and political context dominates criticism in the second half of the twentieth century, there are two distinct approaches within this larger movement (which are sometimes combined): the political–historical perspective outlined above, and a feminist perspective. The latter comprises studies of the role of women in Austen's fiction as well as of her own position as a woman writer in the early nineteenth century – or a combination of the two.

Chapter 6 considers trends in the first decade of the twenty-first century. It sees a continuation of the historicist trends described above, but it also produces studies that go back to an exclusive focus on the text, notably David Miller in his *Jane Austen or The Secret of Style* (2003), in which he argues that the text is absolutely impersonal in that it reveals nothing about gender, age, marital status, social position etc., which renders Austen's narrative a truly omniscient one. Many critics combine a close reading of the texts with placing Austen and her novels in their historical context. An important example here is Peter Knox-Shaw's *Jane Austen and the Enlightenment* (2004). His approach starts with Butler's view of a conservative Austen; he disagrees with this, since he views her as more in line with the Enlightenment. Arguably the most significant study in this decade is Kathryn Sutherland's *Jane Austen's Textual Lives* (2005). Sutherland here shows how Austen has been constructed, through biographies, portraits, films, editions of her novels, illustrations, into what each editor, biographer, etc, believes her to have been.

Chapter 7 discusses studies of the film adaptations of Austen's novels: in the late twentieth century, more people come to Austen through film versions of her novels than through the novels themselves. The chapter looks at the rise in adaptations from the mid-1990s onwards as well as at critics' attitudes towards these translations of Austen's plots.

As the above outline suggests, this Guide offers a chronological account of critical perspectives, which will make it possible to point up developments in criticism and see critics in their respective contexts. This presentation emphasises every reader's being part of an 'interpretive community'[11] and thereby heightens awareness of our own 'horizons of expectations'.[12]

CHAPTER ONE

Contemporary Reviews

REVIEWING IN THE ROMANTIC PERIOD

Reviewing periodicals were at their zenith in the early nineteenth century. Not only were they numerous but they also enjoyed an interest, and therefore a significance, that was new. Most reviewing periodicals appeared monthly, and consisted of a main part, which contained a small number of longer articles, and an end-section called the catalogue, which contained a larger number of short reviews, sometimes only consisting of one sentence. New publications that were regarded as less important but still worthy of inclusion were placed in the catalogue. The fact that a work was reviewed at all was an indication that it was considered to have some merit, and this was qualified by the length and location of the review. *The Critical Review* discussed *Sense and Sensibility*, the first publication by an anonymous female author, in the main part, whereas *The British Critic* noticed it in the catalogue, a difference reflected in the tenor of the overall verdicts on the novel in these two reviews.

The *Edinburgh* and the *Quarterly Review* were the most influential periodicals. They appeared quarterly rather than monthly, which left them more time for careful selection and criticism. Their price of five or six shillings[1] was prohibitive for anyone below the middle classes – but not as expensive as books – and circulation numbers were high: in the 1810s, the *Edinburgh* and the *Quarterly* each achieved print runs of between 12,000 and 14,000,[2] and there were several readers for each copy. By comparison, *The Critical Review* and *The British Critic*, the two periodicals that reviewed Austen's first published novel, achieved monthly print runs of 2,000 in 1813.[3]

Reviewers wrote anonymously, using a corporate 'we', while the editor was responsible for everything published in his Review. This method was supposed to make criticism easier. It also meant, however, that, of all contemporary articles on *Sense and Sensibility, Pride and Prejudice* and *Emma*, we know the author of only one by name: Walter Scott, who wrote a review of *Emma*. With very few exceptions, usually in the more radical periodicals – such as Mary Wollstonecraft (1759–97) writing for *The Analytical Review* – reviewers were male.[4]

The novel as a genre was not highly regarded by reviews, in spite of its general popularity. With the exception of the eighteenth-century novels of Henry Fielding (1705–54), Samuel Richardson (1689–1761), and Laurence Sterne (1713–68), reviewers looked down on the genre. Articles on novels, therefore, comprised only a small part of any reviewing periodical. From its foundation in 1802 to the late 1820s *The Edinburgh Review* included just over thirty novels, while about sixty to eighty novels appeared each year in the first two decades of the nineteenth century and more than eighty in most years in the 1820s.[5] Where novels are reviewed, they are often not included in the main part of a periodical but considered in a short notice in the catalogue at the end of an issue. Articles frequently start off with a justification for reviewing novels at all, insisting on the inclusion of a novel being an exception and their 'not in general attend[ing] to works of this description'.[6] A novel's inclusion in a reviewing periodical, therefore, is already a sign of its being more highly regarded than most other novels.

The novel's low literary status was also influenced by the fact that it was regarded as a female-dominated genre, as regards readers as well as writers. The male reviewers saw themselves as protecting a female readership by selecting suitable novels for them. Authors of novels, too, were believed to be predominantly female, and, as Peter Garside has shown, novel authorship was indeed dominated by women in the 1810s.[7] This view of a female-dominated genre already determined an individual novel's status: even a good novel could not reach great literary significance because it belonged to an entertaining, but intellectually and morally limited, genre. Henry Austen, in the memoir of his sister prefaced to the 1833 'Standard Novels' edition of *Sense and Sensibility*, confirms contemporary expectations:

■ When 'Pride and Prejudice' made its appearance, a gentleman, celebrated for his literary attainments, advised a friend of the authoress to read it, adding, with more point than gallantry, 'I should like to know who i s the author, for it is much too clever to have been written by a woman.'[8] □

In spite of reviewers' attempts to present the novel as an entirely feminine genre, women were not the only readers of novels. Walter Scott in his review of Austen's *Emma* defends novel-reading, emphasises the variety of quality in novels, and believes the genre to appeal to both sexes.[9] He maintains that novels are useful even as light reading. Men as well as women read novels, though because of the genre's cultural stigma they may not admit to it. While a bad novel is far beneath other genres, anyone, including the male members of the republic of letters, is justified in reading a good novel.

However, while novels were not exclusive to one sex, they were socially exclusive. Novels remained luxury items throughout the 1810s, especially at a time of war, when general inflation meant that members of the working classes were even less likely to spend their wages on fiction, and when material restrictions, especially paper shortage, pushed up book prices even further. While working-class men were earning between nine and, very exceptionally, forty shillings a week throughout the period,[10] *Sense and Sensibility* cost fifteen shillings in 1811. High prices meant, as Jane Austen lamented, that 'people are more ready to borrow & praise, than to buy',[11] but even through libraries novels are unlikely to have reached far below the middle class: the most successful circulating library, the Minerva library of William Lane (1745/6–1814), had a subscription fee of between two and five guineas in 1814,[12] well above a working man's means. The libraries open to working-class readers were those funded by benevolent donors, and generally did not include fiction.

While novels were primarily expected to provide amusement, contemporary reviewers could not accept those which provided nothing else. Reviewers in Jane Austen's time applied to novels the criteria formulated for poetry by the ancient Roman poet Horace (65–08 BC): poetry should both instruct and please, combine the sweet with the useful (*prodesse* [*et*] *delectare* [...] *miscuit utile dulci* (lines 333, 343, *Ars Poetica* [*The Art of Poetry*], also known as *Epistula Ad Pisones* [*Letter to the Pisons*])). The philosopher and novelist William Godwin (1756–1836) asserts that the 'first enquiry' he poses when faced with a non-factual work is 'Can I derive instruction from it?'[13] Because of the novel's perceived femininity reviewers did not deem intellectual instruction possible in novels; hence moral instruction became the main criterion a novel had to fulfil. It was not the only criterion for the assessment of novels, however. Apart from moral instruction, criteria that feature most often are amusement, realism in two senses (probable incidents as well as depiction of characters true to nature), storyline, and style. The more of these a novel fulfils, the more positive, usually, is the overall verdict. The criteria are largely content-based, with little or no attention being paid to aesthetic criteria. Literary merit to reviewers consists of a novel's contribution to society. This chapter considers which aspects of *Sense and Sensibility, Pride and Prejudice* and *Emma* fit into reviewers' preconceptions about novels as well as where they see Austen's novels as presenting something new.

CONTEMPORARY REVIEWS OF JANE AUSTEN'S NOVELS

Sense and Sensibility

Sense and Sensibility, Jane Austen's first published novel, came out in October 1811. Its title page specified both that this work was 'a novel' and that it was 'By a Lady'. Notices appeared in two contemporary reviewing periodicals, *The Critical Review* and *The British Critic*. The first to appear was an article of eight pages in *The Critical Review*, in February 1812, followed by a shorter notice of less than one page in *The British Critic* in May 1812.

The *Critical Review*'s article is the first on any of Austen's novels, and gives a favourable judgement on *Sense and Sensibility*. The review starts off with a justification for having included this novel in its main part. Most novels are so similar to each other that it is very easy to predict both incidents and ending, which makes it difficult for reviewers to vary their articles. The reviewer in *The Critical Review* is 'no [enemy] to novels or novel writers, but [he] regrets, that in the multiplicity of them, there are so few worthy of any particular commendation. [... However,] 'Sense and Sensibility' is amongst the few'.[14]

From the start, Austen's novels are categorised as female, as regards authorship as well as content. Like many novels in the early nineteenth century, *Sense and Sensibility* was published anonymously, but, in contrast to most novels' anonymity, that of *Sense and Sensibility* was socially defined as well as gendered, since the title page stated that the novel was 'By a Lady'. Authorship therefore concurs with contemporary assumptions about novels: the genre as a whole was regarded as dominated by women, so that, concerning gender, Austen's novels entered the market as typical productions, which yet needed to distinguish themselves from others.

The criterion that contemporary reviewers of novels most emphasise is morality. It is not what the two reviewers of *Sense and Sensibility* alone are most concerned with, but it remains the most prevalent criterion for all contemporary articles on Austen's novels. Reviewers prefer a novel's moral message to manifest itself in concrete examples throughout the novel, rather than in a general concept. The reviewer in *The Critical Review* is pleased with the contrast between Elinor and Marianne, holding Elinor up as a model of female behaviour:

■ The characters of Elinor and Marianne are very nicely contrasted; the former possessing great good sense, with a *proper quantity of sensibility,* the latter an equal share of the sense which renders her sister so estimable, but blending it at the same time with an *immoderate* degree of sensibility which renders her unhappy on every trifling occasion, and annoys everyone around her.[15] □

According to the reviewer, the moral lies in Marianne's move towards sense and away from her 'delirium of sensibility';[16] the more like Elinor she becomes the more he approves of her. Elinor is never questioned in the review; she is a model of female behaviour, adorned with sense, 'patience and tenderness'.[17] The reviewer understands a novel's morality as constituted in its attitude to love and marriage, which emphasises the author's femininity: she writes about what women should be concerned with, and therefore stays within the field of female propriety and morality. While this field is necessarily limited, reviewers view her writing within it positively as it enhances the novel's moral message. Marianne's and Willoughby's attachment will teach young ladies that such an unbounded sensibility will lead to 'misery [...] inconvenience and ridicule', while it will make young men see the 'folly and criminality'[18] of playing with a young woman's feelings. The underlying assumption is that readers will be of the same social class as the characters depicted, which renders the novel's lesson directly applicable, so that the reviewer highly praises the fact that the characters are 'in genteel life'.[19] Without apparently noticing it himself, the reviewer is attracted to the novel's new kind of realism in its depiction of ordinary – though 'genteel' – characters. The characters in general are highly commended, being 'in genteel life, naturally drawn, and judiciously supported',[20] including minor characters such as John Dashwood and Sir John Middleton. The reviewer praises the novel's realism, and finds the incidents 'probable and highly pleasing, and interesting; the conclusion such as the reader must wish it should be, and the whole [...] just long enough to interest without fatiguing.'[21] Although he therefore still defines the novel's realism as probable incidents, his applying Sense and Sensibility's moral lesson directly to his readers shows that he perceives Austen's different kind of realism, though he does not comment on it. Horace's criteria of 'amusement and instruction' are met because the novel teaches without outright didacticism, and the reviewer can praise the novel as being '[amongst the few that] are worthy of any particular commendation'.[22] This judgment is indirectly based on the novel's realistic depiction of contemporary society, since it is this that makes its message immediately relevant to the reader.

The only negative point the reviewer mentions is brought forward in such a way as immediately to excuse it:

■ The story may be thought trifling by the readers of novels, who are insatiable after something new. But the excellent lesson which it holds up to view and the useful moral which may be derived from the perusal, are such essential requisites, that the want of *newness* may in this instance be readily overlooked.[23] □

The reviewer does not say that he finds the story trifling, but makes it sound as though the reader is not justified in finding it so, as that would mean belonging to a class of 'novel readers who are insatiable after something new'. He also excuses the negative point raised by holding up positive ones that compensate for it. For him, story signifies an exciting plot with new events, which Austen's novel does not offer. Fitting in with his focus on the story's moral message, he concentrates on its plot rather than its construction. His statement shows that, while story was usually one of the criteria applied to novels, its provision of exciting events could be dispensed with, whereas its moral message could not. The 'want of *newness*' in a *novel*, therefore, in itself becomes something new, and his comments testify to his willingness to accept a new kind of fiction that does not conform to his expectations of a novel – provided he can find a moral message in it. Again, he does not appear to realise the link between his remark and the novel's kind of realism: its moral is so useful precisely because it deals with everyday life rather than with exciting events.

Both 'amusement and instruction' may therefore be derived from this 'genteel, well-written novel', and the work 'reflects honour on the writer, who displays much knowledge of character, and very happily blends a great deal of good sense with the lighter matter of the piece',[24] as it instructs without letting the reader feel that it does so.

In this very favourable review, most of the common criteria applied by reviewers (morality, amusement, realism, storyline) are met, while style is not explicitly mentioned.

The review in *The British Critic* raises similar points:

■ We think so favourably of this performance that it is with some reluctance we decline inserting it among our principal articles, but the productions of the press are so continually multiplied, that it requires all our exertions to keep tolerable pace with them.[25] □

This first sentence sets the tone for the review; though the novel is only noticed in a short article, the reviewer still thinks highly of it. Like *The Critical Review*, *The British Critic* stresses the lesson to be learned from the different behaviour of the two sisters in similar situations. While Elinor 'by sober exertion of prudence and judgment sustains with fortitude, and overcomes [her trials] with success', Marianne, because of her excessive sensibility, is plunged by them 'into an abyss of vexation, sorrow and disappointment'. The novel therefore may be read 'not only with satisfaction but with real benefits, for [the female readers] may learn from them, if they please, many sober and salutary maxims for the conduct of life, exemplified in a very pleasing and entertaining narrative'. The characters are well drawn and sustained, and, as in *The Critical Review*, the depiction of John Dashwood is particularly commended. The reviewer finds the novel true to nature and is laudatory about the 'intimate knowledge of life and of the female character'. Like the reviewer in *The Critical Review*, this critic also bases his positive judgment indirectly on the novel's realistic depiction of contemporary society, since this is what makes the novel's message applicable to readers. He further emphasises the gender aspect of this realism, commenting on the author's 'intimate knowledge of life and the female characters'.[26] Again, it is not analysed how the novel displays such insight into female character, so that, while oblivious to technique, reviewers yet recognise that they become more intimately acquainted with Austen's heroines than with those of other authors, which again contributes to the applicability of the moral lesson.

Two negative points are raised: 'the genealogy' in the first chapter is regarded as confusing, and the character of Sir John Middleton is perceived as overcharged. However, there is 'ample compensation' to make up for these 'trifling defects'. Neither the story nor the style of the novel gets mentioned, but the criteria of morality, amusement and realism are met, so that on the whole this is a very favourable review.

Although neither reviewer states it, it is the truthfulness to the quotidian, the everyday, that distinguishes this novel, so that from the appearance of the first review of an Austen novel onwards, domestic realism was perceived as what differentiated hers from other novels. Both reviewers regard *Sense and Sensibility* as a superior novel, but for both, its superiority is based on its containing a 'useful moral'.

Pride and Prejudice

Pride and Prejudice, Austen's next novel to appear, was published in January 1813, again anonymously, and this time stating 'By the author of Sense and Sensibility', rather than 'By a Lady', so that readers would only know for certain that it was written by a woman if they remembered *Sense and Sensibility*'s title page. All her novels followed that pattern from now on of saying 'By the author of...', yet female authorship is hardly ever doubted.

Pride and Prejudice was noticed by three contemporary reviews, *The British Critic* in February 1813, *The Critical Review* in March 1813, and *The New Review* in April 1813. To get reviewed at all was an achievement, since contemporary periodicals included few articles on novels. The main points raised are similar to those *The Critical Review* had already made in its review of *Sense and Sensibility*: the concrete lessons to be learned from the novel, the realistic depiction of everyday life and characters, the pleasure derived from reading the novel, and its being altogether superior to others.

The *British Critic* review starts off by reminding the reader that they 'had occasion to speak favourably of the former production of this author or authoress, [...] and [they] readily do the same of the present.'[27] This sets the tone for the whole review: it is again a favourable one, which justifies the review's former positive verdict. The critic thinks highly of this particular author, and has 'very little doubt' that future 'exertions' will be 'similar' to the ones already produced. Not only does he approve of the volumes before him, he even wishes for more novels. The reviewer is also certain of the novel's pleasing the public and becoming widely read: '[we] entertain very little doubt [of] their successful circulation'.

The *British Critic* emphasises that *Pride and Prejudice* 'is very far superior to almost all the publications of the kind which have lately come before [them]'.[28] Again, being different implies superiority and therefore serves as a justification for inclusion in a serious reviewing periodical like *The British Critic*. The reviewer lists a number of positives against one serious negative point. This weak point is given as a contrast to what the reviewers see as one of the strongest parts of the novel, Elizabeth's character, and is immediately followed by praise for the other characters, which makes the defect appear unimportant:

■ Of the characters, Elizabeth Bennet, the heroine, is supported with great spirit and consistency throughout; there seems no defect in the portrait; this is not precisely the case with Darcy, her lover; his easy unconcern and fashionable indifference, somewhat abruptly changes to the ardent lover. The character of Mr. Collins, the obsequious rector, is excellent.[29] □

Overall, 'the characters are remarkably well-drawn and supported'; even the minor characters 'are exceedingly well-drawn'.

Another criterion that is important to reviewers is the storyline, and the story of *Pride and Prejudice* has 'no great variety'. However, it is 'well told', and 'has a very unexceptionable tendency'.[30] As with the reviews of *Sense and Sensibility*, the moral message of *Pride and Prejudice* is especially emphasised.

Realism is another positive point brought up by the reviewer; the characters depicted are true to nature and the events could happen daily: 'The picture of the younger Miss Bennets, their perpetual visits to the market town where the officers are quartered, and the result, is perhaps exemplified in every provincial town in the kingdom.'[31] Amusement and diversion had to be provided by a novel: 'It is unnecessary to add that we have perused these volumes with much satisfaction and amusement.'

The reviewer in *The British Critic*, therefore, sees the novel as fulfilling three out of the five criteria – morality, realism and amusement – while he is uncertain about the storyline and does not mention style.

The reviewers of both *The British Critic* and *The Critical Review* begin their reviews of *Pride and Prejudice* by saying that it is different from other novels. This elevates *Pride and Prejudice* above the level of other novels, and sets the positive tone of *The Critical Review*'s article, even if in the first sentence the superiority is only mentioned as regards one aspect:

■ Instead of the whole interest of the tale hanging upon one or two characters, as is generally the case in novels, the fair author of the present introduces us, at once, to a whole family, every individual of which excites interest, and very agreeably divides the attention of the reader.[32] □

Though all the characters are interesting, and most are discussed in the review, it is still clear that 'on the character of Elizabeth the main interest of the novel depends'.[33]

The review consists of a lengthy summary of the plot and a few analytical comments and quotations towards the end of the article. Just as the summary began on a laudatory note it also ends on one: 'The above is merely the brief outline of this very agreeable novel.' The summary itself is interspersed with favourable comments, such as that 'Mr. Darcy [...] becomes [...] captivated with the lively and sensible Elizabeth'. The reviewer declares that 'Elizabeth's sense and conduct are of a superior order to those of the common heroines of novels'; although he talks favourably of the other characters as well, particularly of Mr Collins, the reviewer, too, seems to have been captivated by Elizabeth, as so many readers still are 200 years on. He admires her 'independence of character, which is kept within the proper line of decorum, and her well-timed sprightliness'. The novel's superiority to others is emphasised by the main new point that is made in connection with *Pride and Prejudice*: the reviewer in *The Critical Review* not only sees Elizabeth's 'sense and conduct [as being] of a superior order to those of the common heroines of novels',[34] but also links her to 'lively Beatrice',[35] the female protagonist in the play *Much Ado About Nothing* (first published 1600) by William Shakespeare (1564–1616), and twice repeats this comparison. Like Beatrice, Elizabeth is unusually independent and spirited, but it is safe to admire her since she is still within the moral boundaries of female propriety, and it is through this independence and sprightliness that she can humble Mr. Darcy's 'prodigious quantity of family-pride'.[36] Again, the reviewer approves of a new and different element in this novel – which does not violate his sense of morality – and emphasises the unusual element by choosing it to link this author's productions to Shakespeare's. Any comparison with Shakespeare bestows high praise, especially if it concerns the low-status genre of the novel. Here, comparison to Shakespeare also justifies approval of Elizabeth. The comparison that was to recur repeatedly in later years, especially towards the end of the nineteenth and the beginning of the twentieth century, between Austen's and Shakespeare's characterisation, appears for the first time in 1813 – though it is here still based on content rather than technique, since it is the liveliness that is compared, rather than the dramatic representation.

The moral tendency of the novel as a whole is unexceptionable, and in addition to that the novel instructs: both Darcy and Elizabeth learn and see their mistakes; Darcy's speech about having been 'properly humbled' by Elizabeth is quoted, as is her reaction to his letter, when she 'is obliged to condemn herself for her precipitancy in believing the calumnies to which she had given ear'. Furthermore,

■ an excellent lesson may be learned from the elopement of Lydia:- the work also shows the folly of letting young girls have their own way, and the dangers which they incur in associating with the officers who may be quartered in or near their residence.[37] □

This again implies that the novel is realistic, as it can be applied to the daily life of contemporary readers. Realism is further emphasised when discussing Mrs Bennet and Mr Collins: 'Many such silly women as Mrs. Bennet may be found; and numerous parsons like Mr. Collins.'

The reviewer stresses one further aspect that he finds instructive and that he believes should be applied by the readers, especially the 'fair readers', to their own lives: the proper line that is drawn 'between the prudent and the mercenary in matrimonial concerns',[38] quoting a conversation between Elizabeth and Mrs Gardiner about the prudence of Mr Wickham's starting to pay attention to a girl very soon after she has become an heiress. Mr Wickham cannot prudently be fallen in love with as he is not rich enough for someone who does not have any money either. Elizabeth does not, and her prudence is rewarded, as she falls in love instead with Mr Darcy, who is morally far superior to Mr Wickham. She does not have to choose between marrying for love and marrying out of a 'mercenary [...] motive' (p. 120). The moral instruction of this novel is emphasised repeatedly in this review.

The storyline is also commended, especially 'the final *éclaircissement* [explanation or clarification] between Elizabeth and Darcy', which is brought about by the 'fair author' with 'considerable ingenuity'.[39] There are hints that indicate that the reviewer remembers that *The Critical*

Review had noticed a novel by the same author before. He knows the author is a woman, which was not obvious from the title page of *Pride and Prejudice*. The only reference the review makes to having reviewed the former novel is implicit, as it is interspersed in a general laudatory remark: 'The sentiments, which are dispersed over the work, do great credit to the *sense* and *sensibility* of the authoress.'[40]

The last paragraph goes back to some of the points the review has raised: the novel's superiority over other novels, its realistic depiction of everyday life, and its successful drawing of characters.

> ■ We cannot conclude without repeating our approbation of this per-formance, which rises very superior to any novel we have lately met with in the delineation of domestic scenes. Nor is there one character which appears flat or obtrudes itself upon the notice of the reader with trouble-some impertinence. There is not one person in the drama with whom we could readily dispense;-they all have their proper places; and fill their several stations, with great credit to themselves, and much satisfaction to the reader.[41] □

This also implies that the reading of the novel affords amusement, as it is an 'agreeable novel' and gives 'satisfaction to the reader'. No negative point about the novel is raised; instead the reviewer praises it highly.

Overall, then, the articles on *Pride and Prejudice* in both *The British Critic* and *The Critical Review* discuss similar issues to the ones raised about *Sense and Sensibility*: the main points are again the concrete lessons to be learned from it, the realistic depiction of everyday life and characters, the pleasure derived from reading the novel, and its being altogether superior to others.

In contrast to most other reviewing periodicals, *The New Review* endeavoured not to give judgements of the works it reviewed, though the mere inclusion of a novel would usually indicate approval. The review of *Pride and Prejudice* consists of a plot summary, which does not give an opinion, a description of the characters and a lengthy quotation (a dialogue between Elizabeth and Darcy at Lady Catherine's, from chapter 31). The plot summary is in places inaccurate (e.g.: 'on being rejected by the two elder sisters, he [Mr. Collins] marries Miss Lucas'). The article is strictly neutral, perhaps especially so because it is the first novel *The New Review* notices (it was founded early in 1813). However, though it succeeds in summing up the plot without giving judgements, this is more difficult where the portrayal of characters is concerned:

> ■ Their second daughter, Elizabeth, possesses beauty, virtue, intellect, and a lively flow of spirits, with some portion of her father's turn for satire. She is, in fact, the principal personage in the novel, and serves to exemplify the influence of Prejudice over a mind of no common penetration. □

Though not explicit, especially when compared with *The British Critic*'s and *The Critical Review*'s comments that 'Elizabeth Bennet, the heroine, is supported with great spirit and consistency throughout', and that 'Elizabeth's sense and conduct are of a superior order to those of common heroines of novels', to call Elizabeth's mind one 'of no common penetration' is not merely descriptive either. Similarly, Mr Collins is called 'a pompous, prolix, prosing species of prig'. Overall, at least some aspects are approved of, in spite of professed neutrality of judgment.

Emma

Emma was published in December 1815, by John Murray, and received more reviews than any of Austen's other novels: eight British periodicals included an article on the novel. *Emma* was dedicated by permission to the Prince Regent, which would have already singled the novel out. Austen had changed publisher and *Emma* came out with John Murray's imprint, which would have given more importance to the novel: he was a well-known literary figure as the publisher of eminent journals such as *The Quarterly Review* and also Byron's works. The three volumes of *Emma* cost one guinea, and, as Garside points out, this too would have made it 'a different article from contemporary Minerva publications (then generally retailing at about 5s a volume)'.[42] Of the first edition of 2,000 copies 1,250 had been sold by October 1816, earning Austen £221, but since the second edition of *Mansfield Park* (February 1816) had involved a loss she received only £38 for it.[43]

Murray was also publisher of *The Quarterly Review*, which reviewed *Emma* in its October 1815 issue (though the article did not actually appear until March 1816). The review is especially remarkable because *The Quarterly Review* noticed very few novels – in the second and third decades of the nineteenth century the total of articles in the *Quarterly* involving fiction is only about forty.[44] The article on *Emma* is unsigned, but written by the best-selling and famous author Walter Scott. Like many reviews, it deals not only with the latest novel, but also with previous publications by the same author.

Scott starts off by defending the novel genre and discussing its popularity generally. So many readers prefer the light reading of novels to more serious literature such as that by 'the historian, moralist or poet'[45] that even very bad novels will still be read. He owns that he too is well acquainted with novels, and he justifies himself and all other novel readers both for reading and for treating the genre seriously by strongly pleading the novel's cause:

■when [he] consider[s] how many hours of languor and anxiety, of deserted age and solitary celibacy, of pain even and poverty, are beguiled by the perusal of these light volumes, [he] cannot austerely condemn the source from which is drawn the alleviation of such a portion of human misery, or consider the regulation of this department as beneath the sober consideration of the critic.[46] □

These are general arguments in favour of all novels, and he therefore finds himself even more justified to discuss one that 'proclaim[s] a knowledge of the human heart, with the power and resolution to bring that knowledge to the service of honour and virtue' (189). Like many reviewers of Austen, he finds that her novels have justly attracted more attention than average novels, thereby emphasising the superiority of her works.

He discusses Austen's novels in general within the larger development of the genre, so that the novel, from having been the 'legitimate child of the romance',[47] which used to relate what was possible rather than what was probable, with idealised and purified characters, has developed with Austen into a striking and realistic depiction of everyday life. Its realism is:

■ composed of such common occurrences as may have fallen under the observation of most folks and her dramatis personae [persons of the drama, or characters] conduct themselves upon the motives and principles which the readers may recognize as ruling their own and that of most of their acquaintance.[48] □

Readers are thus in a better position to judge this novel's characters and events than those of a romance, which increases Scott's admiration for Austen's successful execution. He emphasises her new kind of realism as the novel's main asset – as had previous reviewers, but Scott does so consciously, whereas they merely perceived it as a side effect of discussing the novel's moral lesson.

Scott points out that this new novel 'must make amends [for a lack of exciting events and characters] by displaying depth of knowledge and dexterity of execution'.[49] He is the first reviewer to be interested in craftsmanship, realising that it is the author's narrative skill that keeps the reader interested, not just the novel's plot. He points out that the advantage of the novel's interest lying in its characters, realism, spirit, style, originality, and dialogue rather than its storyline is that these are elements that the reader can enjoy a second time without getting bored. He thus argues for the validity and even superiority of a novel without an exciting plot, whereas previous reviewers reluctantly, and only as an exception, dispensed with the demand for an exhilarating story in Austen's novels. Her merit 'consists much in the force of a narrative conducted with much neatness and point, and a quiet yet comic dialogue, in which the characters of the speakers evolve themselves with dramatic effect'.[50] Scott praises Austen's detail and her ability to make the familiar interesting, and recognises her technique of letting characters reveal themselves through their speech, rather than describing them herself in the narrative prose. This point about Austen's dramatic qualities would come up repeatedly over the next 200 years.

Like other reviewers, Scott finds the novel's moral lesson particularly useful because it can be directly applied to readers' lives, but, in contrast to other contemporary critics, he is more positive about how this is achieved than about the lesson itself. Like other reviewers, he sees the moral message in Austen's novels primarily in their attitude to love and marriage. However, while other reviewers tend to praise Austen for encouraging a more rational attitude towards love, Scott, who, like them, understands the moral as being in favour of falling prudently rather than passionately in love, sees Austen's heroes and heroines as too much on the side of prudence. While prudent love may encourage selfishness, passionate love can be qualified as the 'tenderest, noblest and best'[51] feeling. (One example he gives is Elizabeth's statement that she fell in love with Darcy on first seeing Pemberley, which he takes at face value.) In spite of not entirely agreeing with the moral message, however, he praises Austen's novels highly, testifying to his placing less emphasis than other reviewers on morality and content, and more on artistic dexterity.

Scott, of course, is an exceptional reviewer; nevertheless, his review is representative in showing a trend towards a less exclusive emphasis on morality, and a recognition that Austen's realism consists of the depiction of everyday life and characters. His interest in her technique is still unique, however.

Because of the popularity of reviews in the early nineteenth century, most magazines carried a reviewing section, though articles in magazines were usually shorter than in Reviews. The Gentleman's Magazine was almost 100 pages long, roughly a fifth of which were taken up by reviews. Out of the works reviewed in The Gentleman's Magazine in September 1816, Emma is the only novel, and it is reviewed on half a page.

The attitude of the reviewer in The Gentleman's Magazine towards novels is a typical contemporary one: 'a good Novel is now and then an agreeable relaxation from severer studies',[52] but it is a trifle, not something serious in itself. The reviewer refers to Pride and Prejudice as having afforded him much entertainment (though The Gentleman's Magazine did not review it), and as having induced him to read Emma, which he also found 'amusing, if not instructive'.[53] He prefers the superior social rank of the characters in Pride and Prejudice to the rank of those in Emma, but he still praises the realism and accuracy with which the middle-class gentry and their habits are depicted, as well as the way they are sustained and organised.

> ■ Every character throughout the work, from the heroine to the most sub-ordinate, is a portrait which comes home to the heart and feelings of the Reader; who becomes familiarly acquainted with each of them, nor loses sight of a single individual till the completion of the work.[54] □

The novel is morally acceptable, as it 'has no tendency to deteriorate the heart' and 'the language is chaste and correct'.[55] As usual, if the moral can be approved of, the overall verdict is positive. *Emma* does not belong to the very best sort of modern novels, but he is willing to give it 'a distinguished degree of eminence'. Within 'that species of composition'[56] only, though, within the novel genre, can *Emma* be commended, which again emphasises the low opinion the reviewer has of the genre as a whole.

The novel affords amusement, has an unexceptionable moral tendency, a commendable style, well-drawn and well-supported characters, and a realistic depiction of the society it deals with, but it does not instruct and will never be more than mere amusement.

It is along these lines that the remaining six reviews of *Emma* run, praising it as above the average novel, but not as culturally or socially significant, and using content-based rather than aesthetic criteria.

The Champion, a weekly Sunday periodical with a regular reviewing section, included an article on *Emma* in March 1816 which was two folio pages long. The reviewer distinguishes realistic from romantic novels and places *Emma* in the former category. It is not action that makes this novel interesting, but the workings of mind, temper, and feeling. He is very positive about the realistic depiction of the characters. The novel has afforded him amusement, style and storyline are commended, but – in contrast to the majority of novel reviews – neither moral tendency nor instruction is discussed.

The Augustan Review was a monthly reviewing periodical which only existed for one year, from 1815 to 1816. It reviewed *Emma* in May 1816, in an article of just over two pages. Because the novel is realistic and deals with everyday occurrences, the reviewer regards it as similar to the author's former works. Though he praises the characters on the whole, he regards Miss Bates as tedious, and he advises the author to include less talk and more incidents in her next novel, without apparently noticing that this would partly undermine the realistic depiction. The reviewer commends the novel's morals, since, by describing realistic happiness, Austen teaches her readers where it may be found, and he particularly praises Emma's sense of duty towards her father. Overall, the novel contains a useful moral as well as humour, evokes interest and is pleasant to read.

The review of *Emma* in *The British Critic*'s July 1816 issue is two pages long, and, as with the two former articles on Austen's novels in *The British Critic*, the superiority of her works over others of the same kind is stressed. The novel amuses and is morally unexceptionable, though it does not instruct. Storyline, style, realism and character depiction are commended. The notice of *Emma* in *The Monthly Review* of July 1816 is only a few sentences long and consists of the reviewer's comments on humour as the novel's sole ingredient. The article in *The British Lady's Magazine* of September 1816 on *Emma* judges the novel on the whole positively, in spite of the repeated claim that Austen's subjects are so limited that they must soon be exhausted. The article on *Emma* in *The Literary Panorama* of June 1817 regards the depiction of characters and the story as the most important criteria for a good novel, and while hitherto the plot has usually been stressed, this novel serves as an example of a new kind of novel that emphasises the delineation of character. *Emma* belongs to a new kind and therefore fulfils this reviewer's two main criteria.

Overall, then, contemporary reviewers regard Austen as superior to most novelists, but not as innovative, genial, or even technically skilled. Her novels rise 'far superior to any novel we have lately met with'.[57] Adverse comments on Austen's novels are rare in these reviews, and generally confined to details. However, compared with Scott, by far the most successful novelist of his time, she produced 'good novel[s]',[58] that were 'amusing',[59] but not significant social contributions.

The main points of appraisal that are raised in these early articles include the novels' moral message and their realism, by which critics come to mean both probable incidents and a realistic depiction of contemporary society; reviewers laud the insight Austen gives us into her characters, especially the female ones, they find the novels amusing, and Scott, as the first reviewer to be interested in this, praises Austen's 'dexterity of execution'. All reviewers agree in seeing Austen's novels as superior to the average novel.

The next chapter moves to the later years of the nineteenth century and looks at how critics view *Sense and Sensibility*, *Pride and Prejudice* and *Emma* in Victorian times, compared with the points raised by reviewers when the novels were first published.

CHAPTER TWO

Victorian Reviews, ca. 1865–80

This chapter outlines the critical trends of a specific period: roughly the years from 1865 to 1880. Few articles had appeared on Austen in the preceding decades, but during this period their number increased, largely as a reaction to the appearance of the first biography of Austen in 1870. The publication of *A Memoir of Jane Austen*, written by Jane Austen's nephew James Edward Austen-Leigh, gave rise to a number of articles, usually overviews of her life and of her oeuvre as a whole rather than discussions of an individual novel. Articles bear titles such as 'Miss Austen'[1] or 'A Memoir of Jane Austen',[2] rather than those of specific Austen novels. This general kind of article means critics include overall estimates of the author, and focus on those elements they believe to be important: biographical events, individual works, and the connection between biography and work.

MORALITY AND AUSTEN'S LIFE

Austen the person as well as Austen the author feature in articles on her and her works. However, the emphasis tends to be on her works, in spite of many of the articles appearing in connection with the *Memoir* of 1870, when a more exclusive focus on Austen's life might have been expected since it was the first full-length biography of Austen to appear.

While reviewers consider Austen's character, they do not discuss her life in much detail. The lack of exciting events in her life, as well as her gender, mean that reviewers focus on the character of a dutiful, kind, domestic daughter, sister, and aunt. Austen is presented as a woman whose life was 'without incidents or passions'.[3]

Reviewers continuously connect life and work. Anne Isabella Thackeray, in an article that first appeared in 1871 and then, as Brian Southam points out, in a revised 1883 version displaying 'heightened sentimentalism',[4] sees Austen's novels in general as describing what she experienced in real life.

> ■ She has a gift of telling a story in a way that has never been surpassed. She rules her places, times, characters, and marshals them with unerring

precision. Her machinery is simple but complete; events group themselves so vividly and naturally in her mind that, in describing imaginary scenes, we seem not only to read them but to live them, to see the people coming and going: the gentlemen courteous and in top-boots, the ladies demure and piquant; we can almost hear them talking to one another. [...] Jane Austen possessed both gifts of colour and of drawing. She could see human nature as it was; with near-sighted eyes, it is true; but having seen, she could combine her picture by her art, and colour it from life. In this special gift for organization she seems almost unequalled. Her picnics are models for all future and past picnics; her combinations of feelings, of gentlemen and ladies, are so natural and life-like that reading to criticize is impossible to some of us – the scene carries us away, and we forget to look for the art by which it is recorded.[5] □

As well as discussing these general elements of Austen's work, Thackeray also draws direct parallels between Austen and her characters. In her sensitivity, sweetness and womanliness she is like some of her heroines, who still have a positive influence on readers. By the end of her life, 'Anne Elliot must have been Jane Austen herself, speaking for the last time'. Both are 'so true, so womanly' that one cannot but love them. Yet Austen, at the end of her life, is also 'the bright-eyed heroine of the earlier novels, matured, chastened, cultivated, to whom fidelity has brought only greater depth and sweetness instead of bitterness and pain'.

Thackeray continues to discuss the *Memoir*, finding that, although Austen's life is shown to have been void of adventure or grandeur, and instead to have been one of tranquillity and 'common events', the biography is yet 'deeply interesting to those who loved the writer of whom it is written'. Indeed, Thackeray argues,

■ as we turn from the story of Jane Austen's life to her books again, we feel more than ever that she, too, was one of these true friends who belong to us inalienably – simple, wise, contented, living in others, one of those whom we seem to have a right to love. Such people belong to all human-kind by the very right of their wide and generous sympathies, of their gentle wisdom and loveableness. □

That such a kind person should have been a novelist for Thackeray necessarily means that the author's character is reflected in the novels. Aunt Jane seems not to have heeded her increasing fame as an author but continued her peaceful and tranquil country life because it suited her gentle character.

■ All this time, while her fame is slowly growing, life passes in the same way in the old cottage at Chawton. Aunt Jane, with her young face and her mob-cap, makes play-houses for the children, helps them to dress up, invents imaginary conversations for them, supposing that they are all grown up the day after a ball. One can imagine how delightful a game that must have seemed to the little girls. She built her nest, did this good woman, happily weaving it out of shreds, and ends, and scraps of daily duty, patiently put together; and it was from this nest that she sang the song, bright and brilliant, with quaint thrills and unexpected cadences, that reaches us even here through fifty years. The lesson her life seems to teach us is this: Don't let us despise our nests – life is as much made of minutes as of years; let us complete the daily duties; let us patiently gather the twigs and the little scraps of moss, of dried grass together; and see the result!-a whole, completed and coherent, beautiful even without the song.

We come too soon to the story of her death. And yet did it come too soon? A sweet life is not the sweeter for being long. Jane Austen lived years enough to fulfil her mission. It was an unconscious one; and unconscious teachers are the highest. They teach by their lives, even more than by their words, and their lives need not reach threescore years and ten to be complete. She lived long enough to write six books that were masterpieces in their way – to make a thousand people the happier for her industry. She lived long enough to be loved by all those of her home.[6] □

Like Austen's earliest reviewers, Thackeray emphasises the moral lesson to be learned from the novels. Unlike earlier critics, however, she connects this moral to Austen's life and sees Austen as teaching through her unexceptionable life even more than through her works. Thackeray's essay was influential in supporting the image that led to the rise of Janeitism; of seeing Austen as an ideal Victorian lady, a paradigm of modesty and essential femininity, whose domestic and family duties were the prime focus of her existence, whose life was 'sweet and peaceful', who wrote unambitiously and achieved great art unconsciously.

Richard Holt Hutton's view of Austen, as expressed in his 1869 review of the *Memoir*, is similar to that of Anne Thackeray. He, too, accepts Austen-Leigh's image of his aunt. Like Thackeray, he links Austen to her heroines, especially to Anne Elliot and Elizabeth Bennet. While Elizabeth was Austen's favourite, Austen herself was yet too much of a lady to be very similar to her heroine, which emphasises just how unconventional Elizabeth must have seemed, not only to contemporary readers but still to readers in late Victorian times. Hutton mentions irony in the novels, but emphasises that it 'had no malice in it' – someone with Austen's gentleness and the calm life that she led could only include 'gentle irony', if irony at all:

■ For Miss Austen's novels and her life, – so far as we learn its tenor from this volume, – was one of perfect calm, and it was to this calm that we owe that fine, sedate humour and gentle irony which imply a settled standard of life, and an estimate of human follies quite unmixed with bitterness of motive or scepticism of inference. There was no mockery in Miss Austen's irony. However heartily we laugh at her pictures of human imbecility, we are never tempted to think that contempt or disgust for human nature suggested the satire. [...]

It is a great comfort to us to have so complete a verification of the theory we have always cherished, – that Miss Austen's personal character was a sort of medium between the heroine of *Pride and Prejudice,* Elizabeth Bennet, and the heroine of *Persuasion,* Anne Elliot, – that she had all the vivacity of the one and all the gentleness and sweetness of the other. Her own great favourite, it appears, among her heroines, was the former; but was she quite aware that there is in Elizabeth Bennet just the very slightest touch of that want of refinement which we may fairly attribute to the influence of such a mother, – and indeed, in some sense of such a father as hers, for Mr Bennet, dry and keen as is his humour, is too indifferent to the feelings of the persons he meets to have the manners of a perfect gentleman, – and to the general effect of the society of Meryton? Anne Elliot, though without the bright and mischievous playfulness of Elizabeth Bennet, is a far more perfect lady, has far more of the grace and refinement which we find from this short biography were the most distinguishing characteristics of the writer. [...]

It is impossible to suppose that the deeper problems of life weighed very oppressively on a mind which touches them so lightly and so gently as Miss Austen's. It is clear she did not at any time arraign either human nature or human society for their shortcomings and positive sins, as our modern novelists, George Eliot [1819–80], or [William Makepeace] Thackeray [1814–63], or even Mrs [Elizabeth] Gaskell [1810–65], either do, or try to do. She was content to take human society and human folly as they were, and to like while she laughed, instead of arraigning because she loved. And this limited work she had to do, she achieved with greater perfection and fineness and delicacy of touch than almost any other English writer with whom we are acquainted. Never was a definite literary field so clearly marked out and so perfectly mastered as by Miss Austen.[7] □

Hutton's description of Austen typifies one of the main aspects that come up in Victorian reviews: she can never be on a very high intellectual level because she is a perfect lady. Her characteristics are refinement and modesty rather than 'depth of intellect', and Hutton approves of her modesty and her knowing 'the limits of her genius'. Again, he sees her life as peaceful and uneventful, which he connects with her fiction necessarily being light, fine, and delicate. Her productions cannot have a significant social impact and are not comparable in strength to the manly works of an author like Thackeray, Eliot or Scott. Other critics, too, connect her biography and work by emphasising her womanly nature and benevolence and seeing this reflected in the novels. Personal

qualities and those of the writer are not distinguished: she is 'so grace-
ful, so affectionate, so fine in observation, so exquisite in touch, so
real in her knowledge of the secrets of the human heart'.[8] The novels
are judged through Austen's personality, and since reviewers only have
the *Memoir* and the novels to judge from, rather than major events that
would shed light on her character, they create an image of her as an
ideal Victorian lady.

Even those critics who see her novels as containing elements of
irony and criticism still regard the woman as sweet and philanthropic,
which demonstrates the critics' desire to approve of this – female –
author's personality when praising the works. She has to be above all
womanly; hence, where Austen's novels are regarded as including cynicism at all, it is 'female cynicism which [...] is something altogether different from the rude and brutal male quality that bears the same name'.[9]
The novelist Margaret Oliphant perceives Austen's work as 'cruel in its
perfection',[10] but offers two excuses for this, thereby making it possible
still to regard the author as sweet, gentle, and feminine. Though there
is cruelty in the novels, this is 'fine-stinging yet soft-voiced contempt
[and] gentle disdain',[11] which is the natural result of the observations
with which a 'young woman, with no active pursuit to occupy her,
spends, without knowing it, so much of her time and youth'. Women
nowadays could find ways of improving their minds, but these opportunities 'were rare in Miss Austen's day'.[12] Female cynicism is thus the
unconscious result of the times not offering women more wholesome
occupations, not of Austen's character. The young woman observes
'without knowing it', and though her work is a 'pitiless perfection of art
[she] was in reality quite unaware of its real power [because] genius [...]
goes a great deal deeper than conscious meaning'.[13] As such, cynicism
can be seen as the result of her genius, without diminishing the gentle
femininity of the woman, so that genius becomes a term distinct from
feminine qualities.

Anne Thackeray asserts that Austen's heroines 'have a certain gentle
self-respect and humour and hardness of heart' which enables them to
take love lightly, and which modern heroines do not possess. Again,
this trait is due to 'the spirit of the age', and, again, it does not mean that
'Jane Austen herself was incapable of understanding a deeper feeling'.[14]
Thackeray, like Oliphant, employs the technique of holding responsible
the times in which the author wrote for traits of the novels that reviewers do not want to ascribe to the author's personality. That her heroines are seen as representing her when they are soft and womanly, but
not where they are hard or pert, reveals the extent to which Victorian
reviewers mould Austen to fit their gender patterns.

Austen's womanly qualities make her an exemplary author, and she is
praised for these as one of those women who 'raise and ennoble all those

who follow after, – true, gentle and strong and tender'.[15] Reviewers
are interested in physical and mental endowments: they describe her as
'healthy'[16] in body and heart, 'personally [...] most engaging',[17] 'at least
pretty',[18] selfless and genteel. Personal qualities dominate over literary
ones. Austen is an ideal not primarily because she wrote high-quality
novels, but because her novels are an image of her own pure self. It is
through her person that her novels make readers 'feel happier and better
for the goodness and charity which is not ours, and yet which seems to
belong to us while we are near it'.[19] Her moral integrity reflects onto
the reader. Austen's 'cheerful healthy tone, the exquisite purity, and the
genuine goodness which are reflected in every line she wrote [leave
the reader] amused, refreshed, benefited'.[20] Reviewers never criticise
Austen's character but present her as a person for whom one cannot help
but feel a 'warm personal regard'.[21]

An unsigned article in *St Paul's Magazine* of 1870 sees Marianne and
Darcy as standing out among Austen's characters. The critic also connects Austen's life to her novels, and sees her 'quiet life' as the reason for
the lack of deep passion or exciting events in her works. 'Her life was
very quiet, affording no subjects for the excitement of emotion, leav-
ing ample time for composition, and by the narrowness of its sphere of
action inducing a habit of minute observation.' Nothing ever occurred
in her life to rouse any passion in her. In fact, only one character in
all the novels shows any kind of violent emotions – Marianne – and
her passions are shown only 'to be rebuked', although Darcy, too, the
reviewer argues, eventually acts driven by passion rather than prudence.
Yet, the critic continues, even here we do not get the 'delirious excitement' which he finds annoying in the novels of his own day.

■ Her delight was in the exercise of her powers of observation and reflection, and in the humour which grew out of them or accompanied them. It
was her special vocation to make fresh combinations out of the peculiarities
of character coming under her immediate notice; and thus to create something new out of something old, and so to bring the diverse parts together
in perfect harmony as to make the new thing seem true. In the art, which
turns fiction into truth, no writer has ever excelled her. Her just sense of
proportion never deserts her, no one portion of her work is ever suffered to
bear down another, the action is always easy, the progress of the narrative
is always smooth, the writer never gets in the way of her characters, they
are never interfered with by unnecessary reflections, the business of the
scene is never disturbed by useless interjections from the dramatist. Her
personages live their own lives in a perfectly natural manner, and the love
stories which arise out of their juxtaposition are such as belong to the ordinary course of things. Only one character through the six novels written by
Miss Austen is moved by any very impetuous emotion. It is that of Marianne,
in *Sense and Sensibility,* and it is exhibited to be rebuked. For the most

part, the men and women love each other rather because circumstances throw them together, than from any passionate predilection. As a balance to the indiscretion of Marianne, however, there is one man whose passion out-runs his prudence; this is Darcy, in the novel of *Pride and Prejudice*. But even when her characters are somewhat carried away by their feelings the authoress maintains her own propriety, and there is a total absence of the delirious excitement which distinguishes the novel writing of the present day. The wild pulsation, the stormy embracing, the hand pressure which bruises, the kiss which consumes, all these things, the essentials of the fiction of our period, are absent from Jane Austen's pages; the strongest expression there permitted to a lover is 'dearest,' and the most ardent exhibition of passion is a shake of the hands.[22] □

Apart from Marianne and Darcy, whom the reviewer sees as the only two characters in any of the novels who display some kind of passion, Austen's characters are prudent and proper, and again the reviewer believes this to be due to her quiet life, which allowed her perfection but lacked deep emotion. In fact, those who read Austen in order to experience 'any exaltation of the imaginative powers, by any deep pathos or stirring passion, will not find their desire fulfilled by Miss Austen', since what Austen gives us is 'a pleasant vein of irony permeating the ordinary scenes of ordinary life, and marking all its follies, vulgarities, vanities, and baseness, with unfailing precision'.

Reviewers' assessments of Austen's character largely reflect the image given in James Edward Austen-Leigh's biography of his aunt. He makes her a model of Victorian femininity and insists that 'there was scarcely a charm in her most delightful characters that was not a true reflection of her own sweet temper and loving heart'.[23] He presents Austen as a kind and sweet woman who wrote novels almost by accident, certainly without an artistic concept. Instead, they reveal her moral principles: the novels

■ were not written to support any theory or inculcate any particular moral, except indeed the great moral which is to be equally gathered from an observation of the course of actual life – namely, the superiority of high over low principles, and of greatness over littleness of mind.[24] □

He connects woman and work and emphasises Austen's unexceptionable sense of morality as well as her drawing her delightful characters and scenes from real life, so that they instruct the reader as an appropriate reading of everyday life itself would. Her general benevolence prevented her from ever playing with the 'serious duties or responsibilities [of everyday life], nor did she ever turn individuals into ridicule.

[...] She was as far as possible from being censorious or satirical'.[25] In Austen-Leigh's biography, Austen becomes a woman adorned with every female virtue who also happens to write novels.

Reviewers react mainly to four points the *Memoir* raises, largely by accepting Austen-Leigh's version: his insistence that the novels reflect Austen's character; connected to that, her general benevolence and sweetness of character; her having written without an artistic concept; and her not having put her novels before her domestic duties. They accept the points regarding Austen's character without hesitation, but differ as regards Austen's artistic consciousness. Yet, in spite of critics seeing Austen as having consciously composed her novels, it is nevertheless Austen-Leigh's image of his aunt as the unconscious artist that was to persist until well into the twentieth century.

REALISM AND LIMITS

Victorian reviewers' treatment of Austen's realism is similar to that of early-nineteenth-century reviewers. They praise the realism of her novels while at the same time censuring the lack of romance (as opposed to ordinary everyday life), finding that even the most perfectly executed realism is insufficient as a substitute. They are especially laudatory about the realism of ordinary people in ordinary circumstances and praise the execution of all of her characters as perfect, but complete perfection in one area is not as great as portraying an ideal mixture of romance and realism.

Victorian reviewers criticise Austen's novels because they 'do not stir the deeper passions'.[26] They maintain, however, the feminine softness of the author. The love in Austen's novels is 'rather an adjunct of the sober common sense than of the impetuous and passionate side of the soul'.[27] Reviewers are critical about her novels' entire lack of emotion, though some, such as the reviewer in *St Paul's Magazine*, compare the lack of sentiment in her works favourably with present-day novels, which are full of 'delirious excitement'.[28] However, he also claims that Austen's realism leads to a 'starving of the higher imaginative faculties',[29] so that for him, too, a perfect depiction of the quotidian is no substitute for a romantic appeal to the imagination.

However, even where he criticises the heroines' behaviour on moral grounds, especially that of Emma and Elizabeth, he still praises Austen's realistic depiction, and blames faults in the characters on the times in which Austen wrote, so that she had no choice but to present them in this way. He also again stresses that he cannot quite approve of Elizabeth, and that therefore Austen cannot really have preferred

Elizabeth to all her other characters, since Austen was a perfect lady, which Elizabeth is not.

■ In cool reflection, Miss Austen would hardly have called the heroine of *Pride and Prejudice* 'as delightful a creature as ever appeared in print;' [as Austen had called Elizabeth in a letter to her sister in January 1813] for her raillery is not without vulgarity, and her vanity and self-satisfaction extend beyond the proper development of those feminine qualities. It is a common fault with Miss Austen's young women that they are remarkably addicted to the contemplation of themselves and their own qualities with special reference to the effect they produce upon men. It is the first aim to be the object of a man's attention, – this desire not springing from a strong preference for some particular man, but from the general ambition of distinction in this kind. Emma wonders whether Frank Churchill will distinguish her before she has seen him, and Elizabeth is greatly fluttered and occupied with thoughts of Mr. Wickham after the first conversation with him, and she is described as going to the ball prepared to win what remains of his heart, without his having given any sign of having a heart at all. Most of the women throughout these novels are ready to arrive at the last conclusion a woman should come to with regard to a man's inclinations towards herself, at the very first possible opportunity, and all the feminine discussions recorded in these volumes generally hover about this single topic. Even the men, who might be supposed to be engrossed with other pursuits, take the village flirtations into anxious consideration, and seem to have few more important interests in life. But this is probably a true picture of village life in England half a century ago, and perhaps even now, though the feminine sphere of thought and action has greatly enlarged with the progress of education, something of the same kind of small gossip, and small agitation, and mean rivalry, and base detraction, might go on wherever there existed a contracted circle, holding within its bounds several young people of different families and opposite sex, with parents to watch over their interests. Only at the present day a girl of higher mind would make an occasional exception to the rule, employing her intellect upon better things, and not, as is the case with Emma, using her superior intelligence to do base things with superior vigour.[30] □

Darcy's and Elizabeth's faults, as well as those of the other heroes and heroines, are excused; even the too strongly emphasised focus of the novels on the single topic of flirtation and marriage is blamed on the times in which Austen wrote. Austen's realism is praised, yet this also emphasises her limits in two ways: it draws attention to her lack of romance and passion, and, because the focus of reviewers' praise of her novels' realism is on the characters, it emphasises her limited social and temporal range. This limited scope prevents her novels from containing instruction – other than through the author's moral integrity – which limits their social relevance.

Victorian reviewers come up with various justifications for this perceived fault, all connected either to Austen's times or to her sex. 'At the time in which Miss Austen wrote, high thinkers – for even Scott was not a high thinker – did not write novels',[31] so that instruction would not have been expected. Similarly, Austen's limitation to only one topic is 'probably a true picture of village life in England half a century ago, and perhaps even now, though the feminine sphere of thought and action has greatly enlarged with the progress of education'.[32] Again, the reviewers' own times are regarded as superior to Austen's. Richard Simpson sees Austen as 'obey[ing] the adage, 'ne gladium tollas mulier' ['Let the woman not carry a sword']'.[33] Instead of condemning her limitations, he praises her for her consciousness of both the limitations of her abilities and the boundaries of female prudence, justifying her by rendering her literary boundaries those of feminine propriety. Writing within these becomes a virtuous necessity for a perfect lady, and it is as a lady that ignorance of 'the great political and social problems'[34] of her day can be excused. The same excuse nevertheless limits the author.

Because of the novels' limited scope, reviewers see them as being 'of a very unambitious character'.[35] Only because of Austen's limits is her artistic perfection possible: 'the very narrowness of her range enabled her to concentrate her intellectual vision upon the few types of character which she did meet',[36] so that, while the circumstances of her life are responsible for the limitations of her novels, they also make her perfection possible by preventing her energies being spent on topics of greater scope. Reviewers regard wide range more highly than technical perfection in a limited thematic field. Leslie Stephen voices this most decidedly: while

> ■ allowing all possible praise to Miss Austen within her own sphere, [he] should dispute the conclusion that she was [because of her great literary skill] entitled to be ranked with the great authors who have sounded the depths of human passion, or found symbols for the finest speculations of the human intellect, instead of amusing themselves with the humours of a country tea-table. Comparative failure in the highest effects is more creditable than complete success in the lower.[37] □

Her realistic depiction of a section of society cannot compete with the all-encompassing realism of Scott, and, by now, Charles Dickens (1812–70) or Thackeray. Because 'her subjects were not grand [...] the employment of unusual art [was] requisite in order to make her work readable'[38] – readable, but not equal in significance.

CONSCIOUS ARTIST AND FEMALE BOUNDARIES

Reviewers unanimously describe Austen's novels as art and, in connection with that, present her as a conscious composer of art rather than as an unconscious genius like the greatly esteemed Walter Scott. This is the main point of deviation between reviewers' and Austen-Leigh's accounts of Austen: he presents her as a writer without an artistic concept, whose excellence is involuntary. Reviewers praise the novels' artistic construction:

> ■ Her just sense of proportion never deserts her, no one portion of her work is ever suffered to bear down another, the action is always easy, the progress of the narrative is always smooth, the writer never gets in the way of her characters, they are never interfered with by unnecessary reflections, the business of the scene is never disturbed by useless interjections from the dramatist.[39] □

The shift from her qualities to those of her novels in this passage emphasises that they are her conscious products, as does the reference to her as a dramatist, since it implies deliberately directing characters.

As the results of 'the technical dexterity of her workmanship',[40] her novels are perfections of composition. This perfection also limits her in Victorian eyes, however: it proves her conscious composition, the opposite of the Romantic notion of an unconscious genius whose workings are unaccountable. Her strength lies in

> ■ the perfect power she has over her wit. [...] she is never carried away [...] she is always perfectly calm, perfectly self-conscious. Her great characteristic is patience, which is notoriously a surrogate genius, the best substitute for it which nature has contrived.[41] □

'Poetic genius is denied' her;[42] instead she labours over her compositions, but she labours with 'an incommunicable gift of humour',[43] and 'a gift for telling a story'.[44] She thus possesses talents, but she employs them consciously to achieve the perfect art she composes. Reviewers tend not to refer to her as a genius, and if they do they limit the extent, calling her a 'real genius in her own line'.[45] She is too feminine to be a genius: 'Miss Austen's nature was not of the highest type; she was not poetical, she was not philosophical, she was not even very noble or highminded; she was amiable and ladylike'.[46]

Austen is held up as an example to the 'scores of young ladies who are at the present moment anxious of rushing into print as novelists [...] to follow her at least in the exercise of [industry and observation] and sparing no pains in cutting down, refining and polishing'.[47] While this reviewer regards Austen's humour as 'impossible to purchase',[48] her attitude and mode of composition are graspable and therefore imitable. Because her novels are the result of labour as well as genius, some of their aspects at least can be copied, which is where reviewers' perception of Austen differs fundamentally from 'true genius', such as that of Shakespeare or Scott, whose geniuses are regarded as inimitable.

Austen fits an ideal Victorian work ethic since what she wrote 'was worked up by incessant labour into its perfect form'.[49] She is seen as labouring to perfection over every detail, 'with a reverence for art itself, and a disregard of immediate popularity as aim'.[50] It is a virtue that she does not write for money, particularly because she is a woman. Her assiduous writing leads to only six novels, but she can be praised as a benevolent soul working hard to achieve a literary ideal.

Austen's femininity makes her writing incompatible with that of men. Using *Sense and Sensibility* as an example, the reviewer in the *EWDM*, in what is overall an appreciative and positive article appearing in 1866, discusses most of the points that also come up in other Victorian reviews: her skill in drawing her characters; the realism of her novels; her writing as art that will be appreciated not by a mass reading public but by the discerning ones; the connection between her life and her work; and her femininity, which leads her to write modestly and for art, rather than for popularity. *Sense and Sensibility* is especially commended, and Lady Middleton used as an example of Austen's skill as regards secondary characters:

■ In *Sense and Sensibility*, the first work she published, we find a great advance in every respect. Greater breadth, greater variety of character and incident, more interest. In some respects we think it unsurpassed by any of her works. She never drew a more humorous character than Mrs. Jennings, nor a more interesting one than Marianne Dashwood. All the characters are several hair's breadth broader than in any other of her books. The book, however, to our mind fails in its intention by making sensibility more attractive than sense. Elinor is too good; one feels inclined to pat her on the back and say, 'Good girl,' but all our sympathy is with the unfortunate Marianne. But for all that, the contrast between the two temperaments, which was, perhaps, the principal aim of the book, is complete, and at the same time subtle and not too violent. The character of Willoughby is one of the best of her male impersonations. But the prevailing merit of *Sense and Sensibility* is in the excellent treatment of the subordinate characters, and in their excellence in themselves. [...] And what is more, such good and thorough work will last, in spite of this want of ready appreciation, when the glamour of false effect has long lost its charm. Those who only write to create excitement sink into oblivion as soon as that excitement is over, but writers who, like Miss Austen, work with a reverence for art in itself and a disregard of immediate popularity as an aim, and are content to labour in the mine of human nature for their material, cannot fail to find the good ore, and to work it into lasting monuments. [...]

Lady Middleton is a good example of those inferior characters on which she has expended so much skill, if not labour – characters of the very slightest structure – mere elementary forms, of which most writers, if they had not disdained to use them, would have made but dreary personifications of abstract stupidity, but which in her hands become lifelike studies of our friends. □

The reviewer discusses Lady Middleton in detail to show Austen's skill in drawing this minor character. He then, however, turns to *Pride and Prejudice*, finding its characters 'on the whole superior to her other works' and even deciding that this is after all her best novel. He goes so far as to argue that the pleasure in reading does not mainly lie in the moral of the story, but in the 'method of its illustration':

■ After much consideration we decide in giving the palm to *Pride and Prejudice*, as the most thoroughly artistic, satisfactory, and amusing of her novels. In construction the book is nearly perfect; the principal theme – the victory over D'Arcy's pride and Elizabeth's prejudice – sprouts at the beginning, flowers in the middle, and, without forcing, bears fine fruit at the end. All the other characters are arranged with the nicest feeling for graduation and variety: there is not one which has not its own peculiar interest perfectly sustained, yet never obtrusive. All the qualities for which Miss Austen is so justly celebrated are here seen in perfection. The one blot in the book is the character of Lydia – one which, however natural, jars with the refined taste usually displayed by the authoress. The moral preached by it is not a very high one, perhaps: it is shortly this – a rich man should not shut his heart against the attractions of a good, pretty girl because she has a vulgar mother and no fortune to speak of; and good and pretty girls with small fortunes and vulgar mothers should not be in too great a hurry to judge the characters of rich men because they are supercilious in demeanour. However, as far as it goes it is quite unexceptionable, and the method of its illustration is so excellent and diverting that the reader cares nothing whatever about the precept at all. □

About *Emma*, the reviewer writes that 'the great fault of this book is that the stupid, unpleasant, and uninteresting nature of most of the characters is unrelieved by much humour', though he does approve of the novel's heroine: 'on the book has been expended an immense amount of labour not without effect. Emma herself is, perhaps, the most elaborate character Miss Austen ever drew'. The review closes with much praise, though it also makes clear that Austen is great only compared with other women writers, and it again links her own ladylike taste and character to her writing in general:

■ For many qualities as we hope we have sufficiently shown, Miss Austen was in her day unrivalled and is now even unsurpassed; but if there is one quality in which she then stood or now stands superior to all writers of her sex, it is in humour. We will not compare her to men, for she never aimed at writing like a man (she is as unapproachable by them as they by her), but as a female humorist she stands almost alone. In satire, humour, wit, and irony, all of a refined and amiable kind, she is excellent; herself a model of refined and cultivated taste, breeding, and sense, even the smallest weakness in any of these points was immediately discerned by her with an infallible but good-natured understanding, and noted for the amusement of her readers. The peculiar refinement which marked the ladies of her day, and which is mirrored in her writings, has been succeeded by another, and, we think, truer refinement, and has lost much of its charm for this generation (though we are sure that it can only increase our reverence for our female ancestors to believe that there were such women as Elizabeth Bennet, Elinor Dashwood, and Anne Elliot), but it is a proof how little that refinement has changed in spirit when we find that the humour which mainly consisted in the exposure of little sins of less cultivated minds against it has still power to make us smile as though committed against one's own pet social code.

Thus the power of Miss Austen to make us smile as she does is an inverse tribute to that delicate, lady-like taste which she must have possessed in so great a degree, and, thus explained, we prefer to rest her highest claim to celebrity on her humour.[51] □

The reviewer is impressed with the realism of Austen's novels and the perfection of their art. *Pride and Prejudice* is his favourite on artistic grounds: the moral message is acceptable but not remarkable, and is especially blotted by the character of Lydia, though even she is drawn with perfect realism. But the construction of the novel and its art is what most recommends it. However, in spite of the positive opinion of *Sense and Sensibility*, *Pride and Prejudice*, and *Emma*, the reviewer still does not see her as great on an absolute scale. He 'will not compare her to men, for she never aimed at writing like a man'.[52] Her scale is too limited to be great, but she is a perfect lady.

Other reviewers are similar: Austen's work is superior to that of other women writers. It is in comparison with men that art alone is not enough: 'as a matter of art, Miss Austen's novels are more perfect than Thackeray's, but they are far from containing as many separate excellencies';[53] yet 'by the side of "Emma" and "Persuasion", "Evelina" [(1778), by Fanny Burney (1752–1840)] as a work of art, is coarse and farcical'.[54] The confinement to art is therefore seen as a feminine quality; greater scope, intellect, and moral and social significance as masculine attributes.

COMPARISON TO SHAKESPEARE AND TO SCOTT

Shakespeare and Scott were the two most highly regarded literary geniuses for most of the nineteenth century, so that any comparison to either of them is a sign of critics' esteem for Austen. Realistic character depiction is what her novels are most praised for in reviews, and it is in this that she is linked to Shakespeare. However, they always make clear in their comparisons that it is only in this one aspect that she can be compared to him, so that 'she is as true to nature (in her limited acquaintance with it) as Shakespeare himself'.[55] The use of the personal pronoun – though the novels are under discussion – emphasises her sex and her limitations.

The Shakespeare scholar Richard Simpson, in his review of the *Memoir*, compares Austen to Shakespeare extensively – her works as well as her abilities and methods. Like Shakespeare, she began by being a critic, and then developed her artistic faculty. As Joseph Cady and Ian Watt point out, Simpson is the first critic to discuss Austen's irony,[56] and he emphasises it by linking it to Shakespeare. Simpson asserts that she deserves to be called a 'prose Shakespeare [because] within her range her characterization is truly Shakespearian; but she has scarcely a spark of poetry'.[57] The link to Shakespeare is limited at the same moment as it is being drawn. Simpson allocates her so high a place in literature on the merit of her characters, and, though she is also deficient in other aspects, it is her lack of a wider variety of characters that limits her most, precisely because the depiction of characters is her greatest strength. While Simpson thus laments her lack of character diversity, he also sees this as an inevitable limitation because she is a woman: 'her benevolent judgement [does not] allow her to paint [rascals]'.[58] Conscious irony in a lady is only possible to a limited extent, and Simpson has no doubt that she is a perfect lady in every respect: even 'her handwriting was beautiful, her needlework delicate'. She was an ideal woman, 'the life of her family', which necessarily informed her writing.

■ It is clear that she began, as Shakespeare began, with being an ironical censurer of her contemporaries. After forming her prentice hand by writing nonsense, she began her artistic self-education by writing burlesques. [...] She began by being an ironical critic; she manifested her judgment of them not by direct censure, but by the indirect method of imitating and exaggerating the faults of her models, thus clearing the fountain by first stirring up the mud. This critical spirit lies at the foundation of her artistic faculty.

Criticism, humour, irony, the judgment not of one that gives sentence but of the mimic who quizzes while he mocks, are her characteristics. If she had set herself to imitate her models seriously, [...] she would never have reached the heights she actually attained. She might have spoiled an intelligible style; she might have clothed her thoughts in a garb totally unfit for them; she might have written much earnest sentiment; but she would never have displayed the subtle humour, the fine sense of the incongruous, the constant presence and alertness of mind, which her writings are full of. [...] And such in her sphere was Miss Austen's growth; she was a critic who developed herself into an artist.

That the critical faculty was in her the ground and support of the artistic faculty there are several reasons for believing. The first reason is her notable deficiency in the poetical faculty. Perhaps there is no author in existence in whom so marvellous a power of exhibiting characters in formation and action is combined with so total a want of the poetical imagination. [John] Heywood [c.1497–c.1580] has been called a prose Shakespeare; Miss Austen much more really deserves the title. Within her range her characterization is truly Shakespearian; but she has scarcely a spark of poetry. [...] And secondly, the paramount activity of the critical faculty is clearly seen in the didactic purpose and even nomenclature of her novels. *Pride and Prejudice* and *Sense and Sensibility* are both evidently intended to contrast, and by the contrast to teach something about, the qualities or acts named in the titles. In *Persuasion* the risks and advantages of yielding to advice are set forth. *Northanger Abbey* exhibits the unreality of the notions of life which might be picked out of [the novels of Mrs. Ann Radcliffe (1764–1823)]; and *Mansfield Park* and *Emma*, though too many-sided and varied to be easily defined by a specific name, are in reality just as didactic as the rest. This didactic intention is even interwoven with the very plots and texture of the novel. The true hero, who at last secures the heroine's hand, is often a man sufficiently her elder to have been her guide and mentor in many of the most difficult crises of her youth. Miss Austen seems to be saturated with the Platonic idea that the giving and receiving of knowledge, the active formation of another's character, or the more passive growth under another's guidance, is the truest and strongest foundation of love. *Pride and Prejudice*, *Emma*, and *Persuasion* all end with the heroes and heroines making comparisons of the intellectual and moral improvement which they have imparted to each other.[59] □

Simpson thus connects the didactic purpose that he sees in Austen's novels with her treatment of the theme of love.

Sense and Sensibility he regards as having been written with the express purpose of showing that 'sudden passion is not the lasting affection'. Instead, again in *Sense and Sensibility*, he argues that 'true love [is] rather an adjunct of the sober common sense than of the impetuous and passionate side of the soul'. In *Pride and Prejudice*, too, Simpson argues, Austen shows how gratitude and esteem can grow into love, and how this is a much more lasting feeling than what may arise at first sight. Both these novels then demonstrate 'her habitual exaltation of judgment over passion, of the critical over the poetical and imaginative faculties'. While 'this is perhaps even more perceptible in the manifest irony of her whole mass of compositions', it is also obvious in her happy endings. Although she takes great care to bring heroes and heroines together and to marry 'them off happily', she also gives the reader to understand that this is not the only possible ending that would have secured happiness, but that other ways might have made the hero or heroine just as happy.

■ Miss Austen believed in the ultimate possible happiness of every marriage. The most ill-assorted couples may get used to one another. Even Willoughby, the nearest approach to a rascal that her benevolent judgment allowed her to paint, is ultimately not unhappy in a marriage that yoked him with a woman he disliked, and separated him for ever from the only one he loved.[60] □

For Simpson, Austen can be connected to Shakespeare because she, like him, was an ironical critic of her surroundings. This critical mind he sees as the basis of her art, which is never passionate but always well thought through and sober. Even love itself is sober in her novels, as can be seen particularly in *Sense and Sensibility* and *Pride and Prejudice*. The didactic purpose of the novels underlines the dominance of judgment over emotion, as does the message that happiness and comfort in marriage are entirely possible even if the relationship is not based on deep emotion. Yet, while analysing her art extensively and introducing irony to Austen criticism for the first time, Simpson finds it just as important to emphasise Austen's personal, ladylike qualities, and is, in this at least, also following Austen-Leigh's portrait.

Austen's contemporary Walter Scott was immensely highly regarded throughout the nineteenth century, by both critics and lay readers, so that comparison of any author to him, just as to Shakespeare, would also bestow high praise. Where reviewers mention him in articles on Austen, they usually see her as approaching him, possibly exceeding him in some aspects, particularly in her character depictions, but being unable to compete with him on any larger scale. The reviewer in *St Paul's* argues that, because Austen's strength was her satire, too much of her might have a negative effect on readers in that they would not be able to appreciate the world around them properly any more but would have too negative a view. This, he argues, is in stark contrast to the novels of Walter Scott.

■ Her special power lay in the satire of the mean and the ridiculous, and this may serve as an instrument of good, if it succeeds in making the contemptible repulsive. The danger in reading too much of Miss Austen, to the exclusion of other works of fiction, would consist in the low estimate of humanity likely to arise from such a study, and from the starving of the higher imaginative faculties; as the danger in reading too much romance would consist in the undue exaltation of the fancy above the level of ordinary life, in the excitation of desires which this world cannot gratify, and the distaste for the real, which is induced by a yearning after the visionary. The novelist who has best united the true with the ideal, who has achieved the most natural amalgamation of the romantic and the real, is Sir Walter Scott. There is hardly a phase of humanity which he has not touched skilfully; his comprehensive glance travels over distant ages, and far-off lands; he extends to all humanity the hand of good fellowship; he recognises the evil as an offset to the good; he has no varnish for vice, but he has a tenderness for the foibles which he satirises, and a genuine pathos underlies his genial humour. [...] It may be urged with truth that Walter Scott has not produced any one character of such complete reality as the feeble Mr. Woodhouse, the caustic Mr. Bennet, the inane Lady Bertram, the chattering Miss Bates, of Miss Austen; his portraits are less elaborately finished, and reveal themselves with less subtlety than hers; but, then, what an immense gallery of human likenesses he has exhibited. It is not to be denied that some of them are mere sketches, invested with no great personal interest, and this is mostly the case with his lovers, male and female, out of whose perplexities his story is built up; but the larger number are portraits vigorously conceived and executed, showing the true lineaments of humanity; and however Miss Austen may excel in the completeness of her representation of a narrow sphere of existence, Scott's is the fairer interpretation of human life, because he gives true suggestions, if not complete pictures, of all its moods, as they vary, according to the infinite variety of time and circumstance.[61] □

His wide range leads to a more realistic image of the world, even if the individual portraits might be more truthful in Austen's novels. The depiction of a section of one social class at a particular time can never be as relevant and instructive as the depiction of all social classes over centuries. Also, reviewers complain that she can only appeal to the reader's head, not heart, whereas Scott appeals to both reason and emotion.

AUSTEN AND THE VICTORIAN PUBLIC

Reviewers distinguish between the public and critical popularity of Austen. The majority agree that she is well known among critics and writers, but see her public popularity as limited.

Critics who assume that the novels are not widely popular give two main reasons for this. One is that, because the novels' emotional and thematic range is limited, they can never become more popular than they are; the other, usually connected to the first, is that only cultivated people can appreciate Austen's high skill. Oliphant states that 'it is scarcely to be expected that books so calm and cold and keen, and making so little claim upon their sympathy, would ever be popular [with the general public]',[62] since an admirer of Austen's novels needs 'a certain amount of culture and force of observation'.[63] Similarly, the reviewer in the *EWDM* warns that only if 'you can appreciate subtle strokes of character, [...] can take pleasure from fineness of workmanship and have patience to examine it, [did] Miss Austen [...] write for you'.[64] Austen-Leigh in the 1870 *Memoir* introduces R.H. Cheney's notion of seeing it as a 'test of ability, whether people *could* or *could not* appreciate Miss Austen's merits'.[65] While reviewers unanimously regard critical popularity as a sign of high literary quality, some, such as Oliphant and the reviewer in the *EWDM*, see Austen's limited public popularity as evidence of her literary excellence.

Direct statements showing reviewers' belief in Austen's popularity with the public are rare, and only occur after the publication of the second edition of the *Memoir* in 1871. Leslie Stephen, in an article on 'Humour' of 1876, mentions 'Austenolatry',[66] already with its connotations of 'intolerant and dogmatic' readers,[67] which implies professional as well as general readers:

■ I never, for example, knew a person thoroughly deaf to humour who did not worship Miss Austen, or, when her writings were assailed, defend themselves by saying that the assailant had no sense of humour. Miss Austen, in fact, seems to be the very type of that kind of humour which charms one large class of amiable persons; and Austenolatry is perhaps the most intolerant and dogmatic of literary creeds.[68] □

Stephen uses Austen as an example of the kind of humour of which he disapproves, and he deprecates all who have a taste for her kind of humour. He also, however, appears to share the view of her as an 'excessively mild' writer, whose books always stay in a proper but unexciting realm and which contain 'not a single flash of biting satire'.

In the period between 1865 and 1880, then, critics generally agree on Austen's high literary status. The majority believe the public at large not to be well acquainted with Austen, but among 'students of literature' she is both known and valued – though still in a female domain. Even Stephen, who condemns her most of all the reviewers, does not doubt her ability:

■ To deny Miss Austen's marvellous literary skill would be simply to convict oneself of the grossest stupidity. It is probable, however, that as much skill may have been employed in painting a bit of old china as in one of [the] masterpieces [of Raphael (Italian painter and architect, properly Raffaello Sanzio (1483–1520))]. We do not therefore say that it possesses equal merit.[69] □

Most late Victorian reviewers approve of *Sense and Sensibility*, *Pride and Prejudice*, and *Emma*, though the degree of admiration varies between the critics. By the 1870s, Austen's critical status is no longer doubted, though she is not regarded as widely popular with the public, mostly because critics cannot imagine the public warming to novels of so limited a scope. Critics connect Austen's life to her novels, arguing that, because she had such a tranquil life and such a gentle character, her novels cannot but display the same gentleness. Her heroines are linked to her, with the possible exception of Elizabeth, who is deemed too unladylike to represent her author. However, reviewers tend to see Austen as a conscious producer of art, which is a view that is forgotten about in ensuing decades and not picked up again until well into the twentieth century. Victorian reviewers also comment on the lack of passion in Austen's novels. Only Marianne and possibly Darcy display any kind of emotion. This, in combination with the novels' limited social scope, means that Austen can never be a true realist because she only ever depicts one detail. Any kind of grandeur of either feeling or social scope is lacking.

The effects of this view of Austen on early-twentieth-century critical developments, especially the insistence that she was a gentle benevolent woman who wrote just the kind of novels one might expect such a person to produce, will be discussed in the next chapter.

CHAPTER THREE

Early to Mid-Twentieth Century Critical Responses

JANEITES

As we have seen, Victorian critics of Austen largely accepted the image James Edward Austen-Leigh drew of his aunt in the *Memoir*. Her life became central to the interpretation of her works, and in subsequent decades her novels continued to be read through judgments of the woman. Leslie Stephen in his 1876 article already uses the term 'Austenolatry', calling it 'the most intolerant and dogmatic of literary creeds', thereby testifying to the existence of Austen-devotees even before the term 'Janeite' was coined.

The term goes back the literary scholar George Saintsbury, who used it in a preface to an 1894 edition of *Pride and Prejudice*, the novel he 'unhesitatingly' declares his favourite: 'It seems to me the most perfect, the most characteristic, the most eminently quintessential of its author's works',[1] emphasising its humour and its ladylike mild cynicism. Austen always remains the perfect lady in the creation of her characters, and Saintsbury her zealous admirer. Through his praise for both Elizabeth and her author, he takes part in the late-nineteenth-century debate about the 'New Woman', a concept that inspired a number of notorious 'New Woman' novels in the 1890s. The debate – as well as the novels – centred on feminist ideas about women's education, family life, and sexual independence. Saintsbury admires Elizabeth's spirit, but makes sure he clarifies that she is not at all like a 'New Woman'. He also compares her to four other female characters from widely-read nineteenth-century fiction, all of whom he highly esteems, and yet none of them can ultimately compete with Elizabeth in his eyes. These women are Diana Vernon, from Scott's *Rob Roy* (1817); Argemone Lavington, from *Yeast: A Problem* (1850) by Charles Kingsley (1819–75); Beatrix Esmond, from Thackeray's *The History of Henry Esmond* (1852); and Barbara Grant, from *Catriona* (1893) by Robert Louis Stevenson (1850–94).

■ Elizabeth, with nothing offensive, [...] nothing of the 'New Woman' about her, has by nature what the best modern (not 'new') women have by education and experience, a perfect freedom from the idea that all men may bully her if they choose, and that most will run away with her if they can. Though not in the least 'impudent and mannish grown' [Shakespeare, *Troilus and Cressida* (first published 1609), 3.3.210], she has no mere sensibility, no nasty niceness about her. The form of passion common and likely to seem natural in Miss Austen's day was so invariably connected with the display of one or the other, or both of these qualities, that she has not made Elizabeth outwardly passionate. But I, at least, have not the slightest doubt that she would have married Darcy just as willingly without Pemberley as with it, and anybody who can read between lines will not find the lovers' conversations in the final chapters so frigid as they might have looked to the Della Cruscans [group of eighteenth-century sentimental poets] of their own day, and perhaps do look to the Della Cruscans of this.

And, after all, what is the good of seeking for the reason of charm? – it is there. There were better sense in the sad mechanic exercise of determining the reason of its absence where it is not. In the novels of the last hundred years there are vast numbers of young ladies with whom it might be a pleasure to fall in love; there are at least five with whom, as it seems to me, no man of taste and spirit can help doing so. Their names are, in chronological order, Elizabeth Bennet, Diana Vernon, Argemone Lavington, Beatrix Esmond, and Barbara Grant. I should have been most in love with Beatrix and Argemone; I should, I think, for mere occasional companionship, have preferred Diana and Barbara. But to live with and to marry, I do not know that any one of the four can come into competition with Elizabeth.[2] □

Saintsbury is the first self-confessed Janeite, seeing himself as a fervent admirer. By contrast, as Deidre Lynch points out, 'Janeite' is 'now used almost exclusively about and against other people'.[3] The term has now come to designate either 'overzealous and unsophisticated' readers, or 'a cohort of cultural purists, who, likewise transgressing against common sense but in their own way, haughtily find fault with all the nice methods of enacting a devotion to Austen.'[4] Even a hundred years ago, though, in spite of a widespread admiration for Austen and of the connotations of 'Janeite' having been different, there was a broad division between fervent admirers of Austen and her works and just as fervent critics. One such critic was Mark Twain, who enjoyed pronouncing himself an anti-Janeite. In a diary entry for 10 April 1896 he notes: 'Jane Austen's books, too, are absent from this library. Just that one omission alone would make a fairly good library out of a library that hadn't a book in it.' In a letter dated 13 September 1898 he writes, 'I haven't any right to criticise books, and I don't do it except when I hate them. I often want to criticise Jane Austen, but her books madden me so that I can't conceal my frenzy from the reader; and therefore I have to stop every time I begin. Every time I read 'Pride and Prejudice' I want to dig her up and hit her over the skull with her own shin-bone.'

In another letter, dated 18 January 1909, Twain states: 'To me his prose is unreadable – like Jane Austin's [sic]. No, there is a difference. I could read his prose on salary, but not Jane's. Jane is entirely impossible. It seems a great pity to me that they allowed her to die a natural death!'[5]

Apart from giving his opinion, these quotations also testify to the widespread Austen admiration that Twain is writing against.

Another decided anti-Janeite was H.W. Garrod, professor of poetry and Fellow of Merton College Oxford, who famously condemned Austen in his 'Jane Austen: A Depreciation' (1928). In fact, as Claudia Johnson states, his text 'is aimed just as much at male Janeites in the audience as at Austen herself: 'There is a time to be born and a time to die, and a time to be middle-aged and read Miss Austen.' A man content to read novels by 'a mere slip of a girl', as Garrod describes her, must be 'a mere slip of a girl himself'[6] Again, as so often in both nineteenth and twentieth-century Austen criticism, it is her gender that determines a reading of her novels.

Consciousness of Austen being regarded by critics and public as 'everybody's dear Jane' is also obvious in 'The Janeites' (1924), a story by Rudyard Kipling (1865–1936), which not only exposes the extent of the Austen cult, but also gives it a nationalistic dimension, as evident from the epigraph:

■ Jane lies in Winchester—blessed be her shade!
Praise the Lord for making her, and her for all she made!
And while the stones of Winchester, or Milsom Street, remain,
Glory, love, and honour unto England's Jane! □

The story was first published in the journals *Story-Teller*, *MacLean's* and *Hearst's International*, and written after Kipling visited Bath, and had a discussion with George Saintsbury 'about the sense of fellowship felt by people who shared a powerful joint experience – whether fighting in war, or membership of a Mason's Lodge, or even familiarity with the works of an author such as Austen'.[7] This sums up the three main themes of the story: soldiers fighting in the trenches in World War I (Kipling's son John had died in the war in 1915), Freemasonry, and admiration for Austen's works. In the story, she is being read and loved by soldiers of different ranks who form what the shell-shocked veteran Humberstall calls 'the Society of the Janeites'. After a barrage, he is the only surviving 'Janeite', and the story shows him telling two friends about the society in 1920, reading the novels during and after the war, and being rescued by a fellow admirer of Jane's:

■ I expect I must ha' been blown clear of all by the first bomb; for I was the on'y Janeite left. We lost about half our crowd, either under, or after we'd got 'em out. The B.S.M. went off 'is rocker when mornin' came, an' he ran about from one to another sayin' : 'That was a good push! That was a great crowd! Did ye ever know any push to touch 'em?' An' then 'e'd cry. So what was left of us made off for ourselves, an' I came across a lorry, pretty full, but they took me in.'

'Ah!' said Anthony with pride. ''They all take a taxi when it's rainin'.' 'Ever 'eard that song?'

'They went a long way back. Then I walked a bit, an' there was a hospital-train fillin' up, an' one of the Sisters—a grey-headed one—ran at me wavin' 'er red 'ands an' sayin' there wasn't room for a louse in it. I was past carin'. But she went on talkin' and talkin' about the war, an' her pa in Ladbroke Grove, an' 'ow strange for 'er at 'er time of life to be doin' this work with a lot o' men, an' next war, 'ow the nurses 'ud 'ave to wear khaki breeches on account o' the mud, like the Land Girls; an' that reminded 'er, she'd boil me an egg if she could lay 'ands on one, for she'd run a chicken-farm once. You never 'eard anythin' like it—outside o' Jane. It set me off laughin' again. Then a woman with a nose an' teeth on 'er, marched up. 'What's all this?' she says. 'What do you want?' 'Nothing,' I says, 'only make Miss Bates, there, stop talkin' or I'll die.' 'Miss Bates?' she says. 'What in 'Eaven's name makes you call 'er that?' 'Because she is,' I says. 'D'you know what you're sayin'?' she says, an' slings her bony arm round me to get me off the ground. ''Course I do,' I says, 'an' if you knew Jane you'd know too.' 'That's enough,' says she. 'You're comin' on this train if I have to kill a Brigadier for you,' an' she an' an ord'ly fair hove me into the train, on to a stretcher close to the cookers. That beef-tea went down well! Then she shook 'ands with me an' said I'd hit off Sister Molyneux in one, an' then she pinched me an extra blanket. It was 'er own 'ospital pretty much. I expect she was the Lady Catherine de Bourgh of the area. Well, an' so, to cut a long story short, nothing further transpired.' [...]

'Well, as pore Macklin said, it's a very select Society, an' you've got to be a Janeite in your 'eart, or you won't have any success. An' yet he made me a Janeite! I read all her six books now for pleasure 'tween times in the shop; an' it brings it all back—down to the smell of the glue-paint on the screens. You take it from me, Brethren, there's no one to touch Jane when you're in a tight place. Gawd bless 'er, whoever she was.'[8] □

Janeites in the world outside the story were, as Johnson points out, 'decried as escapists retreating to the placidity of Austen's world' and it is here that Kipling's Janeites are different. They do not see Austen mainly as a source of ethics and morality, nor is she, as Johnson puts it, connected to 'a feminine elegiac ideal of England whose very vulnerability is what knightly menfolk must fight to protect'. Instead, Humberstall after the war 'reads Austen's novels not because they help him recover the prior world unshaken by war but precisely because they remind him of the trenches'.[9] Kipling's Janeites are therefore different from the image of real-life Janeites. They do not attempt to argue that their way of reading the novels is the only right one. Kipling's story presumes that its readers will know their Jane Austen and recognise references to individual characters such as Miss Bates. The story also testifies to the extent of Janeitism at the time, as well as hinting at Kipling's own appreciation of Austen.

LITERARY AMATEUR

The Janeites' unbounded admiration for the author was an aspect that was also part of the prevalent mode at the beginning of the twentieth century. Austen was held in esteem and affection, and seen as the benevolent maiden aunt who regarded writing as a leisure pursuit. Foremost literati such as Henry James praised her, and, though he wrote against the 'dear Jane' image, his insistence on her having written without an artistic or technical consciousness, as a natural genius and literary amateur, is still patronising: 'Jane Austen, with all her light felicity, leaves us hardly more curious of her process, or of the experience in her that fed it, than the brown thrush who tells his story from the garden bough.' James judges Austen as being now more popular than ever before, partly owing to her 'her intrinsic merit and interest', partly because of the influence of the 'special bookselling spirit'; he defines the latter in this way:

> ■ an eager, active, interfering force which has a great many confusions of apparent value, a great many wild and wandering estimates, to answer for. For these distinctively mechanical and overdone reactions, of course, the critical spirit, even in its most relaxed mood, is not responsible. Responsible, rather, is the body of publishers, editors, illustrators, producers of the pleasant twaddle of magazines; who have found their 'dear', our dear, everybody's dear, Jane so infinitely to their material purpose, so amenable to pretty reproduction in every variety of what is called tasteful, and in what seemingly proves to be saleable, form.

> I do not, naturally, mean that she would be saleable if we had not more or less – beginning with Macaulay [Thomas Babington Macaulay, (1800–59), British historian, writer and politician], her first slightly ponderous amoroso – lost our hearts to her; but I cannot help seeing her, a good deal, as in the same lucky box as the Brontës – lucky for the ultimate guerdon; a case of popularity (that in especial of the Yorkshire sisters), a beguiled infatuation, a sentimentalized vision, determined largely by the accidents and circumstances originally surrounding the manifestation of the genius – only with the reasons for the sentiment, in this latter connection, turned the

other way. The key to Jane Austen's fortune with posterity has been in part the extraordinary grace of her facility, in fact of her unconsciousness: as if, at the most, for difficulty, for embarrassment, she sometimes, over her work basket, her tapestry flowers, in the spare, cool drawing-room of other days, fell a-musing, lapsed too metaphorically, as one may say, into wool-gathering, and her dropped stitches, of these pardonable, of these precious moments, were afterwards picked up as little touches of human truth, little glimpses of steady vision, little master-strokes of imagination.[10] □

It is thus precisely Austen's unconsciousness that makes her art what it is. In the ongoing debate about Austen's art and her realism James – like the majority of Victorian critics – sees her as a perfectly truthful imitator of nature, but at the same time denies her any conscious artistic skill.

CONSCIOUS ARTIST

The beginning of more serious Austen criticism meant a shift from focusing on her life to focusing on her works. As Nicola Trott puts it, 'a critical stance on Austen was acquired, it might be said, just as the criticism of English literature itself became an academic discipline.'[11] English literature became a university subject around the turn of the century, and Austen was established as part of academic courses. A.C. Bradley's lecture on Austen, first given in 1911 to the women at Newnham College, Cambridge, is, as Southam states, 'generally regarded as the starting-point for the serious academic approach to Jane Austen'.[12] Bradley still writes in admiring tones, (e.g., 'In speaking to you of Jane Austen I must assume, not only that you are familiar with her novels, but that, like myself, you belong to the faithful'),[13] but treats Austen as a serious literary author. Bradley compares her to the essayist, poet, biographer, literary critic and lexicographer Samuel Johnson (1709–84) in her capacities as a moralist, humorist, and artist. While Johnson consciously dispenses with mere sentimentalism and favours a realistic mode of depiction, Austen works in a similar way but is far less conscious of it:

■ There are two distinct strains in Jane Austen. She is a moralist and a humorist. These strains are often blended or even completely fused, but still they may be distinguished. It is the first that connects her with Johnson, by whom, I suspect, she was a good deal influenced. With an intellect much less massive, she still observes human nature with the same penetration and the same complete honesty. She is like him in abstention – no doubt, in her case, much less deliberate – from speculation, and in the orthodoxy and strength of her religion. She is very like him in her contempt for mere sentiment, and for that 'cant' of which Boswell [James Boswell, 9th Laird of Auchinleck (1740–95), friend and biographer of Johnson] was recommended to clear his mind. We remember Johnson in those passages where she refuses to express a deeper concern than she feels for misfortune or grief, and with both there is an occasional touch of brutality in the manner of the refusal. It is a question, however, of manner alone, and when she speaks her mind fully and gravely she speaks for Johnson too; as when she makes Emma say: 'I hope it may be allowed that, if compassion has produced exertion and relief to the sufferers, it has done all that is truly important. If we feel for the wretched enough to do all we can for them, the rest is empty sympathy, only distressing to ourselves' (chapter 10). Finally, like Johnson, she is, in the strict sense, a moralist. Her morality, that is to say, is not merely embodied in her plots, it is often openly expressed. She followed a fashion of the day in her abstract titles, *Sense and Sensibility*, *Pride and Prejudice*, *Persuasion*; but the fashion coincides with the movement of her mind, and she knew very well the main lesson to be drawn from the other three novels. Her explicit statements and comments are often well worth pondering, though their terminology is sometimes old-fashioned, and though her novels contain infinitely more wisdom than they formulate. □

Bradley argues generally that our pleasure in reading Austen derives from the fact that 'we constantly share her point of view, and are aware of the amusing difference between the fact and its appearance to the actors'. The characters are regarded 'with ironical amusement, because they never see the situation as it really is and as she sees it'. Austen differs from a cynic or a satirist in that although she, like them, is 'intellectually pleased by human absurdities and illusions', in addition to this she 'feel[s] them to be good'. To Austen, 'so far as they are not seriously harmful, they are altogether pleasant, because they are both ridiculous and right'. In *Emma*, for example,

■ it is amusing, [...] that Knightley, who is almost a model of good sense, right feeling, and just action, should be unjust to Frank Churchill because, though he does not know it, he himself is in love with Emma: but to Jane Austen that is not only the way a man *is* made, but the way he *should* be made. No doubt there are plenty of things that should not be, but when we so regard them they are not comical. A main point of difference between Jane Austen and Johnson is that to her much more of the world is amusing, and much more of it is right. She is less of a moralist and more of a humorist.[14] □

Apart from his comparison of Austen to Johnson, Bradley links Austen to Shakespeare in the depiction of minor characters like Mr Woodhouse and Miss Bates, who 'resemble one another in being the object equally of our laughter and our unqualified respect and affection'. Overall, he especially commends *Emma,* which 'as a comedy, [is] unsurpassed among novels'.

Reginald Farrer, in his 1917 article in *The Quarterly Review* that marked the centenary of Austen's death, writes in similarly admiring tones but again regards Austen as a serious literary author. He starts off by comparing what he sees as her meagre contemporary popularity with her success now, when he is not alone in relating her to Shakespeare. She was 'obviously ill-served by her contemporaries' and took refuge from the toils of her life in her art. To regard her small scope as ' "limitations" is vain, and based on a misapprehension', since it is not because of the width of her subjects or the loudness of any particular mood that he regards her as 'our greatest artist in English fiction'. Rather, he sees her as standing 'supreme and alone among English writers in [...] a most perfect mastery of her weapons, a most faultless and precise adjustment of means to an end'.

Farrer discusses *Sense and Sensibility* first and finds it does not stand comparison to Austen's later works:

■ With 'Sense and Sensibility' we approach the maturing Jane Austen. But it has the almost inevitable frigidity of a reconstruction, besides an equally inevitable uncertainty in the author's use of her weapons. There are longueurs and clumsinesses; its conviction lacks fire; its development lacks movement; its major figures are rather incarnate qualities than qualitied incarnations. Never again does the writer introduce a character so entirely irrelevant as Margaret Dashwood, or marry a heroine to a man so remote in the story as Colonel Brandon. This is not, however, to say that 'Sense and Sensibility', standing sole, would not be itself enough to establish an author's reputation. [...] But its tremendous successors set up a standard beside which 'Sense and Sensibility' is bound to appear grey and cool; nobody will choose this as his favourite Jane Austen, whereas each one of the others has its fanatics who prefer it above all the rest. □

Pride and Prejudice Farrer regards as 'the greatest miracle of English Literature' and Elizabeth as 'literature's most radiant heroine'. Nevertheless, the novel has faults, which Farrer puts down to the youth of its author.

■ Compare the heavy latinised paragraphs of the crucial quarrel between Darcy and Elizabeth (the sentence which proved so indelible a whip-lash to Darcy's pride is hardly capable of delivery in dialogue at all, still less by a young girl in a tottering passion) with the crisp and crashing exchanges in the parallel scene between Elton and Emma. The later book provides another comparison. Throughout, when once its secret is grasped, the reader is left in no doubt that subconsciously Emma was in love with Knightley all the time. In 'Pride and Prejudice' the author has rather fumbled with an analogous psychological situation, and is so far from making clear the real feeling which underlies Elizabeth's deliberately fostered dislike of Darcy, that she has uncharacteristically left herself open to such a monstrous misreading as Sir Walter Scott's, who believed that Elizabeth was subdued to Darcy by the sight of Pemberley.

Emma is the very climax of Jane Austen's work; and a real appreciation of *Emma* is the final test of citizenship in her kingdom. For this is not an easy book to read; it should never be the beginner's primer, nor be published without a prefatory synopsis. Only when the story has been thoroughly assimilated, can the infinite delights and subtleties of its workmanship begin to be appreciated, as you realise the manifold complexity of the book's web, and find that every sentence, almost every epithet, has its definite reference to equally unemphasised points before and after in the development of the plot. Thus it is that, while twelve readings of 'Pride and Prejudice' give you twelve periods of pleasure repeated, as many readings of 'Emma' give you that pleasure, not repeated only, but squared and squared again with each perusal, till at every fresh reading you feel anew that you never understood anything like the widening sum of its delights. But, until you know the story, you are apt to find its movement dense and slow and obscure, difficult to follow, and not very obviously worth the following. For this is *the* novel of character, and of character alone, and of one dominating character in particular. And many a rash reader, and some who are not rash, have been shut out on the threshold of Emma's Comedy by a dislike of Emma herself.[15] □

The view of Austen as a serious author was confirmed by R.W. Chapman's 1923 scholarly edition of her texts – the first scholarly edition of any British novelist. Again, however, while his edition laid the foundation for critical work on Austen's novels, some of the editorial notes reveal his genteel admiration of her. Several times he addresses the readers of this edition as 'admirers' of 'Miss Austen'.[16] He variously refers to her as 'Jane'[17] or as 'Miss Austen'; in an appendix on 'Miss Austen's English' he writes...

■ Miss Austen's language deserves closer attention than is has received. She is not indeed one of the great writers of English prose of the early nineteenth century; but she is one of the greatest, because one of the most accurate, writers of dialogue of her own or any age; and of the writers of her period who furnish good and abundant specimens of polite conversation, she is today by far the most popular.[18] □

Praising her, but taking her seriously, were also novelists such as E.M. Forster and Virginia Woolf. Forster saw himself as 'a Jane

Austenite', yet gave Austen a literary rather than an amateur status in his review of Chapman's edition of the novels in 1924 in *The Nation and The Athenaeum*. In fact, while he describes the Jane Austenite as unable to see any faults in her novels, Chapman's edition has the merit of 'waking the Jane Austenite up', for example as regards *Pride and Prejudice*:

■ I am a Jane Austenite, and therefore slightly imbecile about Jane Austen. [...] She is my favourite author! I read and re-read, the mouth open and the mind closed. Shut up in measureless content, I greet her by the name of most kind hostess, while criticism slumbers. The Jane Austenite possesses little of the brightness he ascribes so freely to his idol. Like all regular church-goers, he scarcely notices what is being said. [...] He does not notice any flatness in this dialogue from *Pride and Prejudice:* 'Kitty has no discretion in her coughs,' said her father; 'she times them ill.' 'I do not cough for my own amusement,' replied Kitty fretfully. 'When is your next ball to be, Lizzy?' Why should Kitty ask what she must have known? And why does she say 'your' ball when she was going to it herself? Fretfulness would never carry her to such lengths. No, something is amiss in the text; but the loyal adorer will never suspect it. He reads and re-reads. And Mr R.W. Chapman's fine new edition has, among its other merits, the advantage of waking the Jane Austenite up. After reading its notes and appendixes, after a single glance at its illustrations, he will never relapse again into the primal stupor. Without violence, the spell has been broken. The six princesses remain on their sofas, but their eyelids quiver and they move their hands. Their twelve suitors do likewise, and their subordinates stir on the perches to which humour or propriety assigned them. The novels continue to live their own wonderful internal life, but it has been freshened and enriched by contact with the life of facts. [...] Observe his brilliant solution of the [difficulty] quoted above. He has noticed that in the original edition of *Pride and Prejudice* the words 'When is your next ball to be, Lizzy?' began a line, and he suggests that the printer failed to indent them, and, in consequence, they are not Kitty's words at all, but her father's. It is a tiny point, yet how it stirs the pools of complacency! Mr Bennet, not Kitty, is speaking, and all these years one had never known! The dialogue lights up and sends a little spark of fire into the main mass of the novel.[19] □

Woolf, in her review of Chapman's edition, praised Austen as 'the most perfect artist among women' as well as criticising aspects of her works, thus again taking Austen seriously as a writer of literature. While Woolf finds 'the balance of [Austen's] gifts [...] singularly perfect', with no failures among her finished novels, she points out that because of Austen's early death, 'at the height of her powers', we do not know what her later writing would have given us: 'she was still subject to those changes which often make the final period of a writer's career the most interesting of all'.

Woolf speculates that a few more years would have seen Austen famous and would have meant her mixing more in society and experiencing a greater range of life that she had done hitherto, which would have changed what she now believed to be all there was to the complexity of human nature and would therefore have made her yet greater.

■ She would have devised a method, clear and composed as ever, but deeper and more suggestive, for conveying, not only what people say, but what they leave unsaid; not only what they are, but what life is. She would have stood farther away from her characters, and seen them more as a group, less as individuals. Her satire, while it played less incessantly, would have been more stringent and severe. She would have been the forerunner of Henry James and of [Marcel] Proust [1871–1922, French writer and critic] – but enough. Vain are these speculations; [the most perfect artist among women, the writer whose books are immortal], died just as she was beginning to feel confidence in her own success.[20] □

Woolf, like Bradley, Farrer, Chapman, Forster, sees Austen as a serious literary author who was a conscious artist.

NARRATIVE COMPLEXITY

Arguably the most significant part in dispelling the notion of Austen as an inartistic and amateurish writer was played by Mary Lascelles' 1939 study *Jane Austen and her Art*, which again has been regarded, for example by Fiona Stafford, as 'the starting point of serious Austen criticism'.[21] A devout Janeite, Lascelles analysed the structure of the novels and showed their artistic complexities. She also studied Austen's reading, looked at the novels in the context of literary history, and 'by revealing Austen's affinities with Burney, [Alexander] Pope [1688–1744], Richardson and Johnson, Mary Lascelles did much to quash the Jamesian view of Austen as a natural genius (i.e. amateur)'.[22]

Lascelles gives several examples to show Austen's conscious narrative art. One is the role of Mr Collins in *Pride and Prejudice*. He is 'a creature born of his author's youthful fancy in its most hilarious mood', yet he also fulfils a structural purpose:

■ As well as making his own contribution to the story, by the comedy he plays out with Elizabeth and her family and neighbours, he has to draw and hold together Longbourn and Hunsford; to bring Hunsford within range of our imagination awhile before we can be taken there (and incidentally to confirm Elizabeth's ill opinion of every one connected with Darcy), to draw Elizabeth to Hunsford when the time is ripe, and eventually to send Lady Catherine post-haste to Longbourn on her catastrophic visit.[23] □

In a similar vein, Lascelles compares the narrative structure of *Sense and Sensibility* and *Pride and Prejudice* and points out that 'even those characters in Jane Austen's novels which might be expected to sit very loosely to the story cannot be studied without reference to it – closer reference as her technique develops'.

■ Certain resemblances and differences between *Sense and Sensibility* and *Pride and Prejudice* illustrate her love and care for nice symmetry in the ground-plan of her stories, and her workmanship in the contrivance of it. [...] There is nothing inconsequent about the plan of *Sense and Sensibility*; in fact, it is a little stiff. [...] There they all stand, formally grouped as for a dance: Marianne and her mother (supported as they imagine by Willoughby) challenging Elinor; while behind Elinor are ranged not merely Edward and Colonel Brandon with their sad moderation, but also the good-humoured worldling, Mrs. Jennings, whose crude raillery comes at length to seem almost like frank common sense, set over against Marianne's excessive sensitiveness and reticence. And this antithetic pattern appears to have imposed itself on all the characters, giving us those capriciously contrasted pairs, the Middletons and the Palmers.

This symmetry is emphasized by the way in which the similarity in the fortunes of Elinor and Marianne points the central opposition, between their tempers and opinions. [...]

Pride and Prejudice is no less deliberately shaped; its pattern shows an equal delight in the symmetry of correspondence and antithesis; but there is a notable difference in the contrivance. This pattern is formed by diverging and converging lines, by the movement of two people who are impelled apart until they reach a climax of mutual hostility, and thereafter bend their courses towards mutual understanding and amity. It is a pattern very common in fiction, but by no means easy to describe plausibly.[24] □

We only get to see Elizabeth's course as a continuous line. 'Elizabeth's chief impetus is due to Wickham; but there is hardly a character in the story who contributes no momentum to it, nor any pressure from without to which she does not respond characteristically.' Lascelles outlines how 'all follows plausibly' from Darcy's and Elizabeth's first meeting: Elizabeth being flattered by Wickham and therefore believing him implicitly, how circumstances seem to confirm rather than dispel this, and how then, 'even when the climax of mutual exasperation is reached, Elizabeth's criticism of Darcy meets some response in his consciousness, his statement of his objections to her family means something to her; and the way is open for each to consider anew the actions and character of the other.' The Pemberley visit adds to the revised impression the two main characters have of each other; it shows 'him at his best on his own estate (a piece of nice observation), and [her] among congenial companions'. Overall, then, Lascelles argues, Darcy's and Elizabeth's better understanding of each other 'had sprung from the very nature of the misunderstanding, from the interaction of character and circumstance'.

Andrew Wright's 1953 close reading of the novels is one of the many studies inspired by Lascelles' work. As Trott points out, Austen's realism tended to be far more emphasised than her artistry, and twentieth-century critics such as Wright have tried 'to redress the balance, often through detailed attention to style or structure'.[25] Similarly to Lascelles, Wright emphasises the structural and character complexities of the novels. With regard to *Sense and Sensibility*, he states that 'the first volume has a symmetrical perfection seldom achieved by Jane Austen or anyone else':

■ So far as the two girls are concerned, there is a clear parallel drawn between the attentions paid them by Edward Ferrars and by John Willoughby. [...] And so ends the first volume. Marianne has had a first and exciting attachment, which has not yet run its course – so has Elinor. In a very superficial way the behaviour of the two sisters is strongly contrasted; but in a profounder sense both sisters are stirred by their respective suitors. Marianne has yet to learn sense, but already the sensibility of Elinor has been awakened. The elder sister may still be able to give counsels of sense; but she has already tasted the values of sensibility. □

Wright goes on to outline the structure of the remainder of the novel. Once Marianne hears the news of Willoughby's engagement, her experience 'exactly parallels Elinor's'. It is when Marianne realises about this parallelism by finding out about Lucy's and Edward's engagement that she can compare her behaviour to that of her sister. She thus learns about 'her sister's fortitude in facing life' and she is able to recover from the Willoughby affair, so that 'her illness leads her to reflect on the impetuosity of her behaviour'. Wright also considers the novel's moral:

■ We are forced to ask ourselves which mode Jane Austen chooses. Does sense solve every problem, does sense deal adequately with life? Elinor, the apotheosis of sense, shows us that it does not: she is not saved the miseries of despair, though outwardly she is able to bear them with greater composure than her sister; she does not make a *mariage de convenance*, but a marriage of love to a far from wealthy clergyman. Marianne, on the other hand, over-compensates for her early want of sense by making a perhaps too eminently sensible marriage. And the 'lesson' of the book is that neither mode is adequate, each contradicts the other – and there is no happy medium.[26] □

REGULATED HATRED

Wright wrote in the 1950s – in the 1930s and 1940s, the dominant view of Austen was still of a benevolent aunt who regarded writing as a pastime and did not aim at producing art. Though there were critical appreciations alongside this, the majority of approaches shared an immense admiration of Austen. Against the prevailing unconditional esteem of the author, D.W. Harding and Marvin Mudrick set their view of Austen as an ungentle writer, critical of her society and readership. In their undeferential approaches they read the texts as brimming with biting irony and 'regulated hatred', and saw her as using this as a defence against her society. They thus turned Austen into an isolated, archetypal modern figure.

Harding argued in his essay 'Regulated Hatred: An Aspect of the Work of Jane Austen' (1940) that the widespread view of Austen was deceptive. He sees the view of Austen as 'expressing the gentler virtues of a civilized social order' and being 'a delicate satirist' who gently mocked the amiable flaws of the people around her as 'seriously misleading'. Yet it is exactly the widespread belief in this false impression of Austen that is part of her multifaceted aim: 'her books are, as she meant them to be, read by precisely the sort of people whom she disliked; she is a literary classic of the society which attitudes like hers, held widely enough, would undermine.'[27] To maintain this misleading image of her, readers would have to misread the novels, but, he argues, Austen took care 'that misreading should be the easiest thing in the world'.[28] A professional psychologist, Harding interlinked her life with her novels to show how she disliked and subverted the society she lived in and wrote for.

■ Jane Austen seems to be on perfectly good terms with the public she is addressing and to have no reserve in offering the funniness and virtues of Mr Woodhouse and Miss Bates to be judged by the accepted standards of the public. She invites her readers to be just their natural patronizing selves. But this public that Jane Austen seems on such good terms with has some curious things said about it, not criticisms, but small notes of fact that are usually not made. They almost certainly go unnoticed by many readers, for they involve only the faintest change of tone from something much more usual and acceptable. □

Harding gives numerous examples, often from *Emma*, which he sees as putting the author's criticism forward more 'quietly and undisguisedly' than the earlier novels. For instance, the description of Miss Bates as enjoying 'a most uncommon degree of popularity for a woman neither young, handsome, rich, nor married', Harding calls 'fairly conventional satire'. The next sentence however, he argues, must have been misunderstood by the majority of readers: Miss Bates 'had no intellectual superiority to make atonement to herself, or frighten those who might hate her into outward respect'. He links Miss Bates to Austen herself, who by the time she wrote *Emma* was 'neither young, handsome, rich, nor married', so that for Harding 'the passage perhaps hints at the functions which her unquestioned intellectual superiority may have had for her':

■ This eruption of fear and hatred into the relationships of everyday social life is something that the urbane admirer of Jane Austen finds distasteful. [...] And it has the effect, for the attentive reader, of changing the flavour of the more ordinary satire amongst which it is embedded. [...] To speak of this aspect of her work as 'satire' is perhaps misleading. She has none of the underlying didactic intention ordinarily attributed to the satirist. Her object is not missionary; it is the more desperate one of merely finding some mode of existence for her critical attitudes. To her the first necessity was to keep on reasonably good terms with the associates of her everyday life; she had a deep need for their affection and a genuine respect for the ordered, decent civilization they upheld. And yet she was sensitive to their crudenesses and complacencies and knew that her real existence depended on resisting many of the values they implied. The novels gave her a way out of this dilemma. This, rather than the ambition of entertaining a posterity of urbane gentlemen, was her motive force in writing.

As a novelist, therefore, part of her aim was to find the means for unobtrusive spiritual survival. [...] She found, of course, that one of the most useful peculiarities of her society was its willingness to remain blind to the implications of a caricature. She found people eager to laugh at faults they tolerated in themselves and their friends, so long as the faults were exaggerated and the laughter 'good-natured' – so long, that is, as the assault on society could be regarded as a mock assault and not genuinely disruptive. Satire such as this is obviously a means not of admonition but of self-preservation. □

Harding does not see this aspect of Austen as limited to *Emma*. He argues that *Pride and Prejudice* also shows up links between Austen's life and novels:

■ The implications of her caricatures as criticism of real people in real society is brought out in the way they dovetail into their social setting. The decent, stodgy Charlotte puts up cheerfully with Mr Collins as a husband; and Elizabeth can never quite become reconciled to the idea that her friend is the wife of her comic monster. And that, of course, is precisely the sort of idea that Jane Austen herself could never grow reconciled to. The people she hated were tolerated, accepted, comfortably ensconced in the only human society she knew; they were, for her, society's embarrassing unconscious comment on itself. [...] Charlotte's complaisance [...] is shown as a considered indifference to personal relationships when they conflict with cruder advantages in the wider social world.[29] □

Harding links Charlotte's situation to Austen herself, who 'spent a night of psychological crisis in deciding to revoke her acceptance of an "advantageous" proposal made the previous evening'. Her letters, too, testify to her convictions. And, after all, Elizabeth does not break with her friend because of the marriage. Charlotte is the kind of friend 'that went to make up the available social world which one could neither escape materially nor be independent of psychologically'.

Marvin Mudrick similarly sees Austen as critical of her society and as using irony as a defence mechanism against it. Like Harding, he connects Austen to her heroines, which allows him to see Austen as both an artist and a realist. Regarding Elizabeth as reflecting and illustrating Austen's views means he can emphasise the importance of social context for both heroine and author:

■ Elizabeth shares her author's characteristic response of comic irony, defining incongruities without drawing them into a moral context; and, still more specifically, Elizabeth's vision of the world as divided between the simple and the intricate is, in *Pride and Prejudice* at any rate, Jane Austen's vision also. This identification between the author and her heroine establishes, in fact, the whole ground pattern of judgment in the novel. The first decision we must make about anyone, so Elizabeth suggests and the author confirms by her shaping commentary, is not moral but psychological, not whether he is good or bad, but whether he is simple or intricate: whether he may be disposed of as fixed and predictable or must be recognized as variable, perhaps torn between contradictory motives, intellectually or emotionally complex, unsusceptible to a quick judgment. □

Mudrick sees *Pride and Prejudice* in contrast to its predecessor *Sense and Sensibility*. He argues that Austen yielded to 'the moral pressures inevitable upon a woman of her time and class' by restricting both Elinor's and Marianne's powers of distinguishing personalities. Elinor can only make the 'solemn and easy discriminations of bourgeois morality', and Marianne's more perceiving mind is finally suppressed.

■ In *Pride and Prejudice*, however, there is no compulsion – personal, thematic, or moral – toward denying the heroine her own powers of judgment. There is, on the contrary, a thematic need for the heroine to display a subtle, accurate, perceiving mind. In *Pride and Prejudice*, as in the previous novels, Jane Austen deals with the distinction between false moral values and true;

but she is also dealing here with a distinction antecedent to the moral judgment – the distinction between the simple personality, unequipped with that self-awareness which alone makes choice seem possible, and the complex personality, whose most crucial complexity is its awareness, of self and others. This distinction, which in her youthful defensive posture Jane Austen has tended to make only between her characters and herself, she here establishes internally, between two categories of personality within the novel. The distinction is, in fact, one that every character in *Pride and Prejudice* must make if he or she can; and the complex characters – Elizabeth and Darcy among them – justify their complexity by making it, and trying to live by its implications, through all their lapses of arrogance, prejudice, sensuality, and fear. Elizabeth is aware because, in the novel's climate of adult decision, she must be so to survive with our respect and interest. □

But, Mudrick argues, Elizabeth has yet to learn that 'the distinction must be made in a social setting'. Human beings are part of their social environment, and the impact of this on each character is stronger than Elizabeth at first realises. Like Harding, Mudrick cites Charlotte's marriage to Mr Collins to illustrate this point:

■ The two girls have been good friends. Charlotte, according to the author, is a 'sensible, intelligent young woman', and she shares Elizabeth's taste for raillery and social generalization. Even when Charlotte offers her altogether cynical views on courtship and marriage, Elizabeth refuses to take her at her word. [...]

It is not that Elizabeth misjudges Charlotte's capabilities, but that she underestimates the strength of the pressures acting upon her. Charlotte is twenty-seven, unmarried, not pretty, not well-to-do, living in a society which treats a penniless old maid less as a joke than as an exasperating burden upon her family. But Elizabeth is inexperienced enough, at the beginning, to judge in terms of personality only. She recognizes Mr. Collins' total foolishness and Charlotte's intelligence, and would never have dreamed that any pressure could overcome so natural an opposition. Complex and simple, aware and unaware, do not belong together – except that in marriages made by economics they often unite, however obvious the mismatching. [...]

Elizabeth's continual mistake is to ignore, or to set aside as uninfluential, the social context. It is a question not merely of individuals and marriage, but of individuals and marriage in an acquisitive society. Elizabeth expects nothing except comfort or amusement from simplicity; but she likes to believe that complexity means a categorically free will, without social distortion or qualification.[30] □

Similarly to Harding, Mudrick shows up the connection between heroines and author especially when judging events in society. In his discussion of *Emma*, he links the heroine's 'offhand cruelty' to 'the malice of Jane Austen, the candid Jane Austen of the letters' (Mudrick on *Emma*, pp.116–17). Citing the example of Austen joking about the death of an acquaintance ('Only think of Mrs Holder's being dead! Poor woman, she has done the only thing in the world she could possibly do to make one cease to abuse her'), he argues that Emma, too, exhibits no tenderness. On Mrs Churchill's death she comments: 'Goldsmith tells us, that when lovely woman stoops to folly, she has nothing to do but to die; and when she stoops to be disagreeable, it is equally to be recommended as a clearer of ill fame.'

Both Harding and Mudrick thus find Austen herself critical, even hateful, of the society she lived in, and see this reflected in her novels, particularly in her heroines' attitude to their world.

ART AND MORALITY

Q.D. Leavis again emphasised the importance of seeing Austen as a serious literary author. She, too, expressed the sense of writing critically against a mass of unintelligent readings of Austen, a stance that was also taken up by F.R. Leavis when allocating her a place in his *The Great Tradition* (1954) among the four who, for him, are the truly great English novelists: Jane Austen, George Eliot, Henry James and Joseph Conrad (1857–1924).

Leavis wrote partly against the Janeite attitudes of Lord David Cecil. In his Leslie Stephen Lecture of 1936, delivered at Cambridge, Cecil voices his admiration for Austen, talking, in Brian Southam's terms, as 'a devotee addressing his fellow-devotees'.[31] To him, 'Jane Austen, it would appear, did not take her work over-seriously'.[32] Cecil rephrases the 'Cheney test', which Austen-Leigh had introduced in the 1870 *Memoir*, according to which it was a 'test of ability, whether people *could* or *could not* appreciate Miss Austen's merits',[33] for the 1930s:

■ There are those who do not like [Austen]; as there are those who do not like sunshine or unselfishness. But the very nervous defiance with which they shout their dissatisfaction shows that they know they are a despised minority. All discriminating critics admire her books, most educated readers enjoy them; her fame, of all English novelists, is the most secure.[34] □

Leavis, as Claudia Johnson remarks, 'dignifies Austen and the great tradition of fiction she originated by insisting on her moral seriousness; accordingly, the leisured enjoyment of Janeites – with their fondness for entertainment, character, and comedy – is hateful to him'.[35] In contrast, however, to anti-Janeites such as Twain, Leavis – similarly to

Harding – nevertheless admires Austen. He insists on her combination of art, life, and moral significance:

■ Jane Austen's plots, and her novels in general, were put together very 'deliberately and calculatedly' (if not 'like a building'). But her interest in 'composition' is not something to be put over against her interest in life; nor does she offer an 'aesthetic value' that is separable from moral signifi- cance. The principle of organization, and the principle of development, in her work is an intense moral interest of her own in life that is in the first place a preoccupation with certain problems that life compels on her as personal ones. She is intelligent and serious enough to be able to impersonalize her moral tensions as she strives, in her art, to become more fully conscious of them, and to learn what, in the interests of life, she ought to do with them. Without her intense moral preoccupation she wouldn't have been a great novelist. □

Leavis sees this combination of art and moral interest as making Austen 'the first modern novelist': 'Jane Austen, in fact, is the inaugurator of the great tradition of the English novel'. He goes on to show that all novelists in that great tradition are concerned with three main issues: with form, with giving a convincing picture of life, and with combin- ing the first two points with moral significance:

■ The great novelists in that tradition are all very much concerned with 'form'; they are all very original technically, having turned their genius to the working out of their own appropriate methods and procedures. [...] As a matter of fact, when we examine the formal perfection of *Emma*, we find that it can be appreciated only in terms of the moral preoccupations that characterize the novelist's peculiar interest in life. Those who suppose it to be an 'aesthetic matter', a beauty of 'composition' that is combined, miraculously, with 'truth to life', can give no adequate reason for the view that *Emma* is a great novel, and no intelligent account of its perfection of form. It is in the same way true of the other great English novelists, [...] they are all distinguished by a vital capacity for experience, a kind of reverent openness before life, and a marked moral intensity.[36] □

This view of Austen as inherently moral, as dealing with human nature and as such being timelessly relevant, was shared by Lionel Trilling. Trilling differed, however, from Leavis in defending Austen against Harding and Mudrick by insisting on the novels' world as idyllic and by going against Mudrick's version of her as 'a writer who may be admired for her literary achievement, but who is not to be loved'.[37] As regards *Emma*, he stresses the characters' goodness:

■ So in *Emma* Jane Austen contrives an idyllic world, or the closest approxi- mation of an idyllic world that the genre of the novel will permit, and brings into contrast with it the actualities of the social world, of the modern self. In the precincts of Highbury there are no bad people, and no adverse judgments to be made. Only a modern critic, Professor Mudrick, would think to call Mr Woodhouse an idiot and an old woman: in the novel he is called 'the kindhearted, polite old gentleman'. Only Emma, with her modern consciousness, comes out with it that Miss Bates is a bore, and only Emma can give herself to the thought that Mr Weston is *too* simple and openhearted, that he would be a 'higher character' if he were not quite so friendly with everyone. It is from outside Highbury that the peculiarly modern traits of insincerity and vulgarity come, in the person of Frank Churchill and Mrs Elton. With the exception of Emma herself, every person in Highbury lives in harmony and peace – even Mr Elton would have been all right if Emma had let him alone! – and not merely because they are simple and undeveloped: Mr Knightley and Mrs Weston are no less innocent than Mr Woodhouse and Miss Bates. If they please us and do not bore us by perfection of manner and feeling which is at once lofty and homely, it is because we accept the assumptions of the idyllic world which they inhabit – we have been led to believe that man may actually live in harmony and peace with himself and the external world.[38] □

Trilling thus sees *Emma* as exhibiting an idyllic world, and argues that it is precisely this overarching feeling of benevolence and harmony that distinguishes Austen's novels.

Whether Janeite or anti-Janeite, regarding Austen as a serious literary figure, focusing on her irony and seeing it as self-defence, or emphasising Austen the moralist, critics in the first half of the twentieth century tend to apply an essentially ahistorical approach. They focus on formal analysis of the novels in the New Criticism mode, with Austen's literary context and her personal character traits occasionally featuring. As will be discussed in the next chapter, a reading of Austen's texts within their historical, social, political, and cultural contexts was yet to come.

CHAPTER FOUR

Later Twentieth-Century Critical Responses: Feminism

In the last fifty years, *Sense and Sensibility*, *Pride and Prejudice*, and *Emma* have provoked more criticism than ever before. Generally, Austen criticism has gone along with the respective larger critical movements in each decade, from New Criticism, Formalism and Structuralism to New Historicism, Feminism and postcolonial readings. While critics writing in the 1960s to 1980s tend to focus on style and form, looking at a text as an aesthetic object, more recent discussions see the text within its original political and social contexts, and connect the text to the author's biography. While there are obviously exceptions, most studies follow the trends of their period, and can therefore be broadly placed into the categories 'earlier', i.e. 1960s to 1980s, and 'later', i.e. 1980s to 2000s.

For the purposes of this Guide, various kinds of critical writings have been considered alongside one another, although there are conceptual differences between them as well as differences in terms of intended readerships. Since the Guide surveys Austen criticism generally, no differentiation has been made between book-length studies, articles, and essays that appear as introductions to editions of the Austen novels. Introductory essays differ from book-length and article-length studies in that they often seek to serve two functions that most critical studies do not need to address – an introduction to the text and an introductory assessment of some criticism – although introductions to recent editions, in particular, often appear more like argumentative essays than ones addressed to first-time readers.

Feminism has been very influential in Austen studies; more so, perhaps, than with many other authors, since Austen was not only herself a woman but also centrally concerned with the lot of women. The biggest change between studies of the 1960s–70s and the 1980s–90s can therefore be directly related to the rise of feminism, both as a political and social movement and as an approach to literature. Earlier studies of Austen's texts tend not to address gender at all, whereas later studies deal with it in depth and connect most other issues to this theme: as a woman, Austen is seen as having necessarily engaged in contemporary feminist debates. Claire Tomalin states in her biography of Austen that 'nobody could live through the 1790s without being aware of [...] *A Vindication of the Rights of Woman*'[1] by the novelist, essayist, educational writer and early feminist Mary Wollstonecraft (1759–97). Yet, as William St Clair has since argued, given the small numbers of copies produced, not many women readers would have had direct access to Wollstonecraft's *Vindication*.[2] Nevertheless, knowledge of Wollstonecraft's ideas is presupposed in many feminist essays. Where Austen is seen as aware of her context, her texts are regarded as participating in contemporary debates.

HERO EDUCATING HEROINE

Scholars writing in the 1960s to 1980s often see the Austen heroine as being educated by the wiser hero. The writer and editor Ronald Blythe (born 1922) in his 1966 introduction to *Emma* sees Knightley as the protector and corrector that Emma needs, as the perfect English gentleman:

■ Mr Knightley is the timeless Englishman, the real thing, modest, unaffected, somewhat inadequate of speech (loquacity is not a masculine virtue in England), just intelligent but not intellectual, loving rather than lover-like, and *landed*. Mr Woodhouse found Frank Churchill 'not quite the thing' and so he would nearly all the gentleman heroes of English fiction. [...] But Mr Knightley *is* the thing. The total acceptability of his status hasn't shifted a fraction since Jane Austen invented him and the success of the novel rests confidently on his broad shoulders. It is noticeable that he takes a precedence over Mr Woodhouse. [...] 'You might not see one in a hundred, with '*gentleman*' so plainly written in', says Emma. His late call on Emma on Miss Taylor's wedding day is casual and gossipy on the surface but beneath the slightly bantering exchange of news vital springs of warmth flood up into the narrative. He is dangerously at home. He has 'walked in' long past the calling hour. He quenches Mr Woodhouse's maudlin solicitudes without snubs. He employs patience and tact easily and never with any sense of having to resort to them. He is well-balanced but not dull; things are what they are and not what they seem when he is present. He has a bluntness which is both sexually aggressive and attractive. [...]

There is a sense of his having shown her right from wrong ever since she was a little girl. He knows the world and she does not – although she doesn't hesitate to exercise her right to rule it. She has not been to school. She has never seen the sea; it is one of her ambitions. ('Thy sea is rarely any use to any body' was her father's opinion.) She hasn't even been to Box Hill, which is only seven miles from Highbury. And when Jane Fairfax plays the piano she is forced to recognize the difference between art and pastime. Such isolation, social, cultural and moral, might already have proved disastrous were it not for Mr Knightley, whose native intelligence and natural goodness have constantly protected her. All the same, Emma's womanhood has been touched off by this wedding [between Miss Taylor and Mr Weston] and Mr Knightley senses this with a mixture of pleasure and fear.[3] □

Blythe thus not only sees Knightley as being responsible for Emma's development towards maturity but also argues that 'the success of the novel rests confidently on his broad shoulders'. While Emma is seen as having to realise her faults, there is no indication of Knightley having to develop at all. Similarly, the novelist and critic David Lodge (born 1935) in his 1971 introduction to the same novel sees Knightley as perfect:

■ How does Jane Austen make us like [Emma]? First of all, by narrating the story very largely from her point of view. We see most of the action through Emma's eyes and this naturally has the effect of making us identify with her interests and of mitigating the errors of her vision – since we *experience* those errors with her, and to some extent share them. Indeed, so powerful is the pull of sympathy exerted by this narrative method, that checks and balances have to be introduced in the form of discreet authorial comments and well-timed interventions from Mr. Knightley. Knightley is the nearest thing to a paragon of virtue in the novel, but Jane Austen has carefully prevented any *female* character from filling the same role and thus putting her heroine in the shade.[4] □

By contrast, Terry Castle (born 1953), who belongs to the later group of critics, in her 1995 essay on *Emma* regards the heroine as fallible, and as coming to recognise her faults, but not as having to be educated by Knightley; instead, Emma and Knightley are equals who are both improved by each other. Emma is 'delightful yet fallible', convinced she understands her world and everyone in it, including herself. Yet, as Castle puts it, 'the central comedy of the book will result from seeing how often this would-be oracle is mistaken', especially as regards love matters, and especially as regards her own heart, so that she is also 'her own victim'. Castle does not immediately see Emma's development as a consequence of Mr Knightley's influence: 'As she comes, over the course of the novel, to recognize her own desires, her own intellectual narcissism will suffer a shock – but end up the better for it.' Castle argues that, for Austen, Emma and Knightley are ideal because they are a couple that is not only good for itself but also contributes to the good of the community, in contrast to couples such as Frank Churchill and Jane Fairfax: 'Austen shows herself deeply suspicious of couples who shut out the rest of the world or pretend to a kind of superior knowledge. She is hostile towards antisocial human pairings.' But Emma and Knightley integrate themselves into the social community:

■ A distinction might be made here between knowingness and what used (in simpler days) to be called wisdom. *Emma* has its knowing couples, but it also has its wise couples – or at least its couples on the way to becoming wise. Emma and Knightley are the most important among the potentially 'wise couples' of course, though Austen also presents the recently married Mr and Mrs Weston (Frank's father and Emma's beloved former governess, Miss Taylor) in a similarly favourable light. Characterizing each of these 'wise' pairings is a kind of positive dynamism: not only do the partners ultimately bring out the best in each other – Emma and Knightley will both be improved by their relationship – their bond in some fashion proves beneficial to others as well as to themselves. The most striking proof of this moral synergy [working together with a beneficial effect] occurs at the end of the novel when Emma and her new husband – at some expense to their own privacy and comfort – decide not to move to Mr Knightley's house, Donwell, but to stay at Hartfield so as not to discompose Emma's father, the invalid Mr Woodhouse. But Austen hints at it earlier too, as in the scene in which Emma and Mr Knightley end their argument over Harriet Smith by playing together with the infant daughter of John and Isabella Knightley. Throughout *Emma* infants and children will figure as living emblems of a world beyond the self. Those who care for them are honoured. Thus when we see Emma and Knightley here together, taking turns at delighting a happy little eight-month-old girl – he will at one point take the baby from Emma's arms 'with all the unceremoniousness of perfect amity' – we have an intimation indeed of the larger good their union portends.[5] □

In contrast to Blythe's and Lodge's earlier view, Castle sees both Emma and Knightley as contributing to each other's development. Also, she makes a point about Emma's intelligence and how it is this, in combination with Emma's mistakes, that amuses the reader.

■ Our vanity is engaged because we can almost hear Austen addressing us *sotto voce*: you and I know just how *wrong* Emma is. Intensifying the feeling of pleasure is in turn the fact of Emma's own intelligence and undeniable (if erratic) moral charm. Austen's novel would not be half so delightful were it retitled *Harriet* and told from Harriet Smith's somewhat befuddled point of view. Gaffes committed by the unintelligent do not, on the whole, amuse us for very long: the spectacle of human error, unenlivened by mental energy, quickly becomes merely tedious or depressing. What truly entertains, on contrary, is the folly of the superior individual – and the more exorbitant the folly the better. We enjoy Emma because she is smart and she is good; but we positively dote on her mistakes, because they allow us to feel superior. At moments of maximum comic absurdity – Emma's farcical coach ride with Mr Elton, for example, or the scene in which the besotted Harriet shares with Emma her precious 'relicks' of Frank Churchill (a grubby sticking plaster and a piece of an old pencil 'without any lead') we seem indeed to gaze down at Austen's heroine from some lofty and pleasant comic Olympus [seat of the Greek Gods].[6] □

In Castle's view, the success of the novel rests on Emma's character, with all its faults, rather than on Knightley's gentlemanly perfection. The focus on the heroine, and the new view of the relationship between hero and heroine, is connected to the aspect that generally most interests later critics: the novels' implications about women and for women, including the advancement of women writers into literary canons, cultural constructions of femininity as revealed in literary texts, women as authors, and women as readers. By making critics more alert to gender issues the rise of feminism has thus substantially altered the perception of *Emma*.

FEMALE SUBMISSION

Sandra M. Gilbert (born 1936) and Susan Gubar (born 1944) in their pioneering *The Madwoman in the Attic* (1979) discuss Austen's situation as a woman novelist as well as how the depiction of her heroines reflects her opinions about women's social position. Austen emerges as a largely conservative, patriarchal writer, yet nevertheless as one who was limited by her circumstances because of her gender – and shows her heroines to be so. She depicts the necessity for women to endorse the status quo, but also the psychological damage this inflicts on them.

■ Aware that male superiority is far more than a fiction, [Austen] always defers to the economic, social, and political power of men as she dramatizes how and why female survival depends on gaining male approval and protection. All the heroines who reject inadequate fathers are engaged in a search for better, more sensitive men who are, nevertheless, still the representatives of authority. [...] Whereas becoming a man means proving or testing oneself or earning a vocation, becoming a woman means relinquishing achievement and accommodating oneself to men and the spaces they provide.

Dramatizing the necessity of female submission for female survival, Austen's story is especially flattering to male readers because it describes the taming not just of any woman but specifically of a rebellious, imaginative girl who is amorously mastered by a sensible man. No less than the blotter literally held over the manuscript on her writing desk, Austen's cover story of the necessity for silence and submission reinforces women's subordinate position in a patriarchal culture. [...] Undoubtedly a useful acknowledgment of her own ladylike submission and her acquiescence to masculine values, this plot also allows Austen to consider her own anxiety about female assertion and expression, to dramatize her doubts about the possibility of being both a woman and a writer. She describes both her own dilemma and, by extension, that of all women who experience themselves as divided, caught in the contradiction between their status as human beings and their vocation as females.[7] □

As regards *Sense and Sensibility*, *Pride and Prejudice* and *Emma*, Gilbert and Gubar come up with two main arguments: the first is the contrast between the two heroines in each novel. One heroine (Elinor Dashwood, Jane Bennet and Jane Fairfax) is docile, reserved and identifies with the 'civil falsehoods' of society; the other (Marianne Dashwood, Elizabeth Bennet, Emma Woodhouse) is imaginative, witty, satirical but eventually 'humiliated, even bullied, into sense'.[8]

Marianne is depicted as imaginative and emotional, admiring nature's beauty and 'impatient with the polite lies of civility'. However, her enthusiasm, although attractive to the reader, is 'always shown to be a sign of immaturity, of a refusal to submit':

■ Finally this [refusal] is unbecoming and unproductive in women, who must exert their inner resources for pliancy, elasticity of spirit, and accommodation. *Sense and Sensibility* is an especially painful novel to read because Austen herself seems caught between her attraction to Marianne's sincerity and spontaneity, while at the same identifying with the civil falsehoods and the reserved, polite silences of Elinor, whose art is fittingly portrayed as the painting of screens.[9] □

In *Pride and Prejudice,* Gilbert and Gubar see the same pairing as in the previous novel, this time between Jane and Elizabeth. Like its predecessor, this novel 'continues to associate the perils of the imagination with the pitfalls of selfhood, sexuality, and assertion'. Elizabeth is witty, 'talkative, satirical, quick at interpreting appearances and articulating judgments'. This contrasts with Jane, who is 'quiet, unwilling to express her needs or desires, supportive of all and critical of none';[10] she is docile, gentle and benevolent and yet suffers for the duration of the whole novel until she is finally rescued by Bingley. While submission to male authority seems the only way a heroine can survive, and marriage the only aim possible, Austen yet 'succeeds in maintaining her double consciousness in fiction that proclaims its docility and restraint even as it uncovers the delights of assertion and rebellion'.[11] The duplicity of Austen's happy endings thus again becomes clear, since the implication here is that 'a girl without the aid of a benevolent narrator would never find a way out of either her mortifications or her parents' house'.[12] At the same time as showing their mortifications and the necessity for submission, Austen celebrates the 'desire for free assertion'[13] and the imagination Emma, Elizabeth and Marianne share.

The same pairing of one quiet and one imaginative heroine is again taken up in *Emma*, with Jane Bennet foreshadowing Jane Fairfax and Elizabeth sharing much with Emma. Furthermore, Gilbert and Gubar see Emma as 'an avatar of Austen the artist', and, as such, as demonstrating 'Austen's ambivalence about her imaginative powers'.

■ More than all the other playful, lively girls, Emma reminds us that the witty woman is responding to her own confining situation with words that become her weapon, a defense against banality, a way of at least *seeming* to control her life. Like Austen, Emma has at her disposal worn-out, hackneyed stories of romance that she is smart enough to resist in her own life. If Emma is an artist who manipulates people as if they were characters in her own stories, Austen emphasizes not only the immorality of this activity, but its cause or motivation: except for placating her father, Emma has nothing to do. Given her intelligence and imagination, her impatient attempts to transform a mundane reality are completely understandable. [...] Yet Austen could not punish her more thoroughly than she does, and in this respect too Emma resembles the other imaginative girls. For all these heroines are mortified, humiliated, even bullied into sense. Austen's heavy attack on Emma, for instance, depends on the abject failure of the girl's wit. The very brilliant and assertive playfulness that initially marks her as a heroine is finally criticized on the grounds that it is self-deluding. [...] Although Emma is the center of Austen's fiction, what she has to learn is her commonality with Jane Fairfax, her vulnerability as a female.[14] □

What Emma thus has to learn in the course of the novel is that her playfulness, be it ever so attractive to the reader, makes her unladylike. She has to submit to a 'realization of her own powerlessness'.

The second argument Gilbert and Gubar make concerns the matriarchs that exist in each of these novels. Mrs Ferrars, Lady Catherine and Mrs Churchill are powerful women who act out 'the rebellious anger so successfully repressed by the heroine and the author'. Although they have a central function in the plot, each of them features a lot less than this role would seem to warrant, so that 'these furious females remain secret presences in the plots'. Furthermore, they are 'buried or killed or banished at the end of the story', and seem to have deserved this because of their unattractiveness:

■ Widows who are no longer defined by men simply because they have survived the male authorities in their lives, these women can exercise power even if they can never legitimize it; thus they seem both pushy and dangerous. Yet if their energy appears destructive and disagreeable, that is because this is the mechanism by which Austen disguises the most assertive aspect of herself as the Other. [...] These bitchy women enact impulses of revolt that make them doubles not only for the heroines but for their author as well.[15] □

In *Sense and Sensibility,* despised Mrs Ferrars extorts the punishment which Elinor must have wished on the man 'who has been selfishly deceiving her for the entire novel':

■ By tampering with the patriarchal line of inheritance, Mrs. Ferrars proves that the very forms valued by Elinor are arbitrary. But even though *Sense and Sensibility* ends with the overt message that young women like Marianne and Elinor must submit to the powerful conventions of society by finding a male protector, Mrs. Ferrars and her scheming protegee Lucy Steele prove that women can themselves become agents of repression, manipulators of conventions, and survivors.[16] □

As regards *Pride and Prejudice,* Gilbert and Gubar argue for the similarity between Lady Catherine and Elizabeth. Both can be sarcastic, stubborn, courageous, and 'these are the only two women in the novel capable of feeling and expressing genuine anger, although it is up to Lady Catherine to articulate the rage against entailment that Elizabeth must feel'. In some ways, Lady Catherine is even 'an appropriate mother to Elizabeth', so that it is fitting both that Elizabeth takes the place which had been intended for Lady Catherine's daughter and that Elizabeth and Darcy invite Lady Catherine to Pemberley. After all, as both hero and heroine realise, Lady Catherine played a central role in bringing them together, first through making it possible for them to meet, and second by trying to separate them, which gave Darcy exactly the encouragement he had been waiting for.

In *Emma,* the 'vitriolic shrew is so discreetly hidden [...] that she never appears at all, yet again she is the causal agent of the plot'. Like Mrs Ferrars and Lady Catherine, Mrs Churchill is 'a proud, arrogant, and capricious woman'. Mrs Churchill is 'a monitory image of what Austen's heroines could be', and she and Emma in fact share characteristics: 'both have the power of having too much their own way, both are convinced of their superiority in talent, elegance of mind, fortune, and consequence, and both want to be first in society where they can enjoy assigning subservient parts'.[17] Gilbert and Gubar thus see the role of women as the central point in Austen's novels, as regards both the heroines and the older powerful woman, and they link these depictions to Austen the artist.

Similarly concentrating on gender, but more focused on Austen's life, is Margaret Kirkham's *Jane Austen, Feminism and Fiction* (1983). She views Austen primarily as woman, then as a writer, and it is consequently only by considering Austen's gender that her texts can be read. Kirkham focuses on Austen's biographical situation but also sees strong connections between the writings of Austen and Wollstonecraft, viewing both as 'feminist moralists of the same school'.[18] For Kirkham, Austen's work – like that of Wollstonecraft – is feminist because it is 'concerned with establishing the moral equality of men and women and the proper status of individual women as accountable beings'.[19] Furthermore, she argues, writing itself at the time Austen wrote becomes a feminist act (although, as Peter Garside has since shown, novel authorship was actually dominated by women in the 1810s[20]). Kirkham grounds Austen's feminism in that of her contemporaries and sees it as English Enlightenment Feminism. In accordance with this, Austen shows her heroines to be rational creatures, beings 'fully representative of human nature'.[21] Instead of having anything in common with male eighteenth-century writers, notably Johnson and Richardson, or indeed with her immediate male contemporaries, the Romantic poets and Scott as a novelist, Austen writes against them wherever she can. Furthermore, she shows patriarchal figures to be 'defective, like Mr. Bennet, and at worst vicious, like General Tilney'.[22] Kirkham therefore goes against Marilyn Butler's view of a conservative Austen and instead sees her as a feminist who expressed ideas similar to those of Wollstonecraft.

Mary Poovey, in her seminal Marxist–feminist study *The Proper Lady and the Woman Writer: Ideology as Style in the Works of Mary Wollstonecraft, Mary Shelley and Jane Austen* (1984), also explores the restrictions Austen would have worked under and the difficulty of combining the activity of writing with an existence as 'a proper lady'. As her title suggests, she again links Austen to Wollstonecraft, as well as to Mary Shelley, and sees all three as writing about women in society, more particularly as criticising ideas about female propriety as expressed in seventeenth and eighteenth-century literature and as applied at the time the three women lived. Through Austen's command of narrative form, she 'completes Wollstonecraft's analysis of female inhibition and perfects Shelley's attempts to make propriety accommodate female desire'.[23] Poovey shows that Austen had a sceptical attitude towards patriarchy, emphasising the novels' subversive qualities. Yet, at the same time, she emphasises how important family was for Austen, especially on a biographical level, supporting her in her writing and representing her first audience. Therefore, 'the notion of the family that served Jane Austen as a model for the proper coexistence of the individual and society was essentially patriarchal, supportive of and supported by the allegiances and hierarchy that feminine propriety implied'.[24] As Robert Clark points out, Poovey is concerned

■ with how Austen's texts mediate between, on the one hand, an established gentry ideology founded in ideas of untransformable hierarchy, organic community and a transcendental view of the value of land, and on the other, the disruptive ideology of a rising, commodifying bourgeoisie that has a much greater respect for individualistic passion and intelligence. For Poovey, Austen's irony stems from the contradictory desire both to reward individual desire and to establish a critical distance from it. Romance has its way, but only within the framework of established hierarchy.[25] □

The heroines are denied any aim other than marriage, and this is something even the financially independent Emma has to accept, being offered instead the hope of 'an emotional intensity that ideally compensates for all the practical opportunities [women] are denied'.[26] Thus, Austen's novels both make use of and subvert the ideology of feminine propriety.

WOMEN IN SOCIETY

Gary Kelly's 'Jane Austen, Romantic Feminism, and Civil Society' (1995) places Austen in the specific context of her times. He maintains that she contributed to a feminism which was conditioned by its historical circumstance in the early nineteenth century, and, more particularly, that 'this was the role of women in creating and sustaining civil society in the aftermath of a political, social, and cultural cataclysm'.[27]

In *Pride and Prejudice*, he argues, Austen envisions a civil society in which 'this alliance of virtuous gentry and meritorious bourgeoisie is motivated by a woman – Elizabeth'. While Elizabeth's consciousness of her own merit is the cause for her first rejecting Darcy, this self-confidence is yet shown to be dangerous if it is excessive. Kelly links this sense of self-worth to the novel's historical context; to the men who 'pushed through the Revolution in France and called for a revolution in Britain during the 1790s, confident of their own rightness – and "right" – in the face of real or apparent upper-class arrogance like Darcy's'. In a similar vein,

■ *Emma* returns to the dangerous saliency of the overconfident woman, though Emma Woodhouse has the social and material standing that Elizabeth Bennet lacks, while lacking the intellectual if not moral merit of the latter. Emma's interference in the civil society of Hartfield is motivated by a paradoxical combination of the same upper-class arrogance that many blamed for arousing Revolutionary resistance and the same self-generated bourgeois enterprise that [Edmund] Burke [1729–1797, British politician who strongly opposed the French Revolution] had condemned as the disruptive driving force of the Revolutionaries in France and their sympathizers in Britain. By contrast Mr. Knightley, her mentor, then lover, and eventually husband, clearly understands civil society as a socially cohesive practice, based on estate management, directing the dominant class to proper exercise of their power in the interests of all classes and thus of social stability, continuity, and prosperity. He also understands the importance of women to this form of civil society, as wives and domestic managers, seen in his concern to find a proper match for his tenant and eventually for himself, in his appreciation of the merits of Jane Fairfax and his contempt for the courtly fecklessness of Frank Churchill, and in his concern that Emma exercise her social leadership in proper ways. □

Kelly argues that all of Austen's works are concerned with 'a reconstruction of civil society for the Revolutionary aftermath, centered critically on the role of women':

■ This centering is not emplotted but represented structurally in Austen's chosen narrative mode – third-person centered narration with extensive use of 'free indirect discourse,' or reported inward speech and thought of the protagonist. The protagonist is a young woman moving from parental family world to her own 'establishment' in society as a wife, or agent in the reproduction and maintenance of local civil society from her base in the home. For Austen, as for many post-Revolutionary social critics, that sphere was the foundational unit of nation, state, and empire. The protagonist's reproduction of civil society is not depicted in the novel but rather prefigured in the crucial act of the plot – the protagonist's choice of (or comical stumbling upon) a husband. This is the major ethical choice of her life, but only one of many that constitute agency in civil society lived daily, at the local level (thereby bypassing demands for constitutional and institutional change). The protagonist is only a figure, however; for a man could as easily read himself into her, as we know many have. Thus the protagonist's situation speaks to all members of the novel reading classes, who were precisely those faced with the task of reconstructing civil society in the Revolutionary aftermath. Ultimately, Austen's dramatization of this situation is based on [...] her liberal Anglicanism, with its stress on both true faith and good works, and the necessary connection between the two, as the path to salvation.[28] □

Austen's novels thus move towards 'social stability, continuity, and prosperity'. The role of the heroine in achieving this aim of 'reconstructing society' in the aftermath of the French Revolution is crucial, not least in her choice of husband, which whom ideally she will act for the common good of all classes of society. The level she can act in, the local level and the home, is after all 'the foundational unit of nation, state and empire'. Kelly places Elizabeth and Emma as well as Austen herself in their historical context to make his argument. He draws on what is known about Austen's life, such as her 'liberal Anglicanism', to connect it to what he sees the novels as propagating: women's significant role in British society after the French Revolution.

One reason why Austen's novels lend themselves to feminist readings is that, no matter which approach one chooses to take and how one reads the novels, they have to be seen as being concerned with women in society and as being largely told from a woman's point of view. Both these features can be translated into other cultures, whether to societies in different geographical locations from those the novels are set in, at different times, or both. In the last few decades of the twentieth century, studies therefore appear that look at the reappearance of Austen's gendered politics in non-Western contexts, tracing plot constellation, characters, and narrative features in some of the literatures of these cultures back to Austen's texts. As Rajeswari Sunder Rajan points out, 'these invocations of Austen in other places are not a consequence of Austen's "universal resonance" as might be easily supposed, but reveal instead the conditions of her work's recuperability in different nation-spaces and historical conjunctures'.[29]

You-me Park in her 'Father's Daughters' compares the marriage plot of *Pride and Prejudice* with that of *A Faltering Afternoon* (1977) by Pak Wansô (born 1931), a contemporary Korean woman writer. The daughters Chohi, Uhi, and Malhi are in a situation similar to that of Jane and Elizabeth since they occupy 'a social and economic position that precariously hovers between rich and poor'.

■ In a patriarchal society that does not offer women any other access to political and economic power, they need to marry right in order not to fall on the wrong side of the fence that they are sitting on. In a postcolonial Korea where there is no stable base for the middle class, the contrast and contradiction between the rich and the poor are much starker than in Austen's England; and these women desire and dream about the world of the rich even more fiercely and desperately than Austen's. Confronting the dilemma of having to make it in the world by presenting themselves as desirable, without cheapening their value by appearing too eager, these three women unsurprisingly choose paths similar to the three sisters who marry in *Pride and Prejudice*. □

Chohi is the Jane figure who adheres to the rules and it is here that Pak's novel 'creates a productive tension with Austen's text, a tension that illuminates the multifaceted relationship of patriarchy and social power in both texts':

■ Chohi, determined to make a leap to the other side of the boundary that divides the poor and the rich, is very well aware that women do not have too many options or chances. She teaches her little sister, Malhi: 'You'd better know this yourself. Women have only one opportunity to jump over the fence around their surroundings and that is when they get married. You should jump over it at the right moment even if it is hard. Why should you marry if you are just to move your butt over within the fence?'. Armed only with her good looks, determination, and the encouragement from her mother who shares Mrs Bennet's sentiment ('I was sure you could not be so beautiful for nothing!'), Chohi charges into the marriage market – only to learn that the negotiation is much more complicated and brutal than she expected. After being rejected by desirable mates a few times due to Hô Sông's small business that does not meet the requirements of wealth and status (read: you should be able to keep your distance from the actual scene of exploitation), Chohi decides to marry a widower twice her age. Anticipating a life of luxury and comfort, Chohi feels desperate about her future obligation to the daily rituals of marriage: 'Chohi felt suffocated thinking she would have to talk to him about something every day when she marries him. That thought is even worse than the prospect of having to sleep with him every day. After marriage, Chohi does succeed in learning about male sexual exploits by heart and satisfying every fantasy of her husband, but fails to retain her sanity. □

Thus Park argues that by reading Pak and Austen side by side we real-ise not only the importance of historical context but also what might have happened to a Jane Bennet figure had she not been rescued by a benevolent narrator.

■ Pak suggests that, in Korea with its frenzy of economic development in the 1970s and 1980s, love has become an impossible concept. Interrogating the validity and the limits of the Austenian paradigm of realist narrative relating to the ideology and practice of the marriage market, I argue that, when put to the test in 'postcolonial' Korea, the realist narrative radically critiques if not sub-verts Austen's explicitly conservative and optimistic vision of the compatibility of 'morality' and the marriage market, and the viability of the concept of civili-zation itself. Here we might have to look for answers outside the literary world and remember the specific conditions of the Korean economy where, due to typically colonial and postcolonial circumstances, the economic transition from pre-modern to postmodern systems became contracted within a span of twenty to thirty years. Austen in a sense was allowed the historical 'limita-tions' of realist novels. She acutely and faithfully portrays the major contra-dictions of the moment – thus 'meeting the requirement of the great realist narrative writer' – without having to confront their ultimate result or long-term consequences. On the other hand, the 'reality' for Pak is a palimpsest forma-tion of postcolonial economy where several major contradictions – from those of industrial capitalism, financial capitalism, imperial capitalism (which Lenin termed the ultimate form of capitalism) to postcolonial, postmodern, and post-industrial capitalism – are concentrated in one geographical and historical site, reinforcing and conflicting with each other.[30] □

Park argues that comparing the two novels makes the reader realise that although Mr Bennet can laugh at the marriage market and its absurdities, it is his daughters who have to 'come up with realistic narratives in order to negotiate their fate in it'. Moreover, Park's argument shows how Austen's plots and the roles her heroines play can be applied in different historical and cultural spaces.

The rise of feminism has thus substantially altered Austen criticism in that this now determines most studies of Austen's novels in some way. The analyses from the later decades of the twentieth century discussed in this chapter all have gender as their main concern, linked to either the author or to her heroines or both. As will be seen in the next chapter, recent critics' approaches are different from those in the 1960s and 1970s, not only as regards feminism but also in terms of their awareness and use of Austen's own and her novels' literary, cultural and historical context. However, the next chapter also shows how even studies appearing from about 1975 that are not expressly feminist are still concerned with the role of women and connect many of the themes they discuss to this issue, thereby testifying to the centrality of feminism to Austen criticism.

CHAPTER FIVE

Later Twentieth-Century Critical Responses: Literary, Cultural, and Historical Context

Devoney Looser states in her 1995 *Jane Austen and Discourses of Feminism* that 'in the thriving industry of Austen criticism, the driving force is arguably feminist',[1] and while this appears to hold, there are of course studies in the second half of the twentieth century that do not explicitly focus on feminism. New Historicism and its concern with a text's historical, cultural, social and political context dominate criticism in this period, but there are two distinct approaches within this larger movement: the feminist focus outlined above, and a political–historical perspective. Of course these two approaches are often combined, not least because of the political–historical dimension of feminism.

CONSERVATIVE AUSTEN

Arguably the most influential study in the second half of the twentieth century is Marilyn Butler's *Jane Austen and the War of Ideas* (1975). She applies a textual approach in combination with an awareness of the author and her context: closely analysing the texts, Butler shows that far from being ahistorical and apolitical, Austen's writings are full of signs that, convey political opinion. The study, therefore, goes against the modes of interpretation hitherto applied to Austen's texts, and it breaks with the view of the novels depicting a timeless world of their own.

From Butler's discussion of each of the novels, Austen emerges as an 'entirely conservative' writer. Butler aligns *Sense and Sensibility* with the conservative anti-Jacobin novels that were meant to counter the Jacobin novels. The term Jacobin derived from the Jacobins, a political group founded in 1789 in Paris, which supported extreme democratic and egalitarian principles. It was soon applied to anyone in favour of radical political reform. William Godwin, for example, was a famous radical as well as a writer of Jacobin novels, such as *Things as they are; or, The*

Adventures of Caleb Williams (1794). Butler links one anti-Jacobin novel in particular to *Sense and Sensibility*, Mrs West's *A Gossip's Story* (1796), to show Austen's conservatism. In *A Gossip's Story*, two sisters, Louisa and Marianne Dudley, illustrate the right and wrong way. Louisa is intelligent, selfless and rational; Marianne is immature and relies on her emotions. Louisa eventually marries Mr Pelham, a man she has been in love with since the start of the novel and who loves her as deeply with a lasting esteem for her virtues. Marianne, by contrast, does not marry the man she is first in love with because he does not live up to her high ideals of passion, and instead hurriedly marries Mr Clermont, with whom she believes herself passionately in love. This passion, however, does not last, so that she and Clermont eventually end up living unhappily together, whereas Louisa and Pelham live in continued contentment and bliss. At a basic level, Butler argues, Austen takes this plot and rewrites it in *Sense and Sensibility*, so that the main difference between the two novels is not the didactic message or the values conveyed but the way it is written:

■ Jane Austen's version of 'sensibility' – that is, individualism, or the worship of self, in various familiar guises – is as harshly dealt with here as anywhere in the anti-Jacobin tradition. Even without the melodramatic political subplot of many anti-Jacobin novels, Mrs Ferrars's London is recognizably a sketch of the anarchy that follows the loss of all values but self-indulgence. In the opening chapters especially, where Marianne is the target of criticism, 'sensibility' means sentimental (or revolutionary) idealism, which Elinor counters with her sceptical or pessimistic view of man's nature. Where the issue is the choice of a husband, Jane Austen's criteria prove to be much the same as Mrs West's: both advocate dispassionate assessment of a future husband's qualities, discounting both physical attractiveness, and the *rapport* that comes from shared tastes, while stressing objective evidence. Both reiterate the common conservative theme of the day, that a second attachment is likely to be more reliable than a first. By all these characteristic tests, *Sense and Sensibility* is an anti-Jacobin novel just as surely as is *A Gossip's Story*.

The sole element of unorthodoxy in *Sense and Sensibility* lies in the execution, and especially in the skilful adjustment of detail which makes its story more natural. □

Sense and Sensibility is 'unremittingly didactic'; the contrast format being chosen 'in order to make an explicit ideological point'. This means that what happens to one character must also happen to the other, so that the reader cannot but compare the two heroines and come to the right conclusion as to whose behaviour is right. Marianne and Elinor advocate two opposing creeds in the 'nature' versus 'nurture' argument: Marianne believes in 'innate moral sense' and sees man as 'naturally good', so that his impulsive actions are also good, whereas Elinor's caution comes from 'the Christian tradition that man's nature is fallible' and who consequently even 'mistrusts her own desires'.

■ It is in keeping with Elinor's objectivity (and also typical of the feminine variant of the anti-Jacobin-novel) that she should advocate a doctrine of civility in opposition to Marianne's individualism. Elinor restrains her own sorrow in order to shield her mother and sister. By her politeness to Mrs Jennings she steadily makes up what Marianne has carelessly omitted. She respects Colonel Brandon for his activity in helping his friends long before Mrs Dashwood and Marianne have seen his virtues. Civility is a favourite anti-Jacobin theme. [...] If *Sense and Sensibility* is compared with other novels of the same genre, and originating at the same time, it can be seen to move in innumerable small ways towards fullness and naturalness. A conception of civility illustrated by gratitude to Mrs Jennings is more natural, for example, than portraying a similar concept in terms of prayers beside a dying father, or fidelity to the death-bed advice of an aunt. In fact, granted the rigidity imposed by the form, the second half of *Sense and Sensibility* is remarkably natural, flexible, and inventive. Both the sisters are presented as plausible individuals as well as professors of two opposing creeds. □

Part of the debate between these two creeds, Butler argues, is the foundation in Christian doctrine. Whereas 'during the first half of the novel Marianne has stood for a doctrine of complacency and self-sufficiency which Jane Austen as a Christian deplored', and failed to question her own conduct, Elinor 'exercised the self-examination prescribed for the Christian, by questioning the state of her heart in relation to Edward, and, even more, her complex and disagreeable feelings about Lucy'.

Nevertheless, and this is one of the problems of the novel, the reader feels drawn to Marianne. This is the case in spite of the 'real technical achievement of *Sense and Sensibility*', the realisation of this Christian self-examination in literary terms: 'Elinor is the first character in an Austen novel consistently to reveal her inner life'.

■ Compared with the common run of anti-Jacobin novels it is a considerable achievement, and yet it has never been found quite good enough. *Sense and Sensibility* is the most obviously tendentious of Jane Austen's novels, and the least attractive. The trouble is not merely that, for all the author's artistic tact, the cumbrous framework and enforced contrasts of the inherited structure remain. It matters far more that the most deeply disturbing aspect of all anti-Jacobin novels, their inhumanity, affects this novel more than Jane Austen's skilled mature work. In a way *Sense and Sensibility* is worse affected than many clumsy works by lesser writers, because it is written naturally, and with more insight into at least some aspects of the inner life. The reader has far too much real sympathy with

Marianne in her sufferings to refrain from valuing her precisely on their account. There is plenty of evidence that Jane Austen, anticipating this reaction, tried to forestall it. As far as possible she tries to keep us out of Marianne's consciousness: Marianne's unwonted secrecy, after Willoughby has left Barton, and after her arrival in London, functions quite as effectively in restricting the reader's sympathy as in restricting Elinor's. Merely to have Marianne's sufferings described after she has received Willoughby's letter is sufficient, however, to revive all the reader's will to identify himself with her. The effort to point up Elinor's feelings instead will not do: either we do not believe in them, and conclude her frigid, or the felt presence of suffering in the one sister helps us to supply imaginatively what we are not told about the inner life of the other. It is difficult, in short, to accept the way consciousness is presented in this novel. □

The reader responds to the strong feelings with which especially Marianne, though also to an extent Elinor, are drawn, yet the novel argues that such feelings 'are not innately good'. But the reader tends to see Marianne subjectively, 'in flat opposition to the author's obvious intention'. She thus has the reader's sympathy, since the reader's reaction to her is 'outside Austen's control':

■ The measure of Jane Austen's failure to get us to read her story with the necessary ethical detachment comes when she imposes her solution. What, innumerable critics have asked, if Marianne never brought herself to love Colonel Brandon? The fact that the question still occurs shows that in this most conscientiously didactic of all the novels the moral case remains unmade.[2] □

Butler's work influenced Austen criticism for decades to come. While critics might disagree with her view of Austen as espousing Tory politics, the majority of them agree with Butler in seeing Austen as a writer deeply conscious of her political, social and literary context, and the novels as reflecting this consciousness.

TIMELESSNESS

Critics writing in the 1960s and 1970s are not much concerned with the literary, cultural, and historical context of Austen and her novels. If context features, it is not usually to trace the influence of her immediate context on her texts, but to place Austen in a general historical setting or her novels in a rough chronological order. She was 'brought up on eighteenth-century thought and was fundamentally loyal to the respect for limits, definition, and clear ideas which it inculcated'.[3] Her literary indebtedness is seen as being to mid-eighteenth-century authors such as Fielding, Richardson and Sterne. Where her contemporary literary context comes up, critics use it to emphasise Austen's originality in being different from or going against contemporary trends in fiction. David Lodge asserts that contemporary fiction only features in Austen to be mocked, since the 'ironic invocation of literary stereotypes is one of the ways by which Jane Austen reinforces the realism of her own fiction'.[4] Realism is not seen as fixing the novels in a certain time and place but as conditioning the works' eternal validity. The issues they deal with are seen as timeless, often connected to issues of morality, such as 'the fallibility of human understanding'[5] or 'the ongoingness of social life'.[6]

Other proofs of Austen's timelessness are links to Shakespeare as well as classic authors. Tanner contends that like Shakespeare's *King Lear* (first published 1608), *Pride and Prejudice* is a 'drama[] of recognition'[7] that deals with the unfolding of 'the 'real character' of both the good and the bad'.[8] King Lear asks his three daughters about the extent of their love for him, and the two eldest, Goneril and Regan, flatter him with compliments. The youngest, Cordelia, however, refuses to flatter him and instead tells him she loves him as a daughter ought to love her father. Lear is incensed and gives power and land to the two eldest and nothing to Cordelia. In the course of the play, he realises his mistake, since both Goneril and Regan turn against him, having secured what he could give them, whereas Cordelia stands by him to the end in spite of having been slighted. When she is killed, Lear dies of grief. Tanner argues that Elizabeth's error is 'of the same kind' as Lear's,[9] since she, like Shakespeare's Othello and Lear, 'ask[s] for the wrong kind of evidence'[10] to assess a character.

Not only is Austen the author is aligned with timeless male authors her characters are also linked to male characters too. Frank Bradbrook, in his introduction to *Pride and Prejudice,* writes:

> ■ It is, partly, in the neatness of the patterns and antitheses formed by the various combinations, comparisons, and contrasts of characters and situations that the wit of Jane Austen is manifest. In this respect, one is reminded that some of her essential allegiances were with the age of Pope. But she looks beyond that to the world of Shakespearian comedy, as well as forwards to the age of romanticism. Shakespeare, too, makes use of pattern, antithesis, and verbal echoes. Despite the fact that Jane Austen has been described, with some justice, as 'a Marxist before Marx', the story of *Pride and Prejudice* is genuinely romantic as well as realistic, with a powerful vein of poetry beneath the surface. When Darcy says, 'I have been used to consider poetry as the *food* of love', misquoting the opening of *Twelfth Night* [first performed c. 1600], Elizabeth replies, 'Of a fine, stout, healthy love it may. Everything nourishes what is strong already.' It is only the robustness of Elizabeth and Darcy which allows them to achieve fulfilment in the world

in which they live. In the novel, the pervading stress on music and dance is a constant reminder of non-materialistic, romantic values. But it is not only the lovers who are seen dramatically and poetically. Mr Collins is the ghost of Malvolio [in Shakespeare's *Twelfth Night*] in his tone and accents, though the character of the steward has been transferred to Wickham's father, who is a good man. Jane Austen has shown in her novel how 'the course of true love never did run smooth.' The Bingleys, the Gardiners, and Mr. Bennet, who, together with Elizabeth and Darcy, constitute 'the happy few', who make up the final idyllic paradise, represent the perfect balance of romance and the realistic appreciation of ordinary, everyday living, which seems to have been Jane Austen's ideal for the good life, in her maturity.[11] □

He sees the novel as romantic and as realistic, and, like Tanner, emphasises 'Shakespearian undertones',[12] finding that Austen's most obvious literary links are to Shakespeare, rather than to any of her contemporaries. Ronald Blythe, too, regards Austen as a pre-Romantic, eighteenth-century author:

■ By allowing Emma to make a genuine emotional progress from brittle head to tender heart and by revealing every step of the way, Jane Austen was to advance the eighteenth-century novel along the road which led to Henry James and [Marcel] Proust.[13] □

Rather than being part of a particular context, Austen's novels pave the way for the nineteenth and twentieth-century novel. Though discussing novels that were begun at different periods, *Pride and Prejudice* and *Emma* respectively, Bradbrook and Blythe do not place Austen's works in the Romantic period regardless of when the respective novel was written and published.

Earlier critics' general unconcern with literary and historical context is connected to their not seeing Austen as including historical circumstances in her novels. Though she may have been aware of changes around her, her novels remain concerned with 'a small section of society locked in an almost timeless present in which very little will or can change'.[14] The novels' greatness is their capacity to apply to any society.

HISTORICAL AND LITERARY CONTEXT

For scholars writing after about 1980, Austen's historical and literary context is relevant to an interpretation of her novels because the texts are seen as engaging with it. The fact that she is a female author who writes about women is the most obvious reason for this preoccupation with context: what other female authors wrote what kind of novels at the time, and what contemporary debates existed about women's role in society, are questions repeatedly addressed. Critics now consider Austen's immediate historical and literary context and then place the novels into that, stressing their reference to other contemporary texts.

The parallels are no longer drawn between Austen and Shakespeare or eighteenth-century authors, but between Austen and near-contemporary women writers such as Burney, Radcliffe, and Wollstonecraft. Their techniques and topics are usually seen as being taken up by Austen. Whether regarding her as breaking with fictional traditions, or as appropriating them, critics after Butler see Austen as engaging with them.

Roger Sales in his 1994 *Jane Austen and Representations of Regency England* shows how Austen's characters need to be seen in the material social history of their author's time, and she herself as a Regency writer who addresses the major issues of her time. Details in the novels have to be related to historical conditions. The extent to which women and men were mobile, for example, needs to be related to the power each gender has. In *Emma*, Mr. Elton and Mr. Knightley are both very mobile characters – they can both ride up to London immediately – and Mr. Elton can journey to Bath to look for a wife.

■ Female characters, by contrast, often have to wait [...] until the necessary travel arrangements have been made for them. According to Miss Bates, Jane Fairfax is unable to fix the time of her arrival in Highbury because her movements are dependent upon those of Colonel Campbell. [...] She continues to be almost totally dependent on others for movement. She is conveyed to and from the dinner party at the Coles in Mr Knightley's carriage. She is brought regularly to the vicarage in the Eltons' new carriage. The Eltons also assume responsibility for taking her to the ball at the Crown. She has to fight hard to assert her right to walk about Highbury on her own. [...] she is closely examined by John Knightley about her walks to the post office. She has to persuade Emma that she is perfectly capable of walking back to Highbury from Donwell Abbey on her own. Emma offers her the use of either a servant or a carriage. The news that she has been 'wandering about the meadows, at some distance from Highbury' reaches Emma, and presumably others, very quickly. Jane's movements are monitored and discussed in ways that are very different from the gossip that surrounds Mr Elton's trip to London. His right to be on the road is not questioned. She is subjected to a different kind of surveillance. □

That Emma is more powerful is reflected in her greater mobility. In fact, she is 'potentially the most mobile of Austen's heroines because of her father's invalidism'. Nevertheless, she does not travel far – she has not made the seven-mile journey to Box Hill before, nor has she seen the sea. When Mr. Elton makes 'violent love to her', this is in a coach when she is unchaperoned.

■ Emma may be powerful and yet even she is momentarily revealed to be in danger when travelling on the public highway. Assaults on women in this period were committed in the home and the workplace as well as on the road. [...] It was nevertheless the attacks on women who were travelling that tended to come to the attention of the public. This conveniently buried the fact that the crime could be much closer to home, as well as reinforcing the notion that women should not travel alone. [...] Another case concerns the activities of the 'monster', who stalked fashionable London streets in 1790 attacking women often in broad daylight. He was a slasher who used a long knife to cut clothing as well as the body. One of his victims, Anne Porter, received a nine-inch-long wound that was four inches deep in places. The attacks were usually accompanied by a torrent of verbal abuse. It seems that he was motivated by a belief that women should not be allowed to walk the streets either on their own or in groups. There are, of course, differences between such cases and the comedy of errors that surrounds Emma's journey with Mr Elton. It would nevertheless be a mistake to ignore some of the broader similarities.[15] □

Sales, therefore, argues for the significance of the novel's historical context, though with a different angle from that of Butler. It is only when considering the precise historical conditions that we come to see the connections between, for example, mobility and power, a connection that would have been immediately obvious to contemporary readers.

Mary Waldron, again like Butler, sees Austen as deeply conscious of her literary contemporaries. Unlike Butler, however, Waldron argues that Austen confronts and challenges the popular novelists of her time. Waldron shows Austen's writing as deliberately disagreeing with that of her contemporaries. In *Sense and Sensibility*, 'Austen is not challenging ideologies but fictions, for the novels that she knew seemed, in making a stand against relativism, to present the problems of living as much too easily solved by the application of theory'. Waldron argues that, in working out Marianne's and Elinor's respective dilemmas and solutions, she 'refers obliquely to two modes of contemporary fiction, the polemical/moral novel of the nineties and the sentimental novel'. The first she sees as a model for the novel's present, i.e. Elinor and Marianne's love stories, and the second as the basis for the past of the novel, i.e. Colonel Brandon's story. 'In tying these stories together Austen enables herself to examine both modes in terms of what she regarded as "probability," and so challenge the simplistic solutions of many of her fellow-novelists.' *Sense and Sensibility* at first looks like a version of the polemical/moral plot, like that of the novels of Austen's contemporaries Mrs. Jane West and Maria Edgeworth – which is, as we have seen, what Butler argues.

These novels often show a pairing of heroines like Marianne and Elinor, for example West's *A Gossip's Story* and Edgeworth's *Letters to Literary Ladies* (1795), and sense is aligned in them with propriety and civility, sensibility with feeling and 'other trendy theories associated with revolutionary politics', and therefore condemned. Austen, however, Waldron argues, 'set out to subvert this simplistic concept very early, and the process continues apace in this novel'; in fact, 'in the final form of *Sense and Sensibility* the oppositional framework is modulated almost to invisibility'. Austen does this partly by relying on the ambiguity of the terms 'sense' and 'sensibility':

■ When the novel came out with its new title in 1811, readers no doubt thought they had got yet another work of fiction trouncing 'feeling', or sensibility, and lauding 'sense' in the familiar mode, and it is quite certain that Austen was aware that this would be so. But she proceeded to shatter this form of novelistic 'cant' by diffracting the impact of received moralistic vocabulary – a process which had engaged her attention very early in her writing life. Both 'sense' and 'sensibility' were extremely slippery concepts throughout the eighteenth and early nineteenth centuries. [During the eighteenth century,] the term ['sense'] had inevitably taken on subjective meanings ranging from humane intelligence and rationality to downright commercial cunning, depending on the speaker's predilections and prejudices. 'A man of sense' meant, more often than not, 'Someone I (an intelligent and sober person, of course) can agree with.' The term 'sensibility' was also used very flexibly; basically it denoted a humane and compassionate attitude to life, but its French provenance had tended to give it a bad name, associating it with all kinds of excess and fashionable affectation. It was quite possible not to know which of its many meanings was being used on any particular occasion. It is this dubiousness of reference which Austen exploits in *Sense and Sensibility*. Different kinds of sense and sensibility are juxtaposed and set against one another in a complex web of relationships, motives and desires in which only the thoroughly unscrupulous can be seen to be able to triumph over intractable circumstance. To achieve this moral uncertainty Austen writes against the grain of novels which she found unsatisfactory, though she often enjoyed them. □

Whereas Butler aligns Austen with West and Edgeworth, Waldron sees Austen as detaching herself from them. With conscious reference to West and Edgeworth, Austen put 'her own gloss on the concept of sensibility, consciously detaching it from the political anxieties it had recently been associated with and reverting to its earlier identification with true civilised behaviour'. After all, Waldron argues, Marianne's sensibility is not entirely 'unsystematic and destructive' but rather combines rationality with feeling, and Marianne believes that 'we ought in reason to be open about our feelings and not give support to the vulgar and commonplace'. The novel does not repudiate this concept altogether, but in fact often represents Marianne's creed as more attractive than Elinor's. However, actually to live by this ideal is shown to be impossible:

■ It is doomed by the overwhelming dominance of the vulgar and commonplace in everyday life, which will, either by stupidity or malice, not only resist the efforts of a few idealists to counter it, but often seek to destroy them. The presence of people like Sir John and Lady Middleton, Robert Ferrars, Mr and Mrs Palmer, and Anne Steele demonstrates clearly what Marianne is up against, not to mention the infinitely more dangerous Ferrars-Dashwood combination and Lucy Steele. Though Elinor's 'sense' – which is like Marianne's – tells her that there is substance in Marianne's view, she is aware of the size of the problem and prefers to try to neutralise it by means which Marianne cannot approve: [...] 'to aim at the restraint of sentiments which were not in themselves illaudable, appeared to her not merely as an unnecessary effort, but a disgraceful subjection of reason to commonplace and mistaken notions.' This is a considered view, not an abdication of reason. Marianne is not presented as corrupted by dangerous political theories. Her opinions are based upon novels of the sixties and seventies in which intuitive reaction is seen as more laudable than obedience to convention because it is more 'natural' – that is, more rational.[16] □

The best known of these novels were *Julie, ou la Nouvelle Héloise* by the Genevan writer and philosopher Jean-Jacques Rousseau (1712–78), which was translated into English in 1761, and *Die Leiden des jungen Werthers (The Sorrows of Young Werther* (1774, revised edn 1787)) by the German writer, humanist and scientist Johann Wolfgang von Goethe (1749–1832), both of which were much imitated, and *Julia de Roubigne* (1777) by Henry Mackenzie (1745–1833) (which was itself a version of *Julie, ou la Nouvelle Héloise*). However, Waldron states, 'Marianne is not portrayed as slavishly following them. Elinor does not have to urge Marianne to *think*', just as the latter's point of view 'is not totally rejected by Elinor as misguided and morally dangerous. [...] The basis of the disagreement between the two is about behaviour rather than morality.'

Marianne and Elinor both have deep feelings, and, while Elinor keeps them to herself, Marianne shows them openly, but, Waldron argues, the novel does not suggest that because Marianne gives vent to her feelings these must necessarily be superficial. Instead, just as Marianne's ideal is not entirely condemned, Elinor 'has by no means all the answers', and it is this fact that shows Austen to be going against the contemporary didactic novel. In these novels of instruction 'Elinor's system would clearly have authorial approval', but in *Sense and Sensibility* this is not always the case; in fact, Elinor is 'in a different way, just as likely to fall into error, just as prone to overdo her convictions, as Marianne'. This dubiousness is what makes the novel 'something new to fiction, for the conventional centre of moral authority, previously thought essential, disintegrates as the story develops'.

In contrast to Butler then, Waldron sees Austen as writing against her literary contemporaries, but, like Butler, Waldron emphasises the importance of Austen's historical and literary context for the analysis of her novels.

Connected to this focus on historical context is another approach, also present in Waldron, which is to identify contemporary meanings and connotations of a term when interpreting Austen's novels. As Waldron defines the terms 'sense' and 'sensibility' in Austen's historical context, Isobel Armstrong draws attention to the complex contemporary significations of the title words of *Pride and Prejudice*, drawing on *A Dictionary of the English Language* (1755) by Dr Samuel Johnson (1709–84). This redefining of terms contributes to Armstrong's aim of showing the complexities behind the novel's 'superficially glittering surface': Armstrong emphasises elements in the text that show how it was originally written in the 1790s but then rewritten in the 1810s.

■ Dr Johnson's *Dictionary*, which would have been authoritative in Jane Austen's time, foregrounds meanings of 'Pride' which are subordinated in modern dictionaries. Johnson's first meaning, for instance, is 'Inordinate and unreasonable self-esteem', whereas a modern dictionary gives the primary meaning of the noun as 'a feeling of honour and self-respect'. Johnson's second definition is 'Insolence; rude treatment of others; insolent exultation', and secondary meanings are 'Dignity of manner, loftiness of air' (3), 'Ornament' (6), and 'Splendour; ostentation' (7). The negative meanings predominate over positive signification – 'Generous elation of heart' (4). As will be seen, the signification of both 'Pride' and 'Prejudice' works in contradictory ways, but it is immediately evident from these definitions and Hume's discussion that *prejudice*, that which pre-judges, must be an inherent attribute of Pride, for in these definitions it is founded on a *pre*-judgement of one's own and one's possessions' worth. For Hume Pride is an object lesson in the way that the human passions work; as ideas and impressions reinforce one another in a self-perpetuating cycle, Pride is confirmed by the Pride it has itself generated. Moral and ideological blindness are virtually inevitable. Just as the medieval sin of pride subsumed all other sins, so pride in this novel subsumes prejudice.[17] □

Again, this analysis emphasises the novels' original political, cultural and economic context.

SENSIBILITY

Another change between critics writing in the 1960s and 1970s and after 1980 is the role given to society in the novels. While earlier scholars discuss the individual in society, later critics specifically look at women in a particular society. Both Margaret Doody and Ros Ballaster in their respective 1990 and 1995 introductions to *Sense and Sensibility* discuss sensibility in its relation to society – as do Tony Tanner and Claire Lamont in their 1969 and 1970 introductions to the same novel. The essential difference is, however, that Doody and Ballaster consider sensibility in its connection with femininity, whereas Tanner's and Lamont's concepts of sensibility can apply to either 'the hero or heroine of sensibility'.[18] Ballaster addresses the relationship between society and specifically 'the bourgeois heroine',[19] finding that, in works by Austen, Wollstonecraft and Edgeworth, 'sensibility is presented as a problematic form of selfhood for women'.[20] Doody argues that sensibility 'poses particular dangers for women'[21] because they live in 'a social and financial system which is so systematically heartless in its treatment of women',[22] She then cites passages from *A Vindication of the Rights of Women* to link Austen to its criticism of women's predicaments in society:

■ Austen and Wollstonecraft both see that delicate feminine sensibility as a mark of upper-class pretension may only mask serious economic disability, and can impede or even damage the female who cultivates it. Economically a cripple, but trained to focus her attention on the flutters of emotion, the young female of sensibility is also a prime target for seduction. For 'sensibility', the capacity for delicate rushes of emotion and enthusiasm, connects itself in the observer's mind with sexual 'sense' – the powerful 'sense' and 'sensibility' hovering behind Austen's pages. Marianne possesses sexual appetite and sensitivity, and she chooses the man she could prefer, blind to the social likelihood that a man in Willoughby's position might truly wish her for a sexual partner for a time, without wishing to marry her. Marianne is spared the trials of the seduced woman – the Elizas stand in for her, undergoing those traumas. But her heart was seduced, and in her ability ultimately to put that past episode behind her and move on, Marianne is one of the strong-minded women presented by liberal or radical writers. Although Austen jokingly complained about the heroine of [*Emmeline* (1788) by Charlotte Smith (1749–1806)] breaking off her engagement to the dashing, impetuous Frederic Delamere, and finding another love, she had obviously taken note of that circumstance. And Smith was a predecessor of the female Jacobin novelists (Mary Wollstonecraft and Mary Hays [1760–1843] among them), who strongly argued a woman's right to find a second love. Austen does not go so far as to argue for the right of the woman already seduced or violated or sexually experienced to find a second love, but she is looking in that direction, and, in making Marianne bid farewell to a fantastic constancy, she is definitely joining in an argument about female sexuality.[23] □

Like Butler, then, Doody discusses *Sense and Sensibility* with reference to other novels of the period, but, where Butler sees Austen as conservative and as writing in the anti-Jacobin mode, Doody argues for the opposite and aligns Austen with Jacobin novelists such as Mary Wollstonecraft.

Also in contrast to Doody, Tanner argues that in *Sense and Sensibility* social codes force compliance to rules. The individual's 'natural sensibility' is at odds with society's values, and Marianne is the embodiment of this conflict. Her 'muffled scream' presents a critique of society's rational ways, but this critique is general, not specific to society's treatment of women. Sensibility 'had to be subordinated'.[24]

■ [Austen] makes it clear that Elinor and Marianne do embody slightly but crucially different notions about how to live and that society will only tolerate one of those notions. [...] It is abundantly clear that she put quite as much of herself into Marianne as into Elinor, so from one point of view we can imagine this to be a psychological parable written partly at least for her own benefit – the two sisters adding up to one divided self. And if the ideal state of affairs would be [a connection between] sensibility and the sense – the actual condition of social living as Jane Austen saw it was that they could not be fully connected but rather one was, and had to be, subordinated. [...] Marianne does suffer from neurosis brought on by repression and her sickness is precisely the cost of her entry into the sedate stabilities of civilized life envisaged at the end. Before her illness her eyes are bright, eager, full of wayward spirit; after her illness – it is the very sign of her recovery – she looks up at Elinor with 'a rational though languid gaze'. [...] Her vision is now clearer; but her energy is turned to languor. She is tamed and ready for 'citizenship'. □

Like many critics and general readers, Tanner proceeds to criticise the ending as 'the weakest part of the book'. He sees Marianne as being married off to Colonel Brandon to satisfy both society's and the novel's need for a harmonious structured ending. With everyone, both society and the author, against her, Marianne has to give in and be 'the reward of all' Brandon's virtues and sufferings. Tanner argues that 'there is something punitive in the taming of Marianne and all she embodies', even that 'something is being vengefully stamped out'. Marianne is 'irreconcilably at odds with society because of her passional intensities'; therefore these need to go. Where later novelists show protagonists with such 'passional intensities', for example George Eliot's Maggie Tulliver in *The Mill on the Floss* (first published 1860), these can only die, pre-cisely because there is no space for them in society.

> ■ And yet Marianne does, in effect, die. Whatever the name of the automa-ton which submits to the plans or its relations and joins the social game it is not the real Marianne, and in the devitalized symmetry of the conclu-sions something valuable has been lost. She 'dwindles' into marriage with a vengeance. [...] The novel has at least shown the existence and power of the inner subterranean life of the emotions but it returns to the surface at the end and is resolved with such brusque manipulation of plot that one wonders if Jane Austen intended that as a last bitter irony. It is certainly hard to know how exactly to respond to the end. Among other things it reminds us that Jane Austen is also a beautiful screen maker and it is hard not to feel that with this ending she is almost wilfully screening something off from herself. One is left with the lurking suspicion that one of the things hidden behind the screen is a potentially tragic ending. On the other hand one might, at the end, applaud the hardheaded realism which recognizes that the consolations of society are only achieved at the cost of a more or less rigorous curbing of the intensities of impulse and a disciplined dimin-ishment in the indulgence of solitary emotional fantasies. Yet one may well wonder what consolations society will have for Marianne after her shatter-ing experience.[25] □

However, Tanner continues, this dubious happy ending once again shows that for Austen 'the structure of society was more powerful than the structure of feeling in any one individual and would always contain it – though, as this novel shows, she was well aware how painful that containment could be.' She did not value society more than the life of individuals, since 'no one before her showed so piercingly the possible miseries of a compulsory social existence'. But for her society was 'the unalterable given', and whatever role sense and sensibility, passion and romance, were going to play, would have to be within society. Austen, like her readers, would have found Marianne charming, but the author also sees her heroine's ideals as 'unwise'.

Both Tanner and Doody regard Marianne's sensibility as prevent-ing her from accessing her sense, and also see sensibility in Marianne as being conquered by the end of the novel, but while Doody sees this as a victory for women's rights and Marianne as a survivor, Tanner sees it as a loss of true self. Doody, therefore, views Austen as making a political statement in the context of debates about gender; Tanner sees Austen as commenting on society's ways and values generally. Analysing the text on its own or in its cultural context leads to different readings.

Austen's femininity means that critics of the later period see the novels in the context of the productions of contemporary women writers. The feminist interpretation of each individual novel as an expression of Austen's political opinions means that writers tend to need to see a consistency between the novels. Though Elizabeth with her spirit and independence most obviously appeals to modern femininity, other Austen heroines embody the same type and therefore have to be seen as meeting similar fates to convey similar political messages, so that Marianne becomes a victor against society's restrictions.

CONSERVATIVE OR REVOLUTIONARY?

Scholars writing in the 1960s and 1970s tend not to see Austen's novels as making political statements, certainly not as challenging the status quo. Through the later critics' preoccupation with women's role in society, the political dimension emerges. The concern with Austen's political position in later texts to an extent replaces the earlier texts' concern with timeless morality. She is variously seen as conservative, progressive, or, for example by Isobel Armstrong and Vivien Jones in their respective 1990 and 1996 essays on *Pride and Prejudice*, as having 'assimilated both positions and moved on'[26] to a post-revolutionary, rather than an anti-revolutionary, position.

In *Jane Austen: Women, Politics and the Novel* Claudia Johnson portrays Austen as a political writer, as mirroring the effect of the French Revolution on contemporary women writers. Like Poovey, she stresses Austen's subversiveness, discussing how Austen's gender would have complicated the expression of political opinion in her writing. Like Butler, Johnson sees Austen as deeply conscious of her political and literary context, but, unlike Butler, Johnson shows Austen to be a liberal and socially critical – but non-radical – writer. Johnson thus reassesses Butler's Austen as one who writes fictions that empower women and are critical of society – to an extent. Again, Johnson does this by connecting Austen to her contemporaries.

As regards *Pride and Prejudice,* Johnson finds that, on the surface, the novel 'corroborates conservative myths', according to which the established social forms guaranteed happiness. The hero is a kind yet sober member of the gentry, the villain an upstart who shows no gratitude whatsoever. The happy ending apparently does not address social problems but is aesthetically pleasing and has a 'fairy-like quality'. Yet, Johnson maintains, 'we should not let our own rather modern preference for ideological conflict predispose us to undervalue Austen's achievement in *Pride and Prejudice*'.

■ To imagine versions of authority responsive to criticism and capable of transformation is not necessarily to 'escape' from urgent problems into 'romance' and to settle for politically irresponsible 'consolations of form' which offer us a never-never land and leave the structures of the 'real world' unchanged. When we recall that Austen's preceding novel could locate her protagonists' contentment only in a retreat from and renunciation of power, Austen's decision here to engage her exceptionally argumentative antagonists in direct, extensive, and mutually improving debates can just as well be viewed as a step towards, rather than an 'escape' from, constructive political commentary. □

While the novel's ending does indeed dodge some of the social realism of its beginning, such as what would have happened to the Bennet sisters after their father's death had they not married well, Johnson argues that 'the novel as a whole certainly does not evade or neutralize social criticism out of a fond or unquestioning allegiance to established forms and the attractive men who embody them.'

■ In fact, the 'conservatism' of *Pride and Prejudice* is an imaginative experiment with conservative myths, and not a statement of faith in them as they had already stood in anti-Jacobin fiction. To be sure, by using these myths, even to hedge, qualify, and improve them, Austen is also [...] unavoidably used by them. But throughout the course of the novel those myths become so transformed that they are made to accommodate what could otherwise be seen as subversive impulses and values, and in the process they themselves become the vehicles of incisive social criticism. □

While Darcy conforms to the conservative ideal of his rank and sex, Elizabeth certainly does not, and 'many social and political issues cluster around her characterization'. It is easy for us, reading 200 years after the novel's publication, to overlook just how outrageously unconventional Elizabeth is. Her behaviour, 'judged by standards set in conduct books and in conservative fiction, constantly verges not merely on impertinence but on impropriety'. To emphasise this point, Austen even has Mr Collins read one such conduct book to the Bennet sisters, *Sermons to Young Women* by the Reverend James Fordyce (1720–96), which was first published in 1766 but remained popular in the 1790s and 1810s when Austen was writing. As Johnson points out, the fact that it is Mr Collins who approves of such a book

■ of itself signals Austen's disaffection with the rules about women promulgated in them. Austen could hardly recommend behavior to her readers through anyone so morally stunted as Collins, a fact not sufficiently reckoned with by critics who argue that Austen's inflexible orthodox morality is anchored in, if not actually derived from, volumes he enjoys. □

And although Lydia might possibly benefit from such books, their rules actually condemn Elizabeth's behaviour just as much as Lydia's. The book may show us from where Mr. Collins draws his ideas about female conduct, but, Johnson states, Fordyce's approval of the '"amiable reserve" of "elegant females," together with his underlying assumption that women's primary desire and duty is to please men, especially through the affectation of modesty, [...] does not provide us with standards flexible and intelligent enough to evaluate Elizabeth's'.

An example of how Austen deals with the tradition of novels of social criticism is the way she handles the confrontation between Elizabeth and Lady Catherine, which is 'simultaneously bold and delicate'. Johnson sees this treatment as 'decisively progressive' because Elizabeth does not regard Lady Catherine's interests, and the interests of the ruling class, as morally binding.

> ■ Convinced that they occupied high ground, progressive novelists seize on the same kinds of distinctions and exploit them for all they are worth, contending, more systematically and more conspicuously of course, that the defenders of money and rank marshal speciously ethical artillery – such as Lady Catherine's 'duty,' 'honour,' and 'gratitude' – in order to sustain their hegemony, and that it is only by force of 'prejudice' that we are either bullied or duped into equating our moral imperatives with their interests. □

This is further emphasised by Lady Catherine's character. Instead of being dignified and as such commanding respect, she is 'every bit as ludicrous as Mrs. Bennet'. It is thus important to note that Elizabeth's resistance to authority is a resistance to Lady Catherine: she is female, and she is ridiculous, and as such 'not the most formidable embodiment' of the patriarchal family.

> ■ Because these surrogates are easier to assail than, say, fathers and uncles, they make it possible to show what is oppressive about the power of rank and wealth, and what is overbearing about their assumptions of superiority. Further, they also make it possible to represent rebellion against the claims of familial authority, because in Austen's novels, at least, female authority figures are invariably defied by their young male relations. Though they may hold some purse strings, they hold virtually no moral sway. Because they cannot enforce obedience, their imperiousness is risible. [...]
>
> If Austen's use of a weak and ridiculous female authority figure makes it possible to dramatize effectual resistance, it is at the cost of minimizing the extent and perhaps even obscuring the object of that resistance. Quite simply, it is left unclear whether all attempts on the part of the high and mighty to meddle in the autonomous choices of others are to be deemed insufferable, or whether it is merely that Lady Catherine's attempts to wield power are incompetent, inappropriate and eccentric. □

Lady Catherine provides a figure at which the critique aimed at Darcy's parents, or indeed the ruling families in general, can be directed. As such she shows 'the advantages as well as the limitations of complying, even critically, with conservative myths about the gentry as Austen does in this novel'. While the insolence of rank is being criticised, this criticism is never strong enough to make the reader doubt their prestige.

■ Austen's attempt to reform gentry myths in *Pride and Prejudice* entailed consenting to most of their basic outlines. The resulting tension is just as conspicuous in her treatment of marriage and family as it is in her treatment of class relations. To most readers, Austen's allegiance to conservative social values is proven by the inevitability of marriage in her novels, for it is marriage that at all times confirms and reproduces established social arrangements, and marriage that, at this particular time, was seen as the best possible arrangement in an imperfect world and, moreover, the sole arrangement by which we can nurture precious moral affections. On some counts, as we have already seen, Austen clearly parts company with the conservative apologists of her own time. Family affections are so far from being considered sufficient or essential to the development of rectitude here, any more than in *Sense and Sensibility*, that Darcy cannot be an acceptable husband until his moral imagination has broadened enough to respect the dignity of those outside his 'family circle'. Furthermore, the wish to subordinate unruly individual passions to prescribed social duties prompts conservative novelists such as [...] West to minimize and even dismiss the importance of love as a precondition of marriage. Austen, on the other hand, puts a premium on it. Not without a touch of self-mockery which seems to imply an awareness that she is the heroine of an extraordinary novel, Elizabeth boasts that the marriage of Darcy and herself can 'teach the admiring multitude what connubial felicity really was'. At least one reason why she is right is that unlike Charlotte's marriage to Collins, her marriage, as well as Jane's, promises 'rational happiness' as well as 'worldly prosperity'.[27] □

Johnson thus shows that *Pride and Prejudice* appropriates conservative gentry myths, while at the same time aligning itself with novels that are socially critical, by itself beginning to criticise these myths.

Isobel Armstrong similarly sees *Pride and Prejudice* as on the one hand 'averting revolution' but on the other 'challenging repression'. While the ending seems to adhere to a conservative plot ideal, this is 'continually questioned by the narrative process'. While it may not be obvious on the surface, the text is 'only too strongly marked by history', and this concern with the politics of Austen's own day signifies the novel's depth. The ending, especially, which seems to appropriate for a comedy, leads the reader to conclude that all problems are resolved, but, Armstrong argues, the novel is in fact not 'unproblematical': 'if it is implicitly about averting revolution, it is just as strongly concerned with challenging repression, and the double programme creates complexities which glance off its superficially glittering surface.'

Austen herself had asked whether 'the novel was not 'rather too light and bright and sparkling', and whether its 'playfulness and epigrammatism' required the contrast of 'anything', such as an interpolated 'history of Buonaparte', to relieve its uniform lightness'. Reminding us of this self-criticism on Austen's part, Armstrong wonders whether perhaps Austen had realized 'that such a 'history' was already covertly present in her novel':

■ On its last pages she remarks that the indigent couple, Wickham and Lydia, continue to be rootless with 'the restoration of peace'. Whether this is the peace settled by the Treaty of Amiens (1802), or one of the much later pauses in the Peninsular War (possibly after the relief of Portugal, 1812), or a hypothetical peace, is unclear. But what is important is the amazing insouciance with which the only overt reference to the major European event of the period, the Napoleonic Wars, occurs when the novel is almost at an end. Contemporary readers would have understood from the presence of the army that this was a novel of the post-revolutionary period set during the Napoleonic Wars, but the uncanny refusal to name these formative events is remarkable. And perhaps this arises less from a willingness to de-historicise her love-story than from a perception that the novel is only too strongly marked by history, however indirectly. The novel's scintillating wit reminds us that the strategy of the joke has come to be seen as a way of displacing aggression, anxiety, or pain. The text knows this: what does Elizabeth do after Darcy's humiliating public rejection of her as a dancing partner – and just as surely as a sexual partner – at the Netherfield ball but joke about it afterwards? In a similar way the displaced anxieties of the post-revolutionary period are at work in this novel. The aesthetic resolution of the 'conservative' plot is continually questioned by the narrative process and subverted by complexities of language.[28] □

Political, social and gender issues are intermingled, since 'political issues are explored through sexual signals', and the novel is 'marked, even scarred, by history', though for the most part it does not name the events directly. Armstrong, like Butler and Johnson, reads the text through the novel's historical context.

Critics writing in the later decades of the twentieth century not only establish her historical context, but also show that Austen engaged with it literarily, socially and politically. Writing by a woman is necessarily marked by the position of women in society. Gender, therefore, becomes a major point of focus, and literary greatness includes engagement with contemporary literary and social debates.

In the context of the general post-structuralist reaction against the previously dominant text-based readings, the approach of critics to Austen and her novels changes. Like the late nineteenth century, the late twentieth century focuses on Austen the woman and looks at the texts via her. However, the new reading is that Austen is no longer a kindly aunt with an exclusively domestic horizon, but a politically aware participant in early-nineteenth-century debates. While there are, of course, exceptions to this general trend, most studies assume that Austen cannot have lived unaware of her political and social context. Though critics vary as to the specific political view assigned to Austen, the majority approach the novels via the author's context, so that the works of an author whose political and social context had in no previous period been seen as having had an impact on her novels are now seen as necessarily reflecting her political opinions, especially as regards the situation of women. She is regarded as politicising her own situation as a woman writer in the 1810s, as well as commenting on women in society through her novels' heroines.

The next chapter looks at developments in criticism in the first decade of the twenty-first century. While this decade sees a continuation of the historicist trend described above, it also produces studies that go back to an exclusive focus on the text. Many critics, however, combine a close reading of the texts with placing Austen and her novels in a historical context.

CHAPTER SIX

The First Decade of the Twenty-First Century

Generally, as we have seen in the preceding chapters, critical trends during the second half of the twentieth century have moved from close reading and an exclusive focus on the text to a historicist reading that concentrated on context. In the first decade of the twenty-first century, Austen's novels have continued to elicit many critical studies as well as new editions for an ever increasing market of readers. Over the last decade, criticism has possibly been yet more diverse than before, combining some of the twentieth-century approaches. While many historicist readings continue to appear, for example coming from a postcolonial or feminist viewpoint, an increasing number of critics are now countering these contextual and politicised readings by going back to the texts themselves, deliberately concentrating on their aesthetic qualities, without taking into account the literary, biographical, historical, or political context of their genesis.

NEW AESTHETICISM

One such example of a critic consciously focusing on the text itself is David Miller in his study *Jane Austen or The Secret of Style* (2003), which offers a close reading of Austen's text. Rather than supplying yet another historicist reading of her novels, though without 'proposing we ignore the impact of cultural forces and form on her work',[1] he wants to bring the focus back to 'the originality of her literary achievement as such'.[2] Miller criticises historicist approaches that merely study Austen in the context of her referents while being indifferent to her actual texts.

Miller's main point is that Austen's Style, which he also calls 'Absolute Style', is an impersonal one that reveals no 'psyche, history, social position',[3] body, age, marital status, or gender. In fact, Austen 'may well be the *only* English example'[4] of a truly omniscient narrator: 'Nowhere else in nineteenth-century English narration have the claims of the "person", its ideology, been more completely denied.'[5] Authors such as Henry Fielding, William Makepeace Thackeray, or even George Eliot, often quoted as examples of omniscient narrators, are in fact very present in the text and thereby humanise their narrations, so that the reader can never forget the narrator's 'earthly origins'.[6] Austen, on the other hand, achieves an 'Austen Neuter',[7] revealing nothing that characterises a person.

One of the reasons for Austen's self-denial in her texts – and this is where Miller self-consciously does bring in biographical detail – is that nowhere in her fictional world do we get a successfully unmarried woman. Because spinsters are pathetic, Austen herself could never appear in her novels: 'Jane Austen's novels will never state what is widely supposed, or at least widely required, to be obvious: that their author is a woman, and an old maid.'[8] Yet, in her novels' world, old maids obviously feature.

■ No doubt good Miss Bates, also known as poor Miss Bates, wins herself some small place of regard by endlessly thanking society for its tolerance (albeit granted in the *irritated* forms of avoidance and ridicule) toward the conjugally irrelevant. She must bear nonetheless [an] unsexed appellation [...]. She is 'a good creature', 'there is not a better creature in the world', she 'thought herself a most fortunate creature'; but she is not a woman in any sense that is interesting either to society or to a novel whose own achievement of social centrality depends on her marginalization.

Far from doing much to alter this state of affairs, Austen refines it into unexceptional consistency. The recorder of Emma's ample inner life categorically refuses to Miss Bates any of the reserve that is its precondition, [...]. The unendurable garrulity typical of these characters, by stimulating our impatience *to get on with the story*, confirms our assent to the old maid's representational limits; indeed, as we ruthlessly skim their speeches, intolerable blemishes on a prose to which we otherwise gladly grant our undivided attention, we take the enforcement of these limits into our own hands. Never are we meant to see Emma as more of an 'imaginist' than when she seeks to prove to Harriet the acceptability of being a rich old maid, and even here, she retains a formidable reality check: 'If I thought I should ever be like Miss Bates! ... I would marry to-morrow!' Besides this temporary self-delusion, nothing contests the common sense of Harriet's opinion: 'To be an old maid at last ... that's so dreadful!'.[9] □

Miller argues that the stigma attached to spinsterhood does not just hold for the world of the novels – witness Charlotte Lucas' marrying Mr Collins rather than becoming an old maid, to the relief of her family – but is also true for Austen's own world. Thus, 'in no way representing herself, [the real old maid] performs the disappearing act of Absolute Style'.[10]

Another point Miller makes about Austen's Style is that it at times splits into two 'mutually exclusive, and definitive, states of being: (god-like) narration and (all-too-human) character'.[11] Characteristic of the Austen heroine is her Style, which in fact becomes her main asset on the marriage market. It is through her Style that she attracts a husband and gets married, thus escaping spinsterhood. However, before she can actually get married, she has to lose Absolute Style and instead become the 'abject subject'.[12] Using Elizabeth and Emma as examples, Miller argues:

■ Style, it would seem, can get a girl married, provided only that she persuades herself into believing she is not using it to that end, or to any end but its own. In fact, though, the relation of style to the marriage plot is far more perverse than such an account suggests. Though the heroine's adoption of style may induce the courtship plot, what brings this plot to fruition – what gets her desire to quicken, too – is a moment of mortification when, the better to acquire the selfhood she had never before wanted, the heroine forsakes style; or rather, what is much more demeaning, she flattens it into a merely decorative reminiscence of itself, like a flower pressed into a wedding album. If at first the novel allows for the naïve belief in a happy match between style and the social (Elizabeth: 'I hope I never ridicule what is wise or good'), its subsequent development of both terms requires, if not their divorce on grounds of mutual incompatibility, then an empathic subordination of style to the social, analogous to the strange, but perfectly ordinary, kind of 'equal' marriage that Mr. Bennet recommends for Elizabeth – and that she gets – in which she will look up to her husband as her superior. [...] So she falls out of the universality of Austen Style – the days of wit and retorts simply pass away – into the particularity of a self hitherto so hidden, so unknown, so barely existing that the pains she now takes to become acquainted with it almost suggest the labor pains of giving it actual birth.[13] □

This change, or 'fall', as Miller terms it, can be seen as resulting in three things: firstly, it immediately puts an end to any kind of ambition the heroine may have had to achieve Absolute Style; secondly, as regards genre, it emphasises the antithesis between narration and character; and thirdly, socially, the heroine now that she gives up style becomes a character and a woman – and as such, a subject to men. However, Miller argues, although this fall 'triply puts [the heroine] in her place',[14] the Austen heroine – and his examples throughout this passage are Emma and Elizabeth – is very willing to give up style and does not show regret at having done so. 'About her presumed deprivation of Darcy or Knightley, she may be miserable and depressed indeed, but as for style, she forfeits it unmourned.'[15] Both Elizabeth and Emma undergo mortification and shame for their aspirations to Absolute Style.

■ Each has exchanged her ambition to Absolute Style for a self of which, in the very first moment of coming to know it, she is 'absolutely ashamed'.

And overshadowing the moral reasons she brings forward to account for this shame – her misjudgment or misconduct – is the chagrin of being a woman who has just discovered that she *does* need to marry. [...] In a word, the Austen heroine chooses to embark on life as a person who already displays in ovo [in the egg, in embryonic form] the most dreadful features of Miss Bates. Like some suddenly disenchanted princess who assumes, as her authentic form, that of a toad unlikely *ever* to be kissed, she gives up style to become the 'bad subject' style had for a time held in abeyance.[16] □

Miller thus shows ways in which a close reading of the works themselves, deliberately eschewing any contextual referents, can result in useful insights. He does however self-consciously refer to the fact of Austen's not having married as one of the factors that contributed to Absolute Style, in that it was her very spinsterhood that was one of the reasons for her absolute self-denial in narrative voice.

John Wiltshire's *Jane Austen: Introductions and Interventions* (2006) is a series of essays on the novels. Some of them, the introductions, are straight close-readings of the novels, intended to introduce readers to some key issues in the novels. The interventions engage with criticism as well as with the novels themselves and make more definite arguments rather than introducing issues.

The 'Intervention' essay on *Pride and Prejudice*, entitled 'Mrs Bennet's Least Favourite Daughter', starts with a contextual reference to eighteenth-century theatre from which, Wiltshire states, some aspects of Mrs Bennet may well have derived. His main focus in the essay, however, is on the relationship between Mrs Bennet and Elizabeth. Much as we may dislike Mrs Bennet, it is

■ not possible merely to dismiss Mrs Bennet as a fool, because the focus of the reader's attention is at least in part on the cost she exacts from those who have to spend their days listening to her. If the reader feels both amusement and contempt at this figure's mindless inanities he or she must also reflect that despising one's mother is a far from comfortable position for a daughter, especially an extremely intelligent one, to be in.[17] □

A scene where Mr Bennet, as so often, addresses his daughter rather than his wife is analysed by Wiltshire:

■ In addressing his daughter in preference to his wife, Mr Bennet is by implication displacing his wife, and favouring Elizabeth with the attention and information he knows she craves. But though *Pride and Prejudice* clearly (and explicitly) suggests that Mr Bennet has a lot to answer for, the overriding implication, I think, is not that, having regard to their economic circumstances Mrs Bennet's psychology is one we can, at a stretch, sympathise with and understand. Instead – and fostered by the narration's close affinity with Elizabeth's point of view – it is to force upon the reader, repeatedly, scenes in which Mrs Bennet's talk and behaviour are felt to be personally offensive, in all nuances of the word. Though the role of mother is certainly the only one her society allows her to claim, she is that worst exemplar of the mother, a woman who cannot separate herself from her offspring because she is in many respects herself still an envious and fractious child.[18] □

And yet, Wiltshire argues, there are similarities between Elizabeth and her mother. One such are Mrs Bennet's sparkling eyes:

■ No other indication of Mrs Bennet as a physical being is given except her 'sparkling eyes'. And this notation occurs in the midst of chapters in which her second daughter's 'fine eyes' catch the attention of Darcy, and are repeatedly kept before the reader by the tiresome and unavailing teasing of him by Miss Bingley. Can this similarity of notation be an accident? Or is it the signal of a consanguinity that the text elsewhere deploys in a more veiled form? Are Mrs Bennet's baffled energies a distorted, bizarre version of her daughter's transgressive high spirits – this daughter who runs everywhere? Elizabeth's provocative social manner remains within the wiry bounding line of decorum, but it surely reproduces, in moderated form, her mother's forwardness. Is Mrs Bennet's embodiment then a more or less pathological variation of her daughter's vitality? One does not press such questions too far. Yet we can begin to see how Austen prompts the reader's imagination to fill in the spaces, the silences of the relation between Elizabeth and her mother. Even Mrs Bennet's comic self-contradictions are echoed, to provide a more subtle amusement for the reader, when Elizabeth tells her mother that she can 'safely promise ... never to dance with Darcy'.[19] □

Precisely because they are also similar, Wiltshire argues that the novel is not just 'a great romantic narrative'[20] but also one that 'enacts in the boldest and most persuasive form the young adult's desire for differentiation and separation from the parent of the same sex'.[21] Because Mrs Bennet is 'a persistent shadow over her daughter's destiny',[22] the novel stresses just how far Elizabeth's future home Pemberley is from the Bennets' home at Longbourn.

Like Miller's, Wiltshire's study is thus primarily a close reading of the text. The majority of studies appearing in the twenty-first century place Austen's novels more obviously into context, even where their main focus is also the text.

TEXT AND CONTEXT

Claire Lamont in her 2003 essay 'Jane Austen and the Old' also offers a close reading of the texts, but with some reference to historical context.

Lamont analyses how Austen, 'a novelist of the contemporary',[23] yet refers to 'things that are old: old people, old families, old buildings and the old objects associated with them, old places and societies, and old ideas and fashions'.[24] However, in the majority of instances Austen's characters prefer the new to the old, with history being turned into something that does not 'make too many claims' on the present.[25] The older generations, and even ancestry, are not what Austen concerns herself with. In *Pride and Prejudice*, we find a family of daughters whose home is entailed onto a male heir. Yet, we do not get any explanation as to the history of the entail or why it was established.

■ The custom of entailing land might be thought to give an opening into the history of the family. Someone wanted to limit the power of an heir to dispose of property, in the interests of preserving the male line. [...] Austen is not concerned with why the entail was established, but with its consequences in the present. Her novels take a feminist view of entails – the inheritance will bypass the daughters, and their fathers, to judge from Mr Bennet and Sir Walter Elliot, will not have the strength of purpose necessary to save money from the property while it is theirs for their daughters' future support. It is amusing to note that only the overbearing Lady Catherine de Bourgh takes a feminist view of entails: 'I see no occasion for entailing estates from the female line. – It was not thought necessary in Sir Lewis de Bourgh's family.'[26] □

Similarly, we have no grandparents, no pictures that are of any interest to anyone, no visits to old or historical locations – characters travel to modern and fashionable places like Bath, Brighton, and London. We therefore notice 'the modernity of Austen's world',[27] since, for the majority of the novels' characters, 'things that are old are boring, irrelevant, and restrictive.'[28] Yet at the same time, the past cannot be entirely ignored, either.

■ Austen's novels describe a modern world in which most of the characters find history tedious to read, irrelevant to their concerns, and limiting to their wishes. But the past cannot be entirely denied, and the novels show several negotiations with it: the past can be imitated, modernized, replaced, or trivialized. A few characters act in ways given legitimacy by their historical inheritance, difficult though that might be. The majority of Austen's characters have moved on into a self-conscious modernity, and for them history is turned into something decorative and consumable which dos not make too many claims. In the language of today her novels show history being rewritten as heritage.[29] □

Through close analysis of the texts Lamont thus shows up Austen's ways of dealing with history and old things. She repeatedly compares Austen's texts to Scott's historical novels and she gives evidence of what

Austen must have known and thought about England's monastic ruins, but otherwise, Lamont takes a close reading approach.

A seminal study on Austen that combines a close reading of her texts with a contextual view is Peter Knox-Shaw's *Jane Austen and the Enlightenment* (2004). Taking his starting point from the observation that Marilyn Butler's view of a conservative and nostalgic Jane Austen still continues, he argues instead that Austen 'is a writer of centrist view who derives in large measure from the Enlightenment, more particularly from that sceptical tradition within it that flourished in England and Scotland during the second half of the eighteenth century'.[30] Knox-Shaw argues for the (life-long) influence of the philosopher and historian David Hume (1711–76) and the philosopher and political economist Adam Smith (1723–90) on Austen and emphasises that it is more this sceptical tradition's criticism of idealisms, its view of the 'irrationality of human nature' and of the 'limits of individual heroism' that Austen adheres to; a movement altogether 'less militant than its French counterpart'.[31]

In his chapter on '*Emma*, and the flaws of sovereignty', Knox-Shaw contends that 'Emma's fitful movement towards self-knowledge is tied [...] to her widening recognition of adjacent lives, so that she is involved in a process of discovery loosely analogous to the reader's, a ploy that was to become increasingly standard for the liberal novelist.'[32] Not only does Austen discuss Emma's view of the importance of her own rank here, she also 'upholds a belief in philanthropy'.[33] Connected to that is the novel's concern with other Enlightenment themes, such as benevolence, but also 'the makings of sociability': because the 'social fabric in country districts' was relatively tightly woven, it is the country that emerges 'as the best mode on offer for the civil'.[34] Highbury thus fits into this scheme, and it is Highbury that teaches Emma and the reader 'not that you have to learn to like everybody, but rather than you have to get on with people you do not like, and that these will never be in short supply'.[35] The novel therefore focuses on 'the provisions and skills that make for affable contact and easy accord'.[36]

Knox-Shaw focuses on the issue of courtship in *Emma*. Wollstonecraft had pointed out in her *Vindication of the Rights of Woman* the shallow education for females, which enables them to reign only during courtship and then be subordinated to their husbands. Mr Elton is an example of this chivalric courtship model and view of women: the charade he writes for Emma, though she believes it to be for Harriet, 'pictures exactly the sort of courtship that Wollstonecraft has in mind',[37] suggesting 'the reign of woman is valid only for the duration of courtship'.[38] Knox-Shaw then contextualises his argument:

> ■ Austen's contemporaries could be relied on to recognize the underlying contours of a stereotype in the character whose 'gallantry [is] always on

the alert' in mixed company, or who displays, as Emma admiringly says, 'the tenderest spirit of gallantry towards us all', for the word so repeatedly applied to Frank Churchill as well as to Mr Elton was replete with cultural clues. Samuel Johnson recorded its French origin in the Dictionary, where he singled out the sense of 'refined address to women' [...]. David Hume had noted that modern gallantry was the true descendant of feudal chivalry, and in a dialogue known to Wollstonecraft had commented on its ascendancy in the France of his time, remarking, in particular, on the way the courtly elevation of women effected a change in general manners – a premium being placed on politeness and gaiety, at the cost of simplicity and good sense. Attention has often been drawn to the association of Frank Churchill's style with things French [...]. When Mr Knightley remarks that Frank (aptly named) can be 'amiable only in French not in English' because he has the 'smooth, plausible manners' that rate as *aimable* while lacking real sensitivity to the feelings of others, his distinction is closely allied to the one made by Hume, and draws on an issue much contested by the Enlightenment. While most historians of civil society treated the original chivalric rescue of women from a subjugated state as a landmark of social development, the *revivalist* chivalry of Versailles, of the latter-day romance [...] was quite a different matter, smacking suspiciously of anachronism.[39] □

As Knox-Shaw points out, Claudia Johnson has persuasively linked 'the portrayal of Frank Churchill and Mr Elton to Wollstonecraft's critique of the effeminized male'.[40] Knox-Shaw argues that Emma and Knightley's courtship stands in opposition to this chivalry, being 'free of the tricks of conventional wooing'.[41] In fact, 'the slow maturation of the lovers' feelings for each other, their unselfconsciousness, and the very unintentionality of their involvement, remain wonderfully fresh and must have been particularly salutary when regulated courting was the order of the day'.[42]

Overall then, Knox-Shaw argues that, of all Austen's novels, *Emma* is steeped in Enlightenment concerns, and this highlights its liberal point of view: 'Enlightenment paradigms run deep in *Emma*, which is perhaps why it, more than any other Austen novel, provides the blueprint for a plan widely used by writers of liberal fiction later in the century.'[43]

An essay collection entitled *The Talk in Jane Austen* (2002), edited by Bruce Stovel and Lynn Weinlos Gregg, would at one time have included mostly essays using a new critical close-reading approach and a few decades later mostly ones applying a new historicist reading. In this collection, the approaches are combined and mixed. Gary Kelly in an essay on 'Jane Austen's Imagined Communities: Talk, Narration, and Founding the Modern State' takes historical context into account through a close-reading of the texts. The dialogues, as well as the omniscient narrator's dialect, 'allow the reader to experience another's subjectivity powerfully – and so to participate in an imagined community of novel readers that reinforces the defining qualities of the emerging nation-state of Great Britain. The aggression and power identified in this essay are those of the novelist herself and the professional class she embodies'.[44]

Jan Fergus in 'The Power of Women's Language and Laughter' looks at what Austen's novels have to say about talk and power. For example, when Elizabeth calls Darcy's judgments into question, 'are we to see Elizabeth as a successful subverter of the social order or is she simply working within it, becoming one of the boys?' (104) Laughter, Fergus argues, 'is a recourse for the disempowered'.[45] Both Elizabeth Bennet and Emma Woodhouse acquire equality and intimacy with Mr Darcy and Mr Knightley through their use of speech and laughter. There are differences between the two relationships, though:

■ Unlike Darcy, Mr Knightley does not have to learn to be laughed at; Emma has long laughed at him, and in their casual encounters [...] I believe it is possible to detect the intimacy that allows them a reciprocal exchange of the kind of irony, and the attendant modification of language, that we see operating only one way between Elizabeth and Darcy. In this sense, too, Mr Knightley may be a new model of an English gentleman whose manliness is defined and modified by woman's language – Emma's, and of course Jane Austen's.[46] □

Jocelyn Harris in her 'Silent Women, Shrews, and Bluestockings' argues that by 'allow[ing] her women characters to speak'[47] Austen undoes 'misogynist constructions of women', who 'have always been discouraged from knowing, speaking, and writing'.[48] In *Emma*, the heroine's openness is better than Jane Fairfax's reserve, even if Emma 'says too much too often'.[49] She, 'like Elizabeth Bennet, speaks too freely because her father's power is weak'.[50] Austen 'shields her outspoken and intelligent heroines from being labeled shrews or bluestockings',[51] partly by using two dramatic devices, the soliloquy and the dialogue overheard:

■ Her last defence is purely technical, for her famous trick of coloured narrative [narrative 'coloured', or influenced by a character's point of view] allows her heroines to think uncomfortable truths that they could never articulate aloud – a daughter's criticism of her parents, for instance. If Elizabeth had said that her mother 'was a woman of mean understanding, little information, and uncertain temper', or pointed out her father's 'continual breach of conjugal obligation and decorum which, in exposing his wife to the contempt of her own children, was so highly reprehensible', we would barely tolerate such unfilial and shrewish remarks.[52] □

As it is, Elizabeth herself is conscious of the all-important difference between 'thinking an uncharitable thought and speaking it'.[53] Through their conscious and powerful speech, then, Austen makes heroines such as Elizabeth and Emma

> ■ def[y] the three thousand years of misogyny that either silenced women or called them shrewish, unequal, inconstant, deceiving, ignorant, and inappropriately learned. [...] The constraints of custom forced her and her characters to adopt dramatic masks. But ultimately she rests her case, for her novels prove indeed that women can know and write.[54] □

These are three examples of the many aspects of talk in Austen's novels that this essay collection discusses. Talk is, after all, as the editors point out in their blurb, 'the principal occupation of Jane Austen's protagonists'.

Penny Gay in her *Jane Austen and the Theatre* (2002) takes a contextual approach, as her title suggests. While Austen's texts are dramatic in themselves and therefore lend themselves easily to adaptation, Gay's main concern is to point up inspirations that Austen may have taken from the plays she knew. During her childhood at Steventon, plays by Shakespeare and Sheridan were studied and eighteenth-century plays were performed by the Austen children. Later, she went to theatres in London, Bath and Southampton. Gay then compares eighteenth-century plays with each of Austen's novels in turn. As regards *Sense and Sensibility*, Gay first points out that 'the drama's contribution to the eighteenth-century debate about sensibility was extensive',[55] and that, of course, Austen would be familiar with many of these contributions. Thus, Elinor and Marianne are seen by Gay as in some ways similar to Kate Hardcastle and Constance Neville in *She Stoops to Conquer* (1773) by Oliver Goldsmith (1730–74), but also to Lydia Languish and Julia Melville in *The Rivals* (1775) by Richard Brinsley Sheridan (1751–1816). Similarly, Charles Marlow from *She Stoops to Conquer* can be regarded in his shyness and self-consciousness as a forerunner of Edward Ferrars. 'Both complain of their education in establishments that kept them from acquaintance with the sophisticated manners of society; both are conscious of their social awkwardness.'[56] Marlow's particular difficulty is that he is extremely awkward around women of his own class, but has no inhibitions when in the society of lower-class women. Gay quotes Edward: 'I have frequently thought that I must have been intended by nature to be fond of low company, I am so little at my ease among strangers of gentility!'

> ■ 'Low company' is not a phrase Austen generally uses, and Edward is probably here deliberately evoking Goldsmith's critique of snobbery [...]. It is a pleasing thought that the novel's tyrannical mother Mrs Ferrars might be construed by contemporary readers to be as foolish and ignorant as Goldsmith's country snob Mrs Hardcastle.[57] □

Similarly, Gay sees *The Rivals* as dealing with themes that recur in *Sense and Sensibility* as well as with characters:

■ Jack Absolute's masquerade as the sentimental Ensign Beverly in order to woo the novel-addicted Lydia Languish is a critique of the hypocrisy that parades as the New Sensitive Masculinity, and it interestingly prefigures Austen's exploration of masculinity in *Sense and Sensibility*. If we read the eloquent but effete Willoughby as 'Beverly', and the frank and honest Colonel Brandon as 'Absolute', it is to have them 'both' wooing the heroine of sensibility and the plain soldier finally winning.[58] □

Gay thus approaches Austen's novels from a biographical and contextual angle, taking into account what she discovers about Austen's knowledge particularly of contemporary plays and finding evidence in the novel's texts for Austen having worked with this knowledge.

Janet Todd in *The Cambridge Introduction to Jane Austen* starts off with chapters on Austen's 'Life and Times' and 'The Literary Context', before moving on to a closer analysis of each the novels. This inclusion again emphasises that introductions, whether to an edition of an individual novel or to Austen's oeuvre as such, tend to include information about the author and her times in historical, political, literary and cultural terms, rather than focusing exclusively on the novels themselves. In her chapter on Austen's literary context, Todd argues both for differences and for similarities. One of the differences is that Austen's novels 'do not insist on a didactic goal, whether politically, radical, or Christian',[59] in contrast to many of the novels of her female contemporaries, which did have a didactic purpose, and which were, because of this, often not very realistic. Similarly, although fully aware of the works of Scott, William Wordsworth (1770–1850) and Byron, she consciously did not attempt to write in Scott's historical vein. Also, her 'main characters are unlike the self-obsessed heroes of Romantic poetry';[60] instead, they are 'embedded in time, place, and fashion; they are endowed with plausible modes of speaking and looking, and given suitable phrases, hairstyles, and clothes'.[61]

In her analysis of *Sense and Sensibility*, Todd applies a typically historicist approach. She focuses on the novel's ending, which so many readers have found unsatisfactory. In Todd's view, both Marianne and Colonel Brandon have suffered losses and disillusionment, Marianne through Willoughby and Brandon through Eliza. Both Marianne and Brandon therefore move away from passion towards esteem, an emotion Willoughby is incapable of and Elinor feels from the start and continuously for Edward. Todd therefore argues that 'the book values and regrets the loss of romantic passion but celebrates the slow-growing love, allowing it to incorporate romantic memory'.[62] She then links

Marianne to Wollstonecraft, stating that 'there is little doubt that Austen knew of her'.[63] (William St Clair argues, however, that, given the small numbers of copies produced, in fact very few women readers would have had direct access to Wollstonecraft's *Vindication*.[64])

■ Wollstonecraft thought women enslaved by sensibility, 'a romantic unnatural delicacy of feeling', so that they remained always childlike and deliciously dependent on men rather than on themselves. However, in her final work, *The Wrongs of Woman* (1798), and in her personal letters, she also saw the illusory feeling of heightened experience as valuable, even when it led to misery.[65] □

Wollstonecraft's husband, William Godwin, published his Memoir of his wife in 1798, immediately after her death, in which he also described her love affair with Gilbert Imlay. Todd argues that Austen 'would not have approved her sexual activity, but in the portrait of Marianne she provides something of the generous and trusting aspects of the Wollstonecraft of the *Memoirs*':[66]

■ Although more extreme, describing two suicide attempts rather than a suicidal illness, Godwin's narrative follows a similar trajectory to Marianne's. but, where Godwin presents closeness to death as part of Wollstonecraft's powerful sensibility, Austen suggests how culturally overwhelmed Marianne is by expectations of female passion leading to death. Two narratives come together again in the conclusion: after 'suffering some of the sharpest struggles that our nature is capable of enduring', Wollstonecraft saw her later and final love for Godwin as one of esteem, of 'sublime tranquility'.[67] □

Todd assumes that Austen must have known the writings of and about her contemporary Mary Wollstonecraft and therefore links the character of Marianne and her experiences to Wollstonecraft's views and life. She thus places *Sense and Sensibility* in not only an historical context but also a literary and cultural one.

TEXT AND BIOGRAPHY

Like David Miller, Bharat Tandon is attentive to aspects of Austen's style in his *Jane Austen and the Morality of Conversation* (2003). In contrast to Miller, however, Tandon mixes his close analysis of conversation in Austen with an historicist approach. While the activity of conversation was regarded as a tool for moral improvement in the eighteenth century, the early nineteenth century was ambiguous in its approach and saw the possibility of deceit and misunderstanding. It is within this framework that Tandon places Austen's ways of working with and playing upon the ideals of polite conversation, showing that Austen not only describes a kind of conversational morality but also represents it as an aim.

Ventriloquism is one conversational mode that Tandon analyses in *Emma*. He first gives the historical and literary context of this phenomenon, then shows how Austen makes use of it. To emphasise his points about Austen's fiction, he cites from her letters. From these, he gives examples that show similar uses of language to those which occur in her novels.

■ Ventriloquial possession – where characters either consciously inhabit others with their words, or find themselves unwittingly mouthing words from elsewhere – has a long literary pedigree [...] and its potential for both comic and uncanny effects does not pass Austen by. In a letter to Cassandra in October 1808, she noted with wry disapproval 'a wedding in the Salisbury paper, which has amused me very much, Dr Phillot to Lady Frances St Lawrence. *She* wanted to have a husband I suppose, once in her life, and *he* a Lady Frances.' The possessiveness which Austen skewers on her indefinite article recurs in *Emma*, where the heroine's first thoughts about Harriet are phrased in just such words: 'She had ventured once alone to Randalls, but it was not pleasant; and a Harriet Smith [...] would be a valuable addition to her privileges.' These coolly rational terms could almost come from *Lady Susan*; they make no distinction between people and things to be collected. Harriet comes to sound like something with which Emma can 'accessorise', a tame lapdog to take out for walks, rather than a human being, let alone a friend. [...] The vocabulary of material possessiveness which pervades *Lady Susan* returns here: for example, after Emma has rejected Elton's advances, she rightly surmises that 'he only wanted to aggrandize himself; and if Miss Woodhouse of Hartfield, the heiress of thirty thousand pounds, were not quite so easily obtained as he had fancied, he would soon try for Miss Somebody else with twenty, or with ten, and, sure enough, we are later told that 'he had gained a woman of 10,000l. or thereabouts'. 'Object', 'obtained', 'gained a woman'; Austen was never one to downplay hard material necessities, but the confluence of 'propriety' with 'property' is shown up in a less flattering light at such moments.[68] □

Tandon here combines close analysis of Austen's language with a consideration of Austen's life, as well as drawing comparisons not only between Austen's use of English in her letters and in her novels, but also between various works in her fictional oeuvre.

This method of applying close analysis together with a contextual approach continues throughout his study. Another example is the discussion of *Emma*'s ending. Tandon argues that Austen's mature works merely hint at questions that in earlier works she still had to spell out, such as *Lady Susan* ending on the narrator's asking whether or not Lady

Susan will be happy in her second choice, and similarly *Northanger Abbey* asking at the end what the moral lesson to be learned from it might be.

■ By the time of *Emma*, Austen can compact such questions into the novel's final silence; plot and narrative, closure and contingency, narrow to an apex in 'the perfect happiness of the union' – then vanish into a blank which is as finally unknowable as the urge to fill it is irresistible. That lifelong scrutiny of the distance and closeness between selves and words, which Austen conducts in her letters, in her epistolary fictions, and on into the mature novels, gives rise in *Emma* to one of the greatest ventriloquial tricks in nineteenth-century fiction: after all the novel's echoes and awkward repetitions, the final phrase of the narrative invites a reader to project his or her own 'ever after', providing a space into which readers can throw their voices, only to echo them straight back, in a final act of novelistic passive resistance. [...] Austen has, throughout the story, threatened the romance by surrounding it with characters unfulfilled within or without marriages, and with possible alternative versions of Emma herself. She then has the audacity to present a romance ending which depends on a marriage, whilst all the time amassing an ever larger weight of equivocal or worrying precedent. [...] Despite all appearances to the contrary, it is as impossible to say definitively how Emma 'turns out' as it is to be wholly at one with the intimacy of others, or to achieve that 'absolute clarity' at which sentimental correspondents aimed – we share the words, but not the timbres which fully give them meaning. The brilliant doubleness of *Emma*'s ending is that it weighs the banality, and the attrition, against which the lovers' hopes are tensed, within the same words. Instead of offering simple oppositions between the 'real' and the 'ideal', the plaited strands of Austen's narrative implicitly recognize the idealizing impulse as part of that reality which novels represent.[69] □

According to Tandon, Austen gives us 'worrying precedent[s]' that make the ending not an unequivocally happy one and cause the reader to doubt that 'perfect happiness' that Emma and Knightley might achieve. Tandon argues that Austen stops 'just before the "ever after"', and remains poised endlessly on the brink',[70] so that we can never be absolutely certain what will follow and instead have to judge 'from probability'. And again, as in the previous example, he backs his analysis up with references to Austen's letters, other novels, and her life.

Linda Bree in her essay on '*Emma*: Word Games and Secret Histories' (2009) gives an introductory account of the novel, and again combines close attention to the text with a biographical/contextual approach. She sets *Emma* in the context of Austen's being 'very familiar with village life', having spent most of her life living in the Hampshire villages of first Steventon and later Chawton.[71] Bree points out how word games 'were a common form of entertainment in Austen's own family',[72] and how this can be seen in *Emma*, for example in Harriet's charade collection.

■ Mr Knightley's distinction between 'amiable' and *aimable* in trying to put his finger on the deficiencies of Frank Churchill's personality [...] is related to this, but hints at extra dimensions of significance in plays on words. And the narrator of the novel has interests in wordplay at her own level, too, for example in the variations rung on significant words such as 'perfection' and 'blunder'. Simple forms of wordplay may hold innocent entertainment for Highbury inhabitants, but they also open up larger questions of words and their meanings, and discrepancy between what is said and what is being conveyed.[73] □

As well as the novel's language, Bree analyses its heroine, and ends on stating that even 'such a lovely, intelligent, self-misleading, self-searching woman as Emma Woodhouse'[74] can aim at nothing but marriage, and ends up 'dwindl[ing] into a Highbury wife'.[75] This is a similar argument to that made by feminist critics who bemoan exactly this aspect of the lives of Austen's heroines, their lack of options and their having to settle for marriage – even Emma Woodhouse, who so decidedly sets out by saying that she has no need to marry.

AUSTEN AND ROMANTIC PERIOD LITERATURE

As Colin Winborn himself points out, his approach in *The Literary Economy in Jane Austen and George Crabbe* (2004) is one that 'combines close reading with fresh contextual and historical insights'.[76] Winborn seeks to show up links between Austen and Crabbe (1755–1832) in their 'common concern with economy [...a] concern [that] was of particular urgency during the period on which they were writing'.[77] Usually, Winborn points out, Austen and Crabbe have been linked through seeing their works as anti-Romantic; published during the Romantic age but not Romantic in the sense of the great Romantic writers of the period. Rather than seeing similarities in what both these writers do not do, he wants to show their similar response to the political context of the Napoleonic Wars, 'in particular the economic pressure of the Napoleonic trade embargo (1806–1812), which transformed the way people conceptualized national space and the appropriate use of resources'.[78] Both writers, Winborn argues, were 'unusually responsive to the economic anxieties of their time'.[79] Part of this common concern can be traced down to their use of similar vocabulary.

   Winborn further contextualises Austen and Crabbe by placing their work in the context of thinkers contemporary to them, among them

Thomas Malthus (1766–1834), who wrote about what he saw as the dangers of overpopulation. He argued against giving any help or support to the poor since their situation was their own fault for over-reproducing themselves. In his *Essay on the Principle of Population* (1798) , Malthus uses the following sentence: 'It is an acknowledged truth in philosophy that a just theory will always be confirmed by experiment.'[80] Winborn argues that the opening sentence of *Pride and Prejudice* ('It is a truth universally acknowledged, that a single man in possession of a good fortune, must be in want of a wife') is 'a definite echo of Malthusian rhetoric':[81]

■ Austen's evocation of Malthusian rhetoric – with the phrase 'It is a truth universally acknowledged'– is suggestive. It mines the economist's gross assumption, sounding out its bases. When Malthus writes sweepingly that 'It is an acknowledged truth in philosophy that a just theory will always be confirmed by experiment', Austen would have us ask *by whom* this is acknowledged to be the case. What local truth is hidden by this implied universality? Austen's novel is interested in the universal only as it is dependent on the local. It suggests how philosophical Truth is composed of smaller domestic truths.[82] □

In the passage following that first sentence of *Pride and Prejudice*, the 'truth universally acknowledged' becomes 'a truth fixed in the minds of the surrounding families' and is thus brought down to the level of the local. Through this, Winborn argues, Austen renders Malthus' argument too general and shows 'the problem of what Malthus neglects in his universalizing rhetoric' since the economist works 'on the broadest possible canvas at the expense of detail and regional colour'.[83] Austen's 'translation from the universal back to the local [...] in fact reverses the intellectual movement of Malthus' *Essay*, and also perhaps brings it into question'.[84]

As regards the 'economy of words', Winborn analyses how both Mrs Bennet and Mr Collins cannot stop talking, whereas Elizabeth and Mr Darcy 'articulate themselves through a tightly regulated economy of words'.[85] To be concise is seen as a strength, 'the strength of a close-guardedness which conceals, makes private, renders self-sufficient'[86] and is placed by Winborn in the context of Rousseau. He therefore combines in his study close-reading with a contextual approach by relating Austen's novels to Crabbe as well as to thinkers contemporary with her.

Another study that places Austen in the context of the British Romantic movement, more specifically in the context of the works of Wordsworth, Samuel Taylor , Coleridge (1772–1834), Scott, and Byron, is *Jane Austen and the Romantic Poets* (2004) by William Deresiewicz. He discusses the differences between the two phases in her career, the first in which *Northanger Abbey*, *Sense and Sensibility* and *Pride and Prejudice* were written (the 1790s), and the second phase, which saw the production of *Mansfield Park*, *Emma*, and *Persuasion* (the 1810s). He argues that we need to pay attention not only to the personal things that changed between these two periods but also to 'the most significant literary event of her lifetime: the flowering of the poetic movement that later became known as British Romanticism'.[87] Rather than looking at specific elements in the novels that might relate to the Romantic movement, he argues 'for a sustained, major influence, one that structures whole novels and pervades an entire phase of her career'.[88] Especially the work of Byron and Scott 'deeply stirred'[89] her, and the fact that she satirises Byron in *Persuasion* and Scott in *Sense and Sensibility* actually shows how much she admired them: 'For Austen, satire was the sincerest form of flattery'.[90] As regards Wordsworth and Coleridge, 'given their great prominence, it is virtually certain that by 1811 a reader such as Austen would have long known their work very well'.[91]

As regards *Emma*, Deresiewicz argues that its 'greatest debt to the British Romantic poets' lies in ideas that Austen drew 'about new possibilities for intimate relationships – their complexity and depth, their freedom from conventional social hierarchies and categories, their transformative potential'.[92] An example is Emma's relationship with Miss Taylor, which he sees as ambiguous – the first description of Miss Taylor refers to her as 'governess', 'mother', 'friend', 'sister'. The number of terms applied here serves 'to capture a relationship of such complexity – of such ambiguity', since it is

■ Austen's purpose here, at the very start of the novel, to expose the inadequacy of such labels to characterize the kinds of relationships she will be concerned to explore, relationships that, in their fruitful, liberating ambiguity, continually push beyond conventional categories, conventional boundaries, conventional roles.[93] □

This ambiguity, he finds, is new to the second-phase novels: 'we have never seen anything like this before in Austen's work. The world of the early novels is one of clearly defined roles – daughter, father, neighbour, suitor'.[94] He explains that 'ambiguous relationships can be found throughout British Romantic literature'.[95] For example, Wordsworth in 'Lines written a few miles above Tintern Abbey' (1798) calls out 'thou, my dearest Friend' (line 115) and only after some lines reveals this friend to be his 'dear dear Sister' (line 122). According to Deresiewicz,

■ Wordsworth means us to understand that such heights of passion can be reached outside the realm of the erotic, that one can feel fraternal or amicable feelings with an erotic intensity. And he also wants us to understand that a large part of what conduces to such intensities is precisely a blending of different kinds of feelings, a dynamic ambiguity of relationship.[96] □

Through close reading of various scenes in *Emma*, Deresiewicz shows a similar ambiguity in almost all the relationships that occur in the novel. For example, the role Knightley occupies towards Emma is hard to define in many of the scenes he has with her,

■ whether [it is] that of neighbor or friend of the family or father figure or any other. The lines between those roles or modes, then, do not so much get crossed and recrossed as effaced. Knightley is not finally all of those things to Emma at once, any more than Miss Taylor was at once a mother, a sister, and a governess. He is, as she was, something else altogether.[97] □

Deresiewicz employs an historicist approach combined with close analysis of the text to claim that 'in *Emma*, under the influence of Wordsworth and Byron, Austen engages the idea of friendship more deeply and complexly than ever before',[98] through her use of ambiguous relationships.

Again, an historicist approach is also taken by Anthony Mandal in his *Jane Austen and the Popular Novel: The Determined Author* (2007). His aim is to show Austen as a determined author in two senses, not only as a writer who was 'self-assured [...] in her calling as a novelist'[99] in spite of not getting published for a long time, but also as a writer who was determined in what she wrote by what was happening in the immediate print culture around her. Mandal focuses on the decade in which Austen actually published all of her novels, the 1810s, to show how she engaged with her literary context, visible in 'the dialogic nature of her texts, which polyvalently appropriated both the radical and the conservative discursive fields as they suited Austen's purpose'.[100] Mandal first establishes the literary context in which Austen publishes, using new data from *British Fiction, 1800–1829: A Database of Production, Circulation and Reception* (2004), to which he contributed. He discusses her publishers, including Cadell & Davies, who rejected the early version of *Pride and Prejudice* and Crosby & Co., who rejected the early version of *Northanger Abbey*, as well as those that did publish her novels, first Thomas Egerton and then John Murray.

Mandal then moves on to show through analytical comparisons how Austen responded in her novels to particular novelists and their output. His chapter on *Emma* is entitled 'Woman as Genius/Genius Loci: *Emma* as an English National Tale', and its subheadings are 'The social and literary contexts for *Emma*', 'National heroinism', 'To be a true citizen of Highbury'. These headings already show just how grounded in context his analysis is, as well as his focus on *Emma* as a tale of nationality. Giving the historical context of the Napoleonic Wars as the context for Scott's hugely successful novels and Austen's later ones, Mandal states that Napoleon's presence 'certainly enabled the formulation of an effective and anti-Continental concept of nationhood'.[101]

■ Specifically, it was one located in the middling classes, supporting Tory-gentry politics, and enshrining Englishness of a particularly 'domestic' – that is, insular and self-reflexive – nature. This nexus of imperatives coincides with the publication of discrete but intertwined definitions of 'Britishness' in *Waverley* and 'Englishness' in *Emma*. Indeed, it is within this synergistic and complex negotiation of conflict and victory between nations that *Emma* is to be located.[102] □

In many ways, then, *Emma* is to be seen in contrast to the 'national heroism'[103] in the novels of Sydney Owenson (1776–1859) and Germaine de Stael (1766–1817), particularly in Owenson's *The Wilde Irish Girl* (1806) and Stael's *Corinne, ou l'Italie* (1807). The national tale is trapped in the conflict between 'a politically conservative accept-ance of the nation's place within an imperial context (the United Kingdom, Napoleonic Europe) [...], and an individualistic, Romantic vision of discrete cultural identity accreted through layers of history and prehistory [...] (Ireland, Italy)'. This results, Mandal states, in a narrative that contrasts the male protagonist who represents 'the mod-ern, metropolitan colonizer' with the heroine, 'the idyllic, enclosed colonized'.[104] There is, therefore, a relation between the woman and the nation: 'being a woman and being Irish are analogical'.[105] The sentimental romance narrative is therefore 'represented as an act of colonization', and consequently Corinne ultimately dies. Not so, however, Emma.

■ Nevertheless, *Emma* is less an instinctive reaction against such 'Continental' conceptions of femininity, as an engaged response to the nov-elistic framework within which such heroines are cast. Austen subtly dis-mantles the apparatus of the national tale by providing a counter-narrative which contrasts melodrama with realism, rather than satire, and grandiose mythmaking with psychosocial depth, rather than bathetic caricature. The static perfections of Glorvina, Ida, and Corinne can be contrasted with the development of the Austenian protagonist. Whereas the enduring accom-plishments of the heroine direct the national romance, Austen's novel is driven by an examination of the heroine's imperfections. *Emma* is the only one of Austen's novels to be published featuring the heroine's name as its title: like the unpublished *Susan*, its focus is on the re-education of a misguided figure who must learn to distinguish romance from reality, fic-tion from fact. The title of the national romances themselves enunciate the correlation between heroine and nation – *Corinne, or Italy* – an act that establishes a dialectical paradigm connecting woman to nation. Is the novel about the heroine or the country? Does a sense of the heroine adumbrate our sense of the nation, or does our reading of the travelogue about Italy open up readings of the heroine? By contrast, the title of Austen's novel ironically reinflects the practices of the national tale, so that eponymity represents not the locus of perfection but the site of social re-education and psychological re-evaluation. Unlike Corinne, there is no parity between heroine and nation here: Emma is certainly not representative of England, and must instead divest herself of excessive individuality, inscribing herself communally within the English provincial world that consistently undercuts Emma's romantic narratives.[106] □

According to Mandal, the most important thing Emma has to learn is 'to integrate herself into the social life of Highbury';[107] she must 'detach herself from her grandiose snobbery and romanticism and integrate herself into community life, symbolized through her union with Knightley'.[108] As a novel, then, *Emma* reinforces 'existing social structures within the broader village community, offering a network of gentry, professionals, and the middle ranks as an alternative to aristocrats and self-inventing heroines of Owenson and Stael'.[109] In contrast to the national tale's romantic individualism, Austen advocates a heroine who learns to lead her life within the social structures of the village community.

HISTORICIST FOCUS

Just as studies have appeared that focus on text more than context, there are also studies that do the opposite and always look at the texts within their original context. *Jane Austen's Textual Lives* (2005) by Kathryn Sutherland is one of the most important studies of Austen written to date. In it, Sutherland discusses how Austen has been constructed, through biographies, portraits, films, editions of the novels and illustrations, into what each editor, biographer, etc., believes – or would like – her to have been. Each historical period, like each individual reader, interprets both author and text differently. In her discussion of Austen biographies, Sutherland shows how the scarcity of material has encouraged biographers to use their imagination.

■ Cassandra Austen did biographers a profound service when she censored or destroyed her sister's private papers and correspondence. Whatever her reasons and whatever was burned, Cassandra licensed the imagining of fact, the dream of history. May not Cassandra's precise dating of her sister's last completed novels (*Emma* and *Persuasion*) point to the existence (and destruction) of a diary, Claire Tomalin speculates intelligently in her 1997 biography? And if the diary contained details of 'the starting and finishing dates' of her novels, what else might it not have contained? Extrapolating more boldly from the paucity of textual clues to the emotional crises of 1796–8, David Nokes, in his 1997 biography, despairingly asks: 'Why do we have no letters from this period? It can hardly be because Jane Austen did not write any ... It can only be that Cassandra ... chose to destroy them ... she preferred to obliterate the memory of a period of such distress.' A favoured strategy is to reconstitute empathetically these 'destroyed' traces. Accordingly, Nokes tells us that 'Cassandra received the news [of her fiancé Tom Fowle's death] with a kind of numbness. Outwardly, she was strangely calm ... Upon Jane the influence of this change in her sister's disposition was no less profound for being, at first at least, unacknowledged and unperceived.' In the interests of recoding the complete life, the biographer appears entitled to recover not only what must have existed and been destroyed but what only appears to be 'unacknowledged and unperceived'. In the hands of the skilful recorder, gaps and silences are even more eloquent than evidence. The form grows strangely fat on such omissions and biography's texts can seem endlessly recessive.[110] □

The 'facts' that are recorded in this way, then, keep being repeated until they seem commonplaces that do not need verification. The other important point Sutherland makes in connection with biographies is that barely any other author's image is so entirely influenced by family, and that we must remember just 'how late Jane Austen's biography remained a family property':[111] yet this family record of Jane Austen is partial and 'reads like myth-making rather than fact'.[112]

Sutherland shows how editors of Austen's texts have also interpreted and, in places, changed them. R.W. Chapman with his edition of the novels in 1923, the first scholarly edition of any British novelist, sought to confer the status of a 'classic' writer onto Austen by giving her texts treatment that until then had been reserved for classical Greek and Roman texts. This edition 'has remained the standard authority ever since',[113] and Sutherland argues for a reconsideration after such a long time, for several reasons. (The only edition that does not take Chapman's as the base text is the Penguin Classics edition of the mid-1990s, with Claire Lamont as the overall textual advisor. This edition goes back to the first edition texts.) One of these reasons is Chapman's at times 'intrusive'[114] way of editing Austen's texts: he suggests emendations where he believes the printer to have been at fault, or conventionalises where he thinks Austen's punctuation is wrong, so that Austen's texts became perfect by early-twentieth-century standards. However, as Sutherland points out, 'Punctuation, in particular, gives voice to the unvoiced text of print and in so doing conditions readers in habits of narrative attention and exerts control over meaning.'[115] She makes a case for going back to the first-edition texts as the ones that are closest to an uncounselled and unchanged Austen, using her study of the few extant manuscripts of Austen's work to give weight to her argument.

Sutherland's study is therefore a combination of an investigation of the primary materials by and relating to Austen and an analysis of how generations of editors, biographers and critics have appropriated them since.

Jane Austen in Context (2005), edited by Janet Todd, is a collection of short essays that illuminate various aspects of Austen's life, the novels, and the times she lived in. It is intended as a reference work, even arranged alphabetically within parts I to III. Part I deals with 'Life and Works', Part II puts the volume itself in context by discussing the novels' 'Critical Fortunes', and the largest section, Part III, discusses the novels' 'Historical and cultural context'. For example, Edward Copeland's chapter on 'Money' points out that

■ the Austen fictional economy draws on a real economy in a state of rapid and unsettling transition: an expanding commercial sector, a rapidly developing consumer culture, an economy tied to the ups and downs of foreign wars, high taxes, scarce capital, inadequate banking and credit systems and large sums of money to be made and spent by those who never had it before. Aggressive enclosure of common lands, consolidation of neighbouring farms and the introduction of modern agricultural improvements had brought enormous wealth and power to the great landholders. These conspicuous and deeply felt changes in the distribution and management of wealth were made even more acute by an unheard of rate of inflation in prices, punctuated by periodic economic depression. In this unstable economy, marriage, Austen's narrative mainstay, was a legitimate and common means of gaining access to all-important capital.[116] □

It is therefore vital to consider this historical contemporary economy rather than applying our modern-day assumptions, and to understand what the consumer power of a certain income would have been. Like many scholars who apply a historicist view, Copeland sees a difference between the treatment of money in the 'early' novels – *Sense and Sensibility, Pride and Prejudice, Northanger Abbey* – and the 'later' ones – *Mansfield Park, Emma, Persuasion*.

Another example of the essays in this volume is Maggie Lane's on 'Food', in which she explains when meals would have been taken and what they would have consisted of in Austen's times and in her novels, who speaks about them, who enjoys them and who does not, and what conclusions the reader is expected to draw from this. For instance:

■ Of all the meals which the characters must consume in *Sense and Sensibility*, the only one of which Austen chooses to specify is Willoughby's

snatched lunch at a coaching inn in Marlborough. We know that this consisted of cold beef and a pint of porter because he tells Elinor so, in order
to refute her imputation that he has had too much to drink. But the menu
does more than that: it has a moral dimension. He is behaving honourably
and with feeling at last; he is not so foolish as to starve himself in his haste
to reach Marianne before she does, but neither will he waste time [...] by
ordering a more elaborate dish. Elinor does not consciously reflect on this
but it undoubtedly contributes to the reassessment of Willoughby's worth in
her estimation and ours. Some of the sterling character associated with the
roast beef of old England attaches to Willoughby now: he is reformed.[117] □

In this way, this essay in particular and the volume as a whole illuminate the context of the novels and as such can enhance our reading of
them.

Feminism continues to play an important part in Austen criticism.
Devoney Looser takes a feminist perspective in her essay ' "The Duty of
Woman by Woman": Reforming Feminism in *Emma*'. She starts off by
explaining that the question of whether or not we see Austen as a feminist depends both on her novels and on our definition of feminism.

■ If we define feminism broadly as a movement attending to how women
are limited and devalued within a culture, then Austen's novels surely participate. When feminism is defined more specifically as a movement to eradi-
cate gender, race, class, and sexual prejudice and to agitate for change, it
is harder to justify so labeling Austen. She was not in the vanguard of social
justice movements by the standards of her time.[118] □

While *Emma* could be regarded as a patriarchal tale in that it embraces a
relationship in which an older, wiser man shapes a younger woman and
helps her develop 'until she is loveable enough – perfected enough – to
marry',[119] Looser argues that it is a novel about women's relationships,
about 'the duty of woman by woman'. 'Austen's descriptions of women's
relationships imply a reformist feminism in her own time; they engage
both conservative and revolutionary views of women's role.'[120] Instead
of viewing the novel as a taming of a spirited woman by marrying her
off, Looser argues 'that it also serves as a corrective to certain kinds of
same-sex exploitation'.[121] In particular, Looser is concerned with the
theme of female patronage:

■ *Emma* functions as a critique of what I call female/female paternalism,
exposing in the process the exploitable structure of companionate relationships; it reveals the ways powerful women wield influence over fellow
females, by uncovering its protagonist's mistakes which [...] are repeated
and exaggerated in Mrs. Elton's behaviour. The novel also implicitly warns
readers about how women of modest means may be (mis)treated by their

more powerful female mentors. Austen did not espouse the revolutionary idea of a feminist sisterhood whereby women from different social
levels would work together for their collective betterment. Instead *Emma*
shows possibilities for establishing greater fairness within existing female
friendships.[122] □

All her novels demonstrate female cruelty to women. Among the female
villains are Mrs Elton, Lady Catherine de Bourgh, and Lucy Steele. All
these women 'relish opportunities to foreclose other women's chances
for happiness in favor of their own self-serving plans'.[123] Yet, while
Austen shows how these women compete unscrupulously in a society
that advances the legal and economic interests of its male members,
and thus shows 'the limits of women's alliances with each other in a
patriarchal culture', she also, at the same time, 'impl[ies] more positive
possibilities of relationships for women'.[124]

   Looser connects *Emma* to the novel *Coelebs in Search of a Wife* (1809),
by Austen's contemporary Hannah More (1745–1833), thus embedding
it even more in its cultural and literary context. Austen's novel

■ diametrically opposes *Coelebs* by centering on a flawed single female,
rather than a flawless single male. Emma is not on a marriage quest for herself – an act considered acceptable in a male but horrifying in a female, who
must remain passive until chosen. She is on a marriage quest on behalf of
others. [...] To counter the advice of More and those like her, Emma is given
precisely the qualities that they would have women guard against: intelligence, confidence, wit, and even some arrogance. That feature alone has
led some critics to suggest that Austen's novels are feminist.[125] □

Emma, therefore, defies convention. Yet she develops in the course of
the novel to understand what was wrong in her patronage of Harriet.
By contrast, Mrs Elton does not show any such understanding about
her female/female paternalism towards Jane Fairfax. In fact, 'Mrs. Elton
is Emma's nemesis but she is also a sign of what Emma – if unrepent-
ant – could become.'[126] The two women share some characteristics,
and, while 'Mrs Elton selects a more class–appropriate and deserving
humble companion in Jane than Emma does in Harriet',[127] she also
'more egregiously oversteps her boundaries as a patron in her attempted
machinations'.[128] Mrs Elton thus represents the negative example of 'the
patroness as bully'.[129] While patronage is defined by an inequality of
economic status, '*Emma* implies that in an equitable companionate relationship economic privilege must be counterbalanced or complemented
by accomplishments and merit'. Both women in a patronage relationship
should bring something valuable with them, and 'each should respect
the gifts and desires of the other'.[130] Austen's feminism is, therefore, a
contemporary one that has to be viewed in its historical context and not

measured by today's standards. *Emma* 'promotes tendencies to respect other women equitably but only if they have proved through education, status, and behavior that they are worthy of such treatment'.[131] 'In her own time', this should be seen as an argument 'for greater fairness among women within the existing social, political, and economic order'.[132] Looser, therefore, regards *Emma* as participating in the feminist debates of Austen's time and argues for reading the novel within its historical and cultural as well as literary context, since such a reading opens up a feminist perspective. She maintains that such a historicist view shows that 'while the novel does not seek to break down received gender and class boundaries, it does encourage more equitable relations among women'.[133]

Vivien Jones' essay on 'Feminisms' appears in Claudia Johnson's and Clara Tuite's *A Companion to Jane Austen* (2009), in a section entitled 'Political, Social, and Cultural Worlds', and this is precisely what Jones consciously sets out to do: she wants to revisit the issue of feminism in the novels 'by locating Austen, in a properly historicist way, in the context of late eighteenth- and early nineteenth-century debates about the role and position of women; but also by invoking modern, necessarily anachronistic terminology to help illuminate her relationship with these debates'.[134] Jones first summarises the main points on which the feminist argument rests, that of Austen depicting the vulnerability of women in early-nineteenth-century society. 'Austen's heroines demonstrate women's condition – in material terms at least – to be one of precarious dependency.'[135] Using *Pride and Prejudice* as an example, Jones asserts:

■ Explicit evidence of that feminist 'line' seems apparent when, at various key moments, Austen's novels echo the Enlightenment-inflected rhetoric of contemporary debates about gender politics and the position of women. In *Pride and Prejudice*, for example, desperately trying to convince Mr Collins that 'no means no' after his unwelcome proposal, Elizabeth Bennet asserts her right to autonomous choice by describing herself in Wollstonecraftian terms: 'Do not consider me now as an *elegant female* intending to plague you, but as a *rational creature* speaking the truth from her heart' (emphasis added).[136] □

The phrase 'rational creature' is not only used by the seventeenth-century philosopher John Locke (1632–1794), but also by Wollstonecraft, in her *Vindication of the Rights of Woman*, who wants woman to be treated as and behave like a 'rational creature', a 'human being'. While Elizabeth is not free economically, she still 'asserts her moral and intellectual independence, at least, and reaches for Wollstonecraftian rhetoric in order to do so'.[137]

Yet, along with this feminist concern, the aim and only fulfilment open to her heroines in the novels is still marriage: both her heroines and her readers have to come to terms with that. There thus exists in Austen, according to Jones, a '"feminist" awareness [and] an essential conservatism'.[138] And, while Austen's novels are not polemical, they are not apolitical either.

■ Rather, they engage indirectly with the agenda of conservative reform through their focus on their heroines' moral rather than formal education, on the ethics of domestic life, and on the right to romantic fulfillment. In doing so, they inevitably engage with contemporary gender politics, putting the language and ideas of Enlightenment feminism to post-Revolutionary effect by representing them in essentially nonthreatening ways.[139] □

It is this aspect of Austen's work, this 'sense that revolutionary feminism has been taken on board and superseded',[140] which Jones terms 'post-feminist': Austen takes the 1790s feminist ideas into consideration, 'but she puts them at the service not simply of individualized fulfillment, but of a conservative agenda of reform'.[141] Her heroines are independent yet they marry romantically, which, Jones argues, suggests that for Austen 'a measure of equality, and certainly happiness, can be achieved'.[142]

In the introduction to the Cambridge University Press edition of *Pride and Prejudice*, Pat Rogers discusses various aspects of the novel. The subsections are headed: 'Inception'; 'Publishing History'; 'The Title'; 'The Heroine'; 'The Author's Reading'; 'Inner Circle'; 'The Entail'; 'Time of the Narrative'; 'Critical History'; 'Artistic Qualities'. As this list indicates, the focus of this introduction is historicist – possibly because Janet Todd's *The Cambridge Introduction to Jane Austen* could be read alongside each of the novels in the Cambridge edition. Nevertheless, it is striking how little interpretation features in this long introductory essay. The section on 'The Title', for example, discusses where the phrase 'pride and prejudice' occurs in eighteenth-century texts, most notably in Fanny Burney's novel *Cecilia* (1782), 'a book Austen unquestionably drew on in her writing'.[143] Rogers then places the title words individually in their historical context and explores what they would have meant in Austen's time, then looks at instances in eighteenth-century texts that have a sentence similar to the first sentence of *Pride and Prejudice*. In her section on 'The Entail', Rogers shows 'Austen's grasp of legal matters', and even in the part on 'Artistic Qualities' he discusses the novel's intertextuality: 'The novel reanimates some of the stalest properties of eighteenth-century writing. Antithesis had sunk into a tired conventional prop in the hands of minor Augustan poets: but Jane Austen gives the Johnsonian formula a new lightness and speed.'[144] Mr Collins is an example: he 'is characterized principally by his language, whether in conversation or in writing. His repetitive, pompous and self-gratulating way with words expresses an entire approach to life, while his self-demeaning vocabulary reveals the conceit that can go with obsequious pose.'[145] Another way of analysing 'Artistic Qualities' for Rogers is to compare Austen to another almost-contemporary: in her combination of romance and satire, of comedy and despair, Austen could be linked to the Austrian composer Wolfgang Amadeus Mozart (1756–91). His mature piano concertos 'were written in the decade preceding Austen's earliest experiments as a novelist, indeed, he composed the last of them only about seven years before she embarked on First Impressions'.[146] The compositions of both artists show 'a minute disposition of parts to create an integrated whole, a cunning choice of appropriate means towards a given end, an innovative use of conventional motifs'.[147] Rogers' introduction therefore places the novel firmly in its historical, political, biographical, literary and cultural context.

Another historicist study that reads Austen's novels, in particular *Emma*, in the political context of their genesis is Gabrielle White's *Jane Austen in the Context of Abolition* (2006). She argues that Austen in her late novels goes against colonialism and slavery and instead celebrates Britain's outlawing of the transatlantic slave trade in 1807. Her main argument in regards to *Emma* is based on the comparison Mrs Elton draws between the task of finding a post for a governesses and the trading of slaves when she discusses Jane Fairfax's situation.

■ Since the respect in which governesses are compared to slaves is in being traded, both may be regarded as commodities. Furthermore, since these objects of trading are said to be victims and to be caused misery, in the case of the slave trade its guilt also being affirmed implies its victims should be freed from their misery.[148] □

Apart from what White sees as textual evidence for Austen's opinions about slavery, she also looks at possible influences on Austen, most notably Samuel Johnson, the poet William Cowper (1731–1800), Thomas Clarkson (1769–1846), a leading campaigner in the abolitionist debate, whose essay on the topic Austen may have seen, and her brother Francis Austen (1774–1865), who was in the navy and 'a fervent abolitionist'.[149] White's study is therefore a reading that sees Austen as making political statements in her later novels, and the texts and their author being necessarily influenced by their political context.

As we have seen, a purely historicist reading of Austen is less dominant than it was during the last decades of the twentieth century, but there are still very few studies in the first decade of the twentieth century that do not refer to context. Instead of an exclusive focus either on text or on context, most critics display a combination of close-reading and relating text and author to their historical, political, cultural and literary contexts.

The final chapter of this Guide looks at film and TV adaptations of Austen's novels and discusses the new aspects that the analysis of adaptations brings to Austen criticism, including the adaptations' ways of presenting Austen's female characters.

CHAPTER SEVEN

Film and Television Adaptations

The earliest film adaptation of an Austen novel was MGM's black and white feature film of *Pride and Prejudice*, with a screenplay by the novelist Aldous Huxley (1894–1963) and the screenwriter and dramatist Jane Murfin (1884–1955), and Greer Garson (1904–96) and Laurence Olivier (1907–89) as Elizabeth and Darcy. A number of adaptations of *Sense and Sensibility, Pride and Prejudice* and *Emma* appeared throughout the twentieth century, but never as many as from the mid-1990s onwards. In 1995 and 1996 alone five adaptations of these three novels came out: *Sense and Sensibility* (1995), directed by Ang Lee (born 1954), with a screenplay by Emma Thompson (born 1959); a BBC TV adaptation of *Pride and Prejudice* (1995), directed by Simon Langton (born 1941) and written by Andrew Davies (born 1936); *Clueless* (1995), loosely based on *Emma*, directed by Amy Heckerling (born 1954); *Emma* (1996), directed by Douglas McGrath (born 1958); and a BBC adaptation of *Emma* (1996), directed by Diarmuid Lawrence (born 1947) and written by Andrew Davies. Not only did existing Austen readers watch them; the films also created an audience that came to Austen through the films. Tie-in editions were produced, and the Austen industry boomed.

AUSTEN'S DRAMATIC QUALITIES

Films usually dispense with the narrative voice and translate the texts' characters and plots into a different medium. Kathryn Sutherland, in her study *Jane Austen's Textual Lives; From Aeschylus to Bollywood*, discusses the transmissions and transformations that Austen's novels undergo in their film versions and the means by which her stories are expressed in this medium, and how far it is in fact possible for 'an equivalent story [to be] told by means of non-equivalent codes'. She explores how Austen's novels in particular can be turned into film versions, and addresses both the specific difficulties Austen's texts pose and the ways in which they suit the screen.

■ Austen's novels are largely plotless (and film relishes action); Austen's text displays a weak dependence on metaphor and figurative language (and film's power lies in the manipulation of image and imagery); Austen's mature art (and, risky word, her 'essence') is a sophisticated aural figuration in which, through free indirect discourse, voice is laid on voice to produce critical (specifically, ironic) connotative effects, and the blurring of character with character and narrator, which are almost impossible to achieve in film whose aural effects, however sophisticated, are subordinated to an immense visual rhetoric. The camera's ability to operate between subjective viewpoint and distance can achieve something, as can other devices of juxtaposition or ironic editing (jump cuts and montage) and voice-over; but the reliance of Douglas McGrath's feature film *Emma* (Columbia1 Miramax, 1996) on the heroine apparently addressing herself in a mirror, or writing in her very un-Austenian diary (used also in [...] the feature film *Mansfield Park* (BBC/Miramax, 1999), [directed by Patricia Rozema born 1958]), and elsewhere the conversion of indirect discourse into direct conversation (between Emma and Mrs Weston), appear clumsily reductive or inapposite by comparison with the novel's subtler ambiguities of voicing. □

A general problem that is particularly relevant when turning Austen's texts into films is, of course, 'the effects we see are always more specific than those we hear and, on occasion, only half hear'. The screen delivers meaning more quickly than words do, in that the viewer gets absorbed at a faster pace than a reader does 'into the illusion of a total environment'.

Regarding the suitability of Austen's texts for the screen, one argument is that her texts already read like drama in many places, which makes them suitable for adaptations. Sutherland contends that it is to a large extent due to the evident dramatic qualities of Austen's texts that they keep being adapted: 'encounters and incidents structured as scenes in a play [...], brisk dialogue, strong characterization [...], a reliance on dramatic entrances and exits [...], her fine use of stage business [...]'.

Another point Sutherland raises is that, while we might think that 'fidelity to detail' would be one of the aspects that could be transferred from one medium to another with comparatively little difficulty, this is in fact not always the case, as 'detail can prove unexpectedly faithless'. One example she gives is that, as Austen's first biographer James Edward Austen-Leigh already points out in his *Memoir* (1870), not only did the dinner table in general look 'far less splendid' than it did in his time, but also 'silver forks had not come into general use' and instead people would use 'the broad rounded end of the knives' as a substitute. The films tend, however, to make Austen's texts take place in grander surroundings and detail than they suggest. That is, if the films err, they err on the side of splendour, never on the side of scantiness: 'we have yet to see an Austen heroine authentically eating peas from her knife in a meagerly furnished room in accordance with Austen-Leigh's memory of how things were among the lesser gentry at the start of the nine-teenth century'. One such example of visual splendour is MGM's 1940 adaptation of *Pride and Prejudice*, starring Greer Garson and Laurence Olivier. The costumes of the Bennet girls are lavish, and the characters move through sets that are 'consciously artificial'. Similarly, typical of many of the 1990s adaptations is a 'visual excess', which turns the novels into depictions of the Prince Regent's 'exuberant materialism. In both cases, the filmic need to make a visually comprehensible psychology renders settings enhanced carriers of meaning in which detail seduces as it proliferates.'

Classic novels now are mostly adapted within 'the heritage movie genre', and these tend to be 'sumptuous affairs drenched with mater-ial significance: not just glamorous costumes but grand sets crammed indoors with priceless art objects and antique furniture, and out-of-doors painstaking period-styled tableaux', in accordance with 'our late capitalist fantasy'.

■ Accordingly, settings became more spectacular: balls grew grander, din-ner tables groaned, houses became more stately. [...] A narrative statement in *Pride and Prejudice* makes it clear that Pemberley is not to be equated with Chatsworth; nevertheless, a British film version currently [2005] in pro-duction will use Chatsworth, ancestral home of the Dukes of Devonshire, for Mr Darcy's estate. □

The films thus turn Austen's texts into systems 'with a higher dispos-able income'. They display 'period magnificence' rather than 'express-ing any specific act of faithfulness' and as such 'detail in film delivers authenticity not so much to the author as to the age in which she lived and which it is presumed she recorded with equal meticulousness'.

■ Period detail in film prioritizes or amplifies some elements over others, and directs us towards the significance we discover in the work as a whole. But more hazardously than this [...] visual detail risks literalizing and pre-empting effects which in the novel take much longer to unfold or are more subtly nuanced for not being seen or fully textualized. The early scene in McGrath's *Emma* where Emma and Mr Knightley practise their archery on a splendid lawn by a lake is not so much troublesome because it does not occur in the novel: as authentic period detail it is as contextually appropriate as Chapman's illustrative plates [in his edition of Austen's novels]; while its embodiment of a visual allusion to a similar scene in the 1940 MGM *Pride and Prejudice* gives it enhanced film-textual authority. The problem is rather that its visual knowingness delivers too quickly and simply (in an arrow's flight) what it takes a reading of the whole novel, with its twists and turns, to know with the same certainty, that Cupid's match is between these two contestants. Visually, it is both splendid and crude.[1] □

The problem is therefore that film, by emphasising visual detail, directs us in a certain way even as regards our reading of the whole. Its visual rendering means that the textual subtleness of things alluded to or 'only half-hear[d]' get turned into much more specific information. Connected to this is film's prioritising of period splendour over faithfulness to the text's detail.

CATERING FOR A LATE TWENTIETH/ EARLY TWENTY-FIRST-CENTURY AUDIENCE

Linda Troost's and Sayre Greenfield's 1998 collection of essays on the Austen adaptations, *Jane Austen in Hollywood*, looks at what changes were made to the novels on their way to the screen and what these changes reveal about our culture and its values. They discuss who the films cater for and show how the films that appeared from the 1990s onwards somehow simultaneously advocate late-twentieth-century feminism, for example through rewriting the novels' heroes, and employ a traditionalist view. One of the main reasons for Austen's popularity in text form and on screen, Troost and Greenfield argue, is her 'devotion to manners'.

■ Our fascination with Austen taps into this fascination with social polish. We may not want to live in this world, but it is fun to visit. An appreciation of manners requires a sophisticated knowledge of social customs, a sensitivity toward others, and [...] self-restraint. [...] In an era of tell-all biographies and talk shows that exploit that all-too-easy impulse for self-exposure, it is difficult not to yearn for some greater degree of reticence in society. □

Troost and Greenfield discuss the specific Austen-adaptation audience. Rather than needing a depiction 'of the individual bursting through all social restraints and all concepts of historical accuracy', such as Hercules, Xena, Warrior Princess, the audience for example of Thompson's *Sense and Sensibility* 'sees less need for, or possibility of, escaping cultural restrictions'.

■ This audience can do without clashes between disparate sections of society or between different nations with mutually incomprehensible social codes and objectives. It wants a game of comprehensible dimensions. Limit the field to a little bit of ivory, two inches wide, and the rules become manageable and reassuring. □

For films with this specific appeal, Troost and Greenfield argue, 'the 1990s audience may be more open than the audience of previous decades'. One reason might be that 'the audience is largely female'. But another is that the films deliberately change some of the aspects of Austen's texts that need not have been changed in the process of the novels' translation onto the screen, such as plot, character, social milieu.

■ In less than two hundred years, the cultural environment has altered enough to require considerable adaptation of the novels (how many of us these days understand the significance of owning a barouche as opposed to a curricle?). These changes from text to film offer us the chance for some sharp cultural self-definition. Certain alterations, of course, derive from the shift in form. Films will shorten the stories, and even a six-hour television miniseries must abbreviate long patches of dialogue or the readings of letters. More important, the translation to a visual medium encourages a far greater reliance on images: words cannot exist without a picture. One sees this already in the 1979 BBC miniseries of *Pride and Prejudice* written by [the novelist] Fay Weldon [born 1933] . The director, Cyril Coke [1914–93], cannot merely have Elizabeth Bennet, after she has rejected Darcy, read his explanatory letter without finding some visual equivalent. Instead, we get long shots of Darcy's receding figure as we hear the letter being read. The 1996 McGrath adaptation of *Emma* must find some action to fill those spaces where Austen herself simply describes the heroine's feelings – and so scenes of *Emma* writing in a journal accompany her voice-over. □

Like Sutherland, Troost and Greenfield point out that the existence of the images themselves will necessarily change the emphasis, and give the example of costumes: while Austen barely mentions what people wear, the film has to show its actors in clothing, and therefore 'cannot avoid placing more value on a superficial concern such as fashion than Austen would'. In addition, the fact that what people wear in these costume dramas is different from our clothing today will also ensure that the audience places greater emphasis on costume than readers of the novels will.

However, while some changes are necessitated by the translation from novel to film, others are invented additions that cater for a 1990s/2000s audience.

■ Often, however, directorial decisions invent images, as when director Simon Langton and writer Andrew Davies remove Darcy's clothes in the 1995 *Pride and Prejudice*. This episode tells us more about our current decade's obsession with physical perfection and acceptance of gratuitous nudity than it does about Austen's Darcy, but the image carves a new facet into the text. □

As the various authors of the essays in Troost and Greenfield's collection contend, 'such scenes empower women by making men the object of the gaze', and enliven Darcy's character. As the critic Amanda Collins suggests, however, films, 'by their natural enough choice of beautiful lead actors, promote the equation of human physical beauty with worth', an attitude which in fact, Collins argues, 'Jane Austen seems directly critical of at times'. Similarly, Deborah Kaplan, in her essay in Troost and Greenfield's volume, argues that 'scenery can intrude into the films as well, transforming Austenian satire on the Picturesque into an outright endorsement of the Picturesque'. The consensus in the volume seems to be that 'the delicate touch of Austen's satire may suffer much in the cinematic transformations of the novels'.

Another change from novel to film regards the depiction of both men and women. Since the importance of romance in the films tends to exceed that given to it in the novels, 'Austen's men are modernized out of their repressions into displays of feeling. Austen generally celebrates male restraint, but film directors cannot tolerate such a value – or at least think the modern viewer cannot.' Even more than the male figures, however, the films change the female characters, mostly, though not always, in a feminist direction. Devoney Looser in her essay in Troost and Greenfield's volume calls these shifts 'mainstreaming of feminism' since the films show heroines 'who can tackle physical activity, social conventions, and love all equally well'. Yet there are also critics, such as Rebecca Dickson and Kristen Samuelian, who find that the screen versions of Austen's heroines ultimately undercut 'the subtle feminism Austen promoted in the novels'.

■ The late twentieth century still has not sorted out women's roles, and the on-screen depictions of Austen's characters echo the ambiguous position of women in the 1990s: feminist, traditionalist, or sometimes both, depending on whom one asks. Each screenwriter, director, and viewer sees the characters as reflecting his or her ideas of womanhood, and that may be the secret of Austen and the film adaptations: they play simultaneously to both camps and reach twice the audience. Both feminists and traditionalists can easily claim Jane Austen as their own.[2] □

VERSIONS OF *EMMA* AND *PRIDE AND PREJUDICE*

In an essay specifically on adaptations of *Emma*, Troost and Greenfield compare the two 1996 versions of the novel, the Miramax McGrath

Emma and the Meridian–ITV Lawrence and Davies *Emma*. The main difference between the McGrath version (with Gwyneth Paltrow (born 1972) as Emma) and the Davies version (with Kate Beckinsale (born 1973) as Emma) versions is the extent to which they focus entirely on Emma, or on Emma within her social circle. For example, the Davies film is more concerned with Jane Fairfax, and 'the shot of Jane Fairfax walking across the fields weeping while being observed sympathetically by Robert Martin makes us interested in her problems and reminds us of his blighted romance'. Both Jane and Robert Martin have been hurt by Emma, and Davies makes the audience interested in them to a larger extent than McGrath does. The latter, by contrast, focuses on Emma's reactions, since McGrath's version 'is really concerned with Emma's feelings and not with the effect Emma has on others'.

Another issue that each film solves differently is how to depict the fact that much of the novel happens in Emma's head, or certainly through her point of view.

■ When we get inside Emma's mind in both scripts, we sense the greater concern with the solitary reactions of the title character in the McGrath version and the more socially enmeshed quality of the Davies version. McGrath accomplishes the trick of admitting us to Emma's private thoughts by showing her writing in her diary and simultaneously giving us a Paltrow voice-over that explains what the young woman is writing: an entry in which she wonders whether she is in love with Frank Churchill. McGrath even [shoots] her reflected in a mirror. We get to watch Emma watch herself as she dreams. In the Davies version, on the other hand, we get to experience Emma's fantasies from her point of view: we see through her eyes (and the camera's lens) as Mr. Elton thank s Emma for uniting her with Harriet, and later we see Frank Churchill's portrait smiling at us (and Emma). We become, for a moment, Emma watching other characters. For McGrath, the reactions are solely Emma's: she remains the end point of a chain of occurrences, and the camera focuses on Paltrow. For Davies, the fantasies require the images of other characters on screen, which grant them a certain importance. [...] Her imaginings place Emma in social situations, surrounded by family and friends. Davies's Emma is not the endpoint of this film or the sole focus of the camera even in the sequences that reveal her hidden thoughts. In other words, the events that occur end with their effect upon Emma in the McGrath film, whereas the implications of events in the Davies version reflect through Emma's mind and back onto society.[3] □

Both renderings, Troost and Greenfield suggest, are 'legitimate visions of the novel', one focusing on the individual, the other on the individual in society. But, whereas 'Austen's novel has the luxury of presenting both visions simultaneously, a film [...] must limit its scope'.

In her 2002 *Jane Austen on Film and Television: A Critical Study of the Adaptations*, Sue Parrill looks at the history of the Austen adaptations and at differences and similarities between them and the novels. She discusses the 1995 BBC Davies adaptation of *Pride and Prejudice* in detail. For example, whereas in the novel the conversation between Mr and Mrs Bennet about Netherfield having been taken by Mr Bingley has no witnesses, in the film it takes place in the hearing of all five daughters on their way home from church. This makes it possible to introduce them all effectively. Elizabeth, for example, gets the author's famous line that 'A single man in possession of good fortune must be in need of a wife', with which her mother is shown to agree gravely and insist on Mr Bennet visiting Mr Bingley.

■ [Mr. Bennet] suggests that the girls go alone, since Mr. Bingley might prefer Mrs. Bennet because she is as handsome as any of them. Lydia laughs loudly at this remark and Elizabeth chides her for laughing. This [whole] scene effectively introduces Mrs. Bennet's foolishness, Mr. Bennet's lack of respect for her, Elizabeth's ironic intelligence, and Lydia's irrepressible nature. □

Parrill also looks at how Darcy is characterised, contending that 'there is no doubt that Colin Firth (born 1960) is the definitive cinematic Mr. Darcy'.

■ Through most of the first episode, Darcy says little. He looks disapprovingly at everyone who is not a member of his group. He spends a lot of time looking out of windows, as if to distance himself from people whom he considers his inferiors. However, he also spends time observing people, especially Elizabeth, whose disregard for him piques his interest. Later, while Elizabeth is playing the pianoforte at Rosings, Davies has provided Darcy with lines from the novel in which he confesses to feeling inadequate to converse easily with strangers. Elizabeth chides him for not making more of an effort. It is a new experience for Darcy to receive instruction from anyone, especially a woman. He is used to the adulation of Miss Bingley (Anna Chancellor [born 1965]) and of his sister. When Elizabeth not only refuses his proposal of marriage but accuses him of wrongdoing, he defends himself in his letter to her, but the anger and hurt which he feels are well conveyed in the scenes in which he labors to write his explanatory letter to Elizabeth. He is in his shirt sleeves, his shirt open at the throat, his hair disheveled and his face drawn.[4] □

Thus Parrill goes on to look closely at how scenes and characters in the novel are rendered on screen.

John Wiltshire in his *Recreating Jane Austen* (2001) uses Austen adaptations to discuss the process of recreation, looking at all of them as 'coherent readings of the original books, which by their public, objective existence, can throw unique light on the nature of reading'.[5] Regarding *Clueless*, a 1995 film loosely based on *Emma*, he shows up the many differences and similarities between the film and the novel. One difference is, for example, that on many levels *Clueless* is a 'fantasy/ burlesque', as signalled for example by Cher's and Dionne's 'exaggerated wardrobes [...], but more importantly in its utopian reinvention of social realities'.

■ Part of *Emma's* realism is the exactness with which it depicts a community in which some are rising into gentility and others are slipping from it, a 'Highbury world' therefore in which the niceties of social discrimination are everywhere woven into the action, but apart from Cher's rebuke to Elton for being 'such a snob' class distinctions appear to have little significance in *Clueless*. □

There are other differences, Wiltshire points out, such as various characters in the novel that do not have an equivalent in the film, and, the other way round, additional characters that occur in the film but do not exist in the novel. However, in spite of all the points of variance between film and novel, 'the many readers who have felt that the film nevertheless has some real affinity with *Emma* are not necessarily mistaken'.

The greatest similarity, Wiltshire contends, is 'Cher's voice-over narration, [which] is an important ingredient in the movie's success'.

■ The contrast between her spoken appraisals and what the screen itself shows parallels Emma's equally mistaken assessments of the world delineated in the novel. Cher's commentary provides continuity for the action, but also supplies unspoken thoughts to supplement the visual images of her face. [...] This voice is sometimes immediate, dramatic, sometimes explanatory, retrospective; sometimes inside, and sometimes outside, Cher's head on the screen. Attending to Cher's unspoken thoughts, the viewer sometimes finds, to their surprise, that this virtual 'inner speech' has become real speech, as the train of thought emerges without a break into the action, or is broken into by someone else's words. [...] Thus the use of the voice-over in *Clueless* avails itself of some of the effects of free indirect speech in the novel. Just as the shifts between narrator and character in the novel make for irony, so does the shifting match or mismatch between verbal and visual representations. □

Apart from the voice, the heroines themselves bear similarities: both are 'beautiful and a natural leader (but not vain), eager, bright, kindhearted, egotistic and intelligent'. But, Wiltshire argues, the real similarity lies in 'the aesthetic treatment that both receive'. Emma, like Cher, 'is a radiant "picture of health",' and in novel and film this comes across partly through sensuous means. 'For the buoyancy and vitality of the imagination that conceives Emma is brought to the reader through the energy and brio, not of metaphor, but of the rhythms of Austen's prose.' And this is reenacted faithfully in *Clueless*, so that the film makes fun of and puts itself into, the tradition of the female *bildungsroman* [novel of development]. Wiltshire concludes that, for him,

■ *Clueless* represents an imaginative absorption of Austen that is perfectly reconcilable with taking liberties and disregarding whole aspects of the original text, and, as I have argued, transforming it into a different genre or order of art. *Clueless* then plays with *Emma* and implicitly too with Jane Austen, the 'classic'. *Emma* is not a mother text that is idealised or revered but an inner presence that has been loved, destroyed in fantasy, survived and can now be treated 'cavalierly'.[6] □

Just as the novels have inspired all kinds of critical attitudes over the years, the films have in recent decades also begun to draw forth a variety of opinions. From a focus on the film's greater splendour as regards houses, costume, and furniture compared with the novels, via an analysis of gender in the adaptations versus the novels, to the comparison of the details of two film versions and the different emphasis this brings out, the study of film has enriched Austen criticism by yet another dimension.

The Conclusion to this Guide sums up the main areas of criticism of *Sense and Sensibility, Pride and Prejudice* and *Emma* to date. It also suggests which factors have been the most influential in each period and draws comparisons among the critical trends over the last 200 years.

Conclusion

As this Guide has shown, Austen's *Sense and Sensibility*, *Pride and Prejudice* and *Emma* continue to inspire ever new critical approaches. In Fiona Stafford's words, the development of readings of Austen criticism demonstrates 'the inexhaustibility of her texts'.[1] However, it is not just with critics that these three novels are outstandingly popular. There is an incessant flow of cheap paperback editions; there are Jane Austen Societies on national and local levels. New biographies keep coming out, which testify to a continuing strong interest in the author's life, and, as discussed in the last chapter, each of these three novels has motivated not one but several film and television versions. *Pride and Prejudice* alone has served as the basis for a screenplay no less than eleven times. This success is partly due to Elizabeth and, out of all the Austen heroines, her coming closest to modern ideas of femininity. Frequently referred to as 'the nation's favourite book',[2] *Pride and Prejudice*'s plot is considered general knowledge. A film such as ITV's *Lost in Austen* (2008), a time-travelling version of *Pride and Prejudice*, emphasises this: large parts of the film only make sense if the viewer understands the jokes and plot twists as the heroine, Amanda Price, does, which presupposes knowledge of the story and the characters of *Pride and Prejudice* – not just Elizabeth and Darcy, but also Jane and Bingley, Charlotte and Mr Collins, and even the 1995 BBC adaptation of the novel, through references to Colin Firth. The making of a film that relies on this plot as known proves how deeply ingrained knowledge of the plot and characters of *Pride and Prejudice* is in general culture. From having been read by some of the few who could afford novel-reading in the early nineteenth century, *Sense and Sensibility*, *Pride and Prejudice* and *Emma* have achieved a popular as well as critical status that not many novels can boast.

A main factor that has been influencing Austen criticism and her general popularity is the issue of gender, as regards her readership/audience, herself, and her characters. In the last few years this may have become more obvious than before: the majority of viewers of the screen versions in cinemas are female, and the advertisements during the adaptations are typically aimed at women. Austen herself is female, and this fact is constructed in some articles, films and books into a picture of an independent woman who consciously chose to write instead of marrying. Her heroines appeal to women in the late twentieth/early twenty-first century; Elizabeth in particular, with her unconventional behaviour, independent spirit, liveliness and pride, seems to fulfil current needs. She appears to have it all: she is able to stand up for herself, not defer to anything she cannot respect, nor marry where she does not love, and is rewarded for all this with a fairy-tale Mr Darcy of Pemberley.

Gender was already an influencing factor in the reception of *Sense and Sensibility*, *Pride and Prejudice* and *Emma* when they first appeared. Fiction was regarded as a female-dominated genre, and therefore as one with a lower intellectual level than other kinds of writing, such as history or poetry. Contemporary reviewers, like the one writing for *The Critical Review* in 1813 in his article on *Pride and Prejudice*, see Austen's works as 'very superior to any novel we have lately met with in the delineation of domestic scenes'.[3] This judgement emphasises the novel's feminine sphere, so that, while critics see Austen as superior to most female novelists, they do not regard her as innovative or artistically skilled. The main points early reviewers raise concern the novels' moral message, their realism, and the insight the reader gains into the characters, especially the female ones (though critics do not discuss how this is achieved, which again emphasises that Austen's novels – like the novel genre in general – were not regarded as meriting a discussion of their artistry). Scott is the first reviewer who is interested in Austen's craftsmanship: in his article on *Emma* he praises the author's 'dexterity of execution',[4] but he, of course, is an exceptional reviewer in many ways, so that his view cannot be taken to represent that of the majority of early-nineteenth-century critics. The dominant view of Austen, then, as it emerges from the reviews of *Sense and Sensibility*, *Pride and Prejudice* and *Emma* when they first appeared, is one of pleasant, amusing pieces of writing that are superior to most novels the reviewers know but that cannot compare to more serious genres. Even within the novel genre, Austen's works are judged as better than most works of fiction, but a long way beneath the by far most popular novels of the time, Walter Scott's Waverley Novels.

Gender continues to play a dominant role in Victorian readings of Austen's three novels. Most late Victorian reviewers approve of *Sense and Sensibility*, *Pride and Prejudice* and *Emma*. By the 1870s, however, while Austen's critical status is no longer doubted, reviewers maintain that she can never be widely popular with the public because of her novels' limited scope. Neither politics, history, nor passion feature in her novels, which must limit her overall significance as an author since it prevents her from being a true realist. One of the main elements her novels are found to lack is the display of passion. Only Marianne and Darcy are seen as showing any kind of emotion and as acting accordingly. Any kind of grandeur of either feeling or larger social scope is lacking, which is in part linked to Austen's gender: the Shakespeare scholar Richard Simpson in his essay on J.E. Austen-Leigh's *Memoir* is one of the critics who comment on the limitations of Austen's novels, but justifies them by rendering her literary boundaries those of feminine propriety. Writing within these becomes a virtuous necessity for a perfect lady, and it is as the work of a lady that the limitations of her novels as regards 'the great political and social problems'[5] of her day can be excused. While this deficiency is excused, it is nevertheless seen as a deficiency and therefore as limiting her works.

However, Simpson is also the first scholar who sees irony in Austen's works. He links Austen to Shakespeare in being an ironic observer of her contemporaries. 'She began by being an ironical critic; she manifested her judgment of them not by direct censure, but by the indirect method of imitating and exaggerating the faults of her models.' Like Shakespeare, she began by observing, and then developed her artistic faculty. Instead of being grand, her novels are thus perfect in their minute field.

With Victorian critics in general, Austen's life and her gender tend to influence readings of her novels. Anne Isabella Thackeray, for example, finds that, because of Austen's calm life and her kindness, her novels cannot but display the same gentleness. Since she describes what she experiences, her novels display sensitivity, sweetness, womanliness. Richard Holt Hutton argues in a similar way by connecting Austen's heroines to her character. Both he and the reviewer in *St Paul's Magazine* puzzle a little over Elizabeth having been Austen's favourite heroine, and maintain that the author herself was far too much of a lady to be like her preferred heroine. The reviewer in *St Paul's* finds that Elizabeth's 'vanity and self-satisfaction extend beyond the proper development of those feminine qualities', which is in direct opposition to how these reviewers see Austen's own character.

The Victorian admiration for the woman feeds into the early-twentieth-century phenomenon of 'Austenolatry' and the emergence of Janeites. George Saintsbury is the first self-confessed Janeite, a critic proud of his fervent admiration of the author as well as of her heroines – especially Elizabeth, the only heroine in literature he can think of that he would want to marry. The existence of Janeites led to self-professed anti-Janeites such as, famously, Mark Twain, but also academics such as H.W. Garrod.

The twentieth century also saw the development from a Henry James view of Austen as a realistic imitator of nature but a literary amateur to an approach that took her seriously as a conscious artist. This was linked to a shift away from a focus on her life towards an analysis of the texts alone, as well as to the rise of English Literature as an academic discipline at universities, with Austen as an established author on the syllabus. Critics such as Bradley or Farrer still write in admiring tones, but take Austen seriously as an author of literature. They also distinguish between the novels, and Farrer in particular holds *Sense and Sensibility* as bearing no comparison to her more mature novels, above all to *Emma*, the 'very climax' of Austen's work. Another factor that established Austen's importance was Chapman's scholarly edition of her works. However, arguably the most significant factor that dispelled the notion of Austen the literary amateur was Mary Lascelles' study of the novels' narrative complexity. Lascelles showed, for example, that characters such as Mr Collins were not just hilarious but also served an important structural purpose, which emphasises that the novels are in fact carefully crafted.

Another approach that belongs to this period is that of Harding and then Mudrick. Both saw Austen as writing to survive emotionally since she despised the society that surrounded her and that read her novels. Charlotte Lucas' marriage to the 'comic monster' Mr Collins shows this hatred of people who were tolerated and accepted by the society that Austen knew, so that she had to write in order to 'find some mode of existence for her critical attitudes'. Yet another view is that of Leavis and Trilling, who regarded Austen as part of the great tradition of English Literature, partly because they saw her as an inherently moral writer, and therefore timelessly relevant.

The main trends that occur in the first half of the twentieth century are those connected to Janeites and anti-Janeites, viewing Austen as a serious literary figure, focusing on her irony and seeing it as self-defence, or emphasising Austen the moralist. What these critics have in common with one another as well as with mid-century critics is an essentially ahistorical approach, which comprises a more formal analysis of the novels in the New Criticism mode, an approach quite distinct from what had happened in the nineteenth century, as well as from what was to follow in the later decades of the twentieth century, and therefore possibly the period that was least influenced by Austen's gender. Critics writing in the 1960s and 1970s expand this focus on the texts on their own terms, separated from both the biographical and the socio-political context of the texts' origin. They are not usually concerned with Austen's personal character traits, views, and aims.

In keeping with general critical and cultural trends, roughly the last twenty-five years of the twentieth century see the influence on Austen criticism of New Historicism and its emphasis on an author's historical, political and social context. Biography again becomes an important factor in the analysis of the novels. However, in contrast to how Victorian critics viewed Austen, she is now perceived as a politically aware participant in early-nineteenth-century debates, a woman who is necessarily aware of and writes about her political and social context. *Sense and Sensibility*, *Pride and Prejudice* and *Emma* had not been read in

any previous period as having been shaped by the political and historical context in which they were written. In the late twentieth century,
however, while the specific political view critics assign to Austen varies, the dominant mode is to analyse the novels as reflecting her political views, particularly as regards the situation of women.

Marilyn Butler sees Austen as an 'entirely conservative' writer whose
novels convey her political opinions. Like most critics writing after
Butler's study, Gilbert and Gubar pick up on this and also see Austen as
a conservative writer, but as one who endorses the status quo because
she has to. She is herself limited by her gender and shows her heroines
also to suffer from having to defer to 'the economic, social, and political
power of men'. Austen's strength is her dramatisation of 'the necessity of
female submission for female survival' – including heroines as romantic
as Marianne, as sprightly as Elizabeth, as independent as Emma.

Though almost all critics in the late twentieth century regard
Austen as politically aware, they do not all accept Butler's conservative Austen. Terry Castle, for example, sees *Sense and Sensibility* as a
revolutionary novel because it asserts 'a woman's right to find a second
love'. Austen, in Castle's view, makes a statement about women's rights
through Marianne's survival, whereas earlier critics, for example Tony
Tanner, see Marianne's marriage to Brandon as a loss of true self and
do not connect it to gender issues but to the pressures of society on the
individual.

The first decade of the twenty-first century sees a continuation of
the historicist trends described above. Alongside that, however, studies
appear that go back to a focus on the text itself. David Miller in his *Jane
Austen or The Secret of Style* argues that Austen's style is absolutely impersonal because it reveals nothing about gender, age, marital status, social
position etc., so that Austen's narrative is a truly omniscient one. Many
critics combine a close reading of the texts with placing Austen and her
novels in their historical context. Peter Knox-Shaw's study starts with
Butler's view of a conservative Austen but disagrees with it: he regards
Austen as deriving mostly from the Enlightenment. Arguably the most
significant study in this decade is Kathryn Sutherland's *Jane Austen's
Textual Lives*. Sutherland shows here how Austen has been constructed,
through biographies, portraits, films, editions of her novels and illustrations, into what each editor, biographer, etc., believes her to have
been.

From the 1990s onwards there has been a abundance of adaptations of
Sense and Sensibility, Pride and Prejudice and *Emma*. Sutherland analyses
which elements in Austen's novels fit the screen and which are not so suitable, one obvious problem being that a reader of the text is for large parts
in the heroine's consciousness. The artistry of Austen's texts is therefore
difficult to convey. Another point Sutherland makes is that even where

fidelity to the texts would be easier, for example as concerns the depiction of period detail, the viewer gets 'period magnificence' instead of faithfulness to the texts' detail. Troost and Greenfield are among the critics who look at the differences in the gender portrayal between novel and adaptation, concluding that both men and women are often modernised. While Austen's novels are thus already being read as texts with contemporary relevance partly because they are concerned with the situation of women, this issue is also taken up in the discussion of film adaptations, though critics reach different conclusions, some seeing the films as making the heroines feminist, some arguing for them being traditionalist.

Overall, then, it would appear that the single most influential factor in Austen criticism over the last 200 years has been, and still is, the author's gender, and, connected to that, the depiction of her heroines, in particular Marianne, Elizabeth and Emma. But this is not to say that this main concern excludes all others. On the contrary, the appearance of ever-new adaptations and the mass production of paperback editions, and the incessant flow of studies of both the novels and the adaptations, show the continuing popularity and inexhaustibility of Austen's *Sense and Sensibility*, *Pride and Prejudice* and *Emma* in their various forms.

Notes

INTRODUCTION

1 Wherever possible, dates have been given for authors and other significant figures, and for titles. In some cases, however, dates were unavailable.

2 Peter Garside, 'The English Novel in the Romantic Era: Consolidation and Dispersal', in *The English Novel 1770–1829: A Bibliographical Survey of Prose Fiction Published in the British Isles*, Peter Garside, James Raven and Rainer Schöwerling (eds), 2 vols (Oxford: Oxford University Press, 2000), II, pp. 15–103, p. 51.

3 All numbers of copies for the first editions of Austen's novels are taken from Gilson.

4 Garside (2000), p. 39.

5 David Gilson, *A Bibliography of Jane Austen* (New Castle: Oak Knoll Press, 1997), p. 16.

6 Gilson (1997), p. 24.

7 Gilson (1997), p. 36.

8 Janet Todd, *The Cambridge Introduction to Jane Austen* (Cambridge: Cambridge University Press, 2006), p. 6.

9 Gilson (1997), pp. 68, 69.

10 *The Quarterly Review* in October 1815, *The Champion* in March 1816, *The Augustan Review* in May 1816, *The British Critic* in July 1816, *The Monthly Review* in July 1816, *The Gentleman's Magazine* in September 1816, *The British Lady's Magazine* in September 1816, *The Literary Panorama* in June 1817, and *Morgenblatt für gebildete Stände* in June 1816, *Jenaische Allgemeine Literaturzeitung* in June 1816, and *Vestnik Europi* in June 1816.

11 Stanley Fish, 'Interpreting the Variorum', in *Reader-Response Criticism: From Formalism to Post-Structuralism*, Jane Tompkins (ed.) (Baltimore; London: Johns Hopkins University Press, 1988), pp. 164–84, p. 184.

12 Hans Robert Jauss, *Toward an Aesthetic of Reception*; translated from German by Timothy Bahti; introduction by Paul de Man (Brighton: Harvester Press, 1982), p. 21.

1 CONTEMPORARY REVIEWS

1 John Gross, *The Rise and Fall of the Man of Letters, Aspects of English Literary Life since 1800* (London: Weidenfeld and Nicolson, 1969), p. 2.

2 William St Clair, *The Reading Nation in the Romantic Period* (Cambridge: Cambridge University Press, 2004), p. 573. Also see Altick, Richard D., *The English Common Reader, A Social History of the Mass Reading Public 1800–1900* (Chicago: University of Chicago Press, 1957), p. 392.

3 St Clair (2004), p. 574.

4 I therefore refer to individual reviewers as 'he' throughout; read 'he or she' each time.

5 Peter Garside, 'The English Novel in the Romantic Era: Consolidation and Dispersal', in *The English Novel 1770–1829: A Bibliographical Survey of Prose Fiction Published in the British Isles*, Peter Garside, James Raven and Rainer Schöwerling (eds), 2 vols (Oxford: Oxford University Press, 2000), II, pp. 15–103, p. 16, p. 38.

6 *BC* (January 1812), p. 39.

7 Garside (2000), p. 74.

8 1833 edition of *SS*, p. viii.

9 *The Quarterly Review*, (by Walter Scott), (October 1815), pp. 188–201, p. 188. (The article did not in fact appear until March 1816.)

10 Kathryn Sutherland, '"Events…have made us a world of readers": Reader Relations 1780–1830', in *The Romantic Period*, David B. Pirie (ed.) (London: Penguin, 1994), pp. 1–48, p. 9.

11 Jane Austen, Letter to Fanny Knight, November 1814; in *Jane Austen's Letters;*, ed. and coll. by Deidre Le Faye (Oxford: Oxford University Press, 1995), p. 287.

12 Sutherland (1994), p. 12.

13 William Godwin, 'Essay of History and Romance', in *Political and Philosophical Writings of William Godwin*, Mark Philip (ed.) (London: Pickering, 1993), v: *Educational and Literary Writings*, Pamela Clemit (ed.) (1993), pp. 291–301, p. 297.

14 *CR* (1812), p. 149.

15 *CR* (1812), p. 149.

16 *CR* (1812), p. 153.

17 *CR* (1812), p. 153.

18 *CR* (1812), p. 153.

19 *CR* (1812), p. 149.

20 *CR* (1812), p. 149.

21 *CR* (1812), p. 149.

22 *CR* (1812), p. 149.

23 *CR* (1812), p. 149.

24 *CR* (1812), p. 149.

25 *The British Critic* (1812), p. 527.

26 *BC* (1812), p. 527.

27 *BC* (February 1813), pp. 189–90.

28 *BC* (1813), p. 189.

29 *BC* (1813), p. 190.

30 *BC* (1813), p. 189.

31 *BC* (1813), p. 189.

32 *CR* (March 1813), pp. 318–19.

33 *CR* (1813), p. 323.

34 *CR* (1813), p. 323.

35 *CR* (1813), p. 324.

36 *CR* (1813), p. 322.

37 *CR* (1813), p. 324.

38 *CR* (1813), p. 324.

39 *CR* (1813), p. 323.

40 *CR* (1813), p. 324.

41 *CR* (1813), p. 324.

42 Garside (2000), p. 45.

43 David Gilson, *A Bibliography of Jane Austen* (New Castle: Oak Knoll Press, 1997), pp. 68–9.

44 Garside (2000), p. 17.

45 Walter Scott in *The Quarterly Review*, (October 1815), pp. 188–201, p. 188.

46 Scott (1815), p. 189.

47 Scott (1815), p. 189.

48 Scott (1815), p. 193.

49 Scott (1815), p. 193.

50 Scott (1815), p. 199.

51 Scott (1815), p. 201.

52 *The Gentleman's Magazine* (September 1816), pp. 248–9, p. 248.

53 *GM* (1816), p. 248.

54 *GM* (1816), p. 249.

55 *GM* (1816), p. 249.

56 *GM* (1816), p. 249.

57 *CR* (1813), p. 324.

58 *BC* (1818), p. 296.
59 *GM* (1816), p. 249.

2 VICTORIAN REVIEWS, CA. 1865–80

1 Anonymous, 'Jane Austen', *St Paul's Magazine*, 5 (1870), pp. 631–43; cited from reprint in *The Critical Heritage*, vol. 2, 226–40.

2 Edith Simcox, 'A Memoir of Jane Austen, 2nd edition', *The Academy* (1 August 1871), pp. 367–8.

3 Edith Simcox, 'A Memoir of Jane Austen and Sense and Sensibility', *The Academy*, 1 (12 Februray 1870), pp. 118–19.

4 Brian Southam (ed.), *Jane Austen: The Critical Heritage*, 2 vols (London: Routledge and Kegan Paul, 1968 and 1987), vol. 2, p. 164.

5 Anne Isabella Thackeray, 'Jane Austen', *Cornhill Magazine*, 34 (1871), pp. 158–74 cited from reprint in *The Critical Heritage*, vol. 2, pp. 164–70, p. 166.

6 Thackeray (1871), *CH II*, pp. 167–9.

7 Richard H. Hutton, 'The Memoir of Miss Austen', *The Spectator*, 25 (1869), 1533–5; cited from reprint in *The Critical Heritage*, vol. 2, 160–4, pp. 162–4.

8 Henry F. Chorley, 'A Memoir of Jane Austen and The Life of Mary Russell Mitford', *The Quarterly Review*, 128 (1870), 196–218, p. 204.

9 Margaret Oliphant, 'Miss Austen and Miss Mitford', *Blackwood's Edinburgh Magazine*, 107 (1870), pp. 290–313, p. 294.

10 Oliphant (1870), p. 300.

11 Oliphant (1870), p. 294.

12 Oliphant (1870), pp. 294–5.

13 Oliphant (1870), pp. 301–2.

14 Thackeray (1871), p. 166.

15 Thackeray (1871), p. 167.

16 Thomas E. Kebbel, 'Jane Austen', *Fortnightly Review* 13 (1870), pp. 187–93, p. 191.

17 Chorley (1870), p. 203.

18 Kebbel (1870), p. 189.

19 Thackeray (1871), p. 167.

20 Kebbel (1870), p. 191.

21 Simcox (15 August 1871), p. 394.

22 Anonymous, 'Jane Austen', *St Paul's Magazine*, 5 (1870), pp. 631–43; cited from reprint in *The Critical Heritage*, vol. 2, pp. 226–40, pp. 227–9.

23 James Edward Austen-Leigh, *A Memoir of Jane Austen*, Kathryn Sutherland (ed.) (Oxford: Oxford University Press, 2002), pp. 9–10.

24 Austen-Leigh (2002), p. 116.

25 Austen-Leigh (2002), p. 73.

26 Kebbel (1870), p. 190.

27 Richard Simpson, 'A Memoir of Jane Austen', *North British Review* 52 (1870), pp. 129–52; cited from reprint in *The Critical Heritage*, vol 1, pp. 241–65, p. 245.

28 *St Paul's* (1870), p. 228.

29 *St Paul's* (1870), p. 235.

30 *St Paul's* (1870), pp. 231–2.

31 Anonymous, 'Miss Austen', *Englishwoman's Domestic Magazine*, 2 (1866), 238–9, 278–82; cited from reprint in *The Critical Heritage*, vol. 2, 200–14, p. 204.

32 *St Paul's* (1870), p. 232.

33 Simpson (1870), *CH I*, p. 264.

34 Simpson (1870), *CH I*, p. 250.

35 Anonymous, 'Jane Austen', *Month*, 15 (1871), pp. 305–10, p. 372.

36 Kebbel (1870), p. 188.

37 Leslie Stephen, 'Humour', *Cornhill Magazine*, 33 (1876), pp. 318–26, cited from reprint in *The Critical Heritage*, vol 2, pp. 173–5, pp. 324–5.
38 *EWDM* (1866), *CH I*, p. 204.
39 *St Paul's* (1870), *CH I*, pp. 227–8.
40 Simcox (12 February 1870), p. 118.
41 Simpson (1870), *CH I*, p. 252.
42 Simpson (1870), *CH I*, p. 252.
43 *Month* (1871), p. 310.
44 Thackeray (1871), p. 162.
45 Anonymous, 'Life of Jane Austen', *Month*, 12 (1870), pp. 371–2, p. 372.
46 *EWDM* (1866), *CH I*, p. 203.
47 *Month* (1871), p. 310.
48 *Month* (1871), p. 310.
49 Simpson (1870), *CH I*, p. 253.
50 *EWDM* (1866), *CH I*, p. 207.
51 *EWDM* (1866), *CH I*, pp. 206–12.
52 *EWDM* (1866), *CH I*, p. 212.
53 Simcox (12 February 1870), p. 118.
54 Chorley (1870), p. 200.
55 James Payn, 'A Glimpse at a British Classic', *Chambers Journal*, 47 (1870), pp. 157–60, p. 153.
56 Joseph Cady and Ian Watt, 'Jane Austen's Critics', in *Jane Austen: critical assessments*, Ian Littlewood (ed.) (Mountfield: Helm Information, 1998), pp. 231–45, p. 233.
57 Simpson (1870), *CH I*, p. 243.
58 Richard Simpson, 'A Memoir of Jane Austen', *North British Review* 52 (1870), 129–52; cited from reprint in *The Critical Heritage,* vol. 1, pp. 241–65, p. 246.
59 Simpson (1870), *CH I*, pp. 242–5.
60 Simpson (1870), *CH I*, pp. 242–6.
61 *St Paul's* (1870), *CH I*, pp. 235–6.
62 Oliphant (1870), p. 204.
63 Oliphant (1870), p. 204.
64 *EWDM* (1866), p. 201.
65 Austen-Leigh (2002), p. 105.
66 Stephen (1876), p. 174.
67 Stephen (1876), p. 174.
68 Stephen (1876), p. 174.
69 Stephen (1876), pp. 174–5.

3   EARLY TO MID-TWENTIETH CENTURY CRITICAL RESPONSES

1 George Saintsbury, Preface to *Pride and Prejudice* (London: George Allen, 1894), cited from reprint in Southam (1987), pp. 214–18, p. 215.
2 Saintsbury, p. 218.
3 Deidre Lynch, 'Sharing with our Neighbours', in Deidre Lynch (ed.), *Janeites: Austen's Disciples and Devotees* (Princeton: Princeton University Press, 2000), pp. 3–24, pp. 13–14.
4 Lynch (2000), pp. 12–13.
5 Mark Twain, comments collected in Southam (1987), pp. 232–3, p. 232.
6 Claudia Johnson, 'The Divine Miss Jane: Jane Austen, Janeites, and the Discipline of Novel Studies', in Deidre Lynch (ed.) *Janeites: Austen's Disciples and Devotees* (Princeton: Princeton University Press, 2000), pp. 25–44, p. 30.
7 Andrew Lycett, *Rudyard Kipling* (London: Weidenfeld & Nicolson, 1999), pp. 513–14.
8 Kipling, Rudyard, *The Janeites*, in *Story-Teller, MacLean's* and *Hearst's International*, May 1924, cited from http://www.telelib.com/words/authors/K/KiplingRudyard/prose/DebtsandCredits/janeites.html [last accessed 14 August 2009].

9 Johnson (2000), p. 32.

10 Henry James, *The Lesson of Balzac* (Boston and New York: Houghton & Mifflin, 1905), cited from reprint in Southam (1987), pp. 229–31.

11 Nicola Trott, 'Critical Responses, 1830–1970', in Janet Todd (ed.), *Jane Austen in Context* (Cambridge: Cambridge University Press, 2005), pp. 92–100, p. 93.

12 Brian Southam (ed.), *Jane Austen: The Critical Heritage* vol. 2 (London: Routledge and Kegan Paul, 1987), p. 233.

13 A.C. Bradley, 'Jane Austen: A Lecture', *Essays and Studies by Members of the English Association*, 2 (1911), pp. 7–36, cited from reprint in Southam (1987), pp. 233–9, pp. 233–4.

14 Bradley (1911), pp. 234–8.

15 Reginald Farrer, 'Jane Austen', *The Quarterly Review*, 228 (1917), pp. 1–30, cited from reprint in Southam (1987), pp. 245–72, pp. 250–60.

16 R.W. Chapman (ed.), *The Novels of Jane Austen*, 5 vols (Clarendon Press: Oxford, 1923), preface to vol 1, pp. i–ii.

17 Chapman (1923), preface to vol. 1, p. xiii.

18 Chapman (1923), vol. I, p. 389.

19 E.M. Forster, Review of Chapman's edition in *Nation and Athenaeum* (5 January 1924), cited from reprint in Southam (1987), pp. 279–80.

20 Virginia Woolf, 'Jane Austen at Sixty', in: *Athenaeum* (15 December 1923), cited from reprint in *The Critical Heritage*, vol. 2, pp. 281–3.

21 Fiona Stafford, 'Jane Austen', in *Literature of the Romantic Period: A Bibliographical Guide*, Michael O'Neill (ed.) (Oxford: Clarendon Press, 1998), pp. 246–268, p. 251.

22 Stafford (1998), p. 254.

23 Mary Lascelles, *Jane Austen and her Art* (Oxford: Clarendon Press, 1939), pp. 149–50.

24 Lascelles (1939), pp. 157–63.

25 Trott (2005), p. 95.

26 Andrew Wright, *Jane Austen's Novels: A Study in Structure* (London: Chatto & Windus, 1953), pp. 98–9.

27 D.W. Harding, 'Regulated Hatred: An Aspect of the Work of Jane Austen', *Scrutiny*, 8 (1940), pp. 346–62, p. 347.

28 Harding (1940), p. 347.

29 Harding (1947), pp. 349–54.

30 Marvin Mudrick, *Jane Austen: Irony as Defense and Discovery* (Princeton: Princeton University Press, 1952). Quotations on *PP* taken from reprint: 'Irony as Discrimination: Pride and Prejudice', in *Jane Austen, A Collection of Critical Essays*, Ian Watt (ed.) (London: Prentice Hall 1963), pp. 76–97, pp. 77–86.

31 Southam (1987), p. 121.

32 David Cecil, *Jane Austen* (1935), cited from reprint in Southam (1987), pp. 119–21, p. 121.

33 James Edward Austen-Leigh, *A Memoir of Jane Austen*, Kathryn Sutherland (ed.) (Oxford: Oxford University Press, 2002), p. 105.

34 Cecil, cited from Southam (1987), p. 120.

35 Johnson (2000), p. 35.

36 F.R. Leavis, *The Great Tradition* (Garden City, NY: Doubleday and Co, 1954), pp. 7–9.

37 Lionel Trilling, '*Emma* and the Legend of Jane Austen' (1957), reprinted in Lodge (1969), pp. 148–169, pp. 149–50.

38 Trilling (1957), pp. 165–6.

4 LATER TWENTIETH-CENTURY CRITICAL RESPONSES: FEMINISM

1 Tomalin, Claire, *Jane Austen: A Life* (London: Viking, 1997), pp. 138–9.

2 St Clair, pp. 277–8.

3 Ronald Blythe, Introduction to *Emma* (Penguin 1966), pp. 16–20.

4 David Lodge, Introduction to *Emma* (Oxford: Oxford University Press, 1971), p. x.

5 Castle, Terry, Introduction to *Emma* (Oxford: Oxford University Press, 1995), pp. viii–xxviii, pp. xv–xviii.

6 Castle, pp. xi–xii.

7 Gilbert, Sandra M., and Susan Gubar, *The Madwoman in the Attic: The Woman Writer and the Nineteenth-century Literary Imagination* (New Haven: Yale University Press, 1979), pp. 154–5.

8 Gilbert and Gubar (1979), p. 159.

9 Gilbert and Gubar (1979), p. 157.

10 Gilbert and Gubar (1979), p. 157.

11 Gilbert and Gubar (1979), pp. 168–9.

12 Gilbert and Gubar (1979), p. 169.

13 Gilbert and Gubar (1979), p. 162.

14 Gilbert and Gubar (1979), pp. 158–9.

15 Gilbert and Gubar (1979), p. 170.

16 Gilbert and Gubar (1979), p. 172.

17 Gilbert and Gubar (1979), p. 174.

18 Kirkham, Margaret, *Jane Austen, Feminism and Fiction* (Brighton: Harvester, 1983), p. xi.

19 Kirkham (1983), p. 3.

20 Garside, Peter, 'The English Novel in the Romantic Era: Consolidation and Dispersal', in *The English Novel 1770–1829: A Bibliographical Survey of Prose Fiction Published in the British Isles*, Peter Garside, James Raven and Rainer Schöwerling (eds.), 2 vols (Oxford: Oxford University Press, 2000), II, pp. 15–103, p. 78.

21 Kirkham (1983), p. 87.

22 Kirkham (1983), p. 32.

23 Poovey, Mary, *The Proper Lady and the Woman Writer* (Chicago: Chicago University Press, 1984), p. 173.

24 Poovey (1984), p. 203.

25 Clark, Robert (ed.) *Sense and Sensibility and Pride and Prejudice: Contemporary Critical Essays* (London: Macmillan, 1994), p. 12.

26 Poovey (1984), p. 237.

27 Gary Kelly, 'Jane Austen, Romantic Feminism, and Civil Society', in: Looser, Devoney (ed.), *Jane Austen and Discourses of Feminism* (Basingstoke: Palgrave, 1995), pp. 19–34, p. 19.

28 Kelly (1995), pp. 26–30.

29 Rajeswari Sunder Rajan, 'Austen in the World: Postcolonial Mappings', in: You-Me Park and Rajeswari Sunder Rajan, eds., *The Postcolonial Jane Austen* (London: Routledge, 2000), p. 4.

30 Park, You-Me "Father's daughters", in You-Me Park and Rajeswari Sunder Rajan, eds., *The Postcolonial Jane Austen* (London: Routledge, 2000), pp. 205–17, pp. 213–16.

5   LATER TWENTIETH-CENTURY CRITICAL RESPONSES: LITERARY, CULTURAL, AND HISTORICAL CONTEXT

1 Devoney Looser (ed.), *Jane Austen and Discourses of Feminism* (Basingstoke: Palgrave, 1995), p. 1.

2 Marilyn Butler, *Jane Austen and the War of Ideas* (Oxford: Clarendon Press, 1975), pp. 182–96.

3 Tony Tanner, Introduction to *Pride and Prejudice* (London: Penguin, 1972), pp. 368–408 (cited from Appendix to 2003 Penguin Edition), p. 405.

4 David Lodge, Introduction to *Emma* (Oxford: Oxford University Press, 1971), pp. vii–xvi, p. xiii.

5 Lodge (1971), p. ix.

6 Tanner (1972), p. 369.

7 Tanner (1972), p. 369.

8 Tanner (1972),p. 381.

9 Tanner (1972), p. 377.

10 Tanner (1972), p. 381.

11 Frank Bradbrook, Introduction to *Pride and Prejudice* (Oxford: Oxford University Press, 1970), pp. vii–xvi, pp. xv–xvi.

12 Bradbrook (1970), p. xvi.

13 Ronald Blythe, Introduction to *Emma* (London: Penguin, 1966), pp. 7–32, p. 14.

14 Tanner (1972), p. 369.

15 Roger Sales, *Jane Austen and Representations of Regency England* (London: Routledge, 1994), pp. 155–8.

16 Mary Waldron, *Jane Austen and the Fiction of her Time* (Cambridge: Cambridge University Press, 1999), pp. 63–8.

17 Isobel Armstrong, Introduction to *Pride and Prejudice* (Oxford: Oxford University Press, 1990), pp. vii–xxvi, p. xii.

18 Claire Lamont, Introduction to *Sense and Sensibility* (Oxford: Oxford University Press, 1970), pp. vii–xxi, p. vii.

19 Ros Ballaster, Introduction to *Sense and Sensibility* (London: Penguin, 1995), pp. xi–xxxi (quoted from 2003 Penguin edition), p. xviii.

20 Ballaster (1995), p. xx.

21 Margaret Anne Doody, Introduction to *Sense and Sensibility* (Oxford: Oxford University Press, 1990), pp. vii–xxxix, p. xiii.

22 Doody (1990), p. xi.

23 Doody (1990), pp. xiv–xv.

24 Tony Tanner, Introduction to *Sense and Sensibility* (Penguin 1969), pp. 355–83 (cited from Appendix to 2003 Penguin Edition), p. 378.

25 Tanner (1969), *SS*, pp. 378–81.

26 Armstrong (1990), p. xxviii.

27 Claudia L. Johnson, *Jane Austen: Women, Politics and the Novel* (Chicago: University of Chicago Press, 1988), pp. 74–90.

28 Armstrong (1990), p. viii.

6   THE FIRST DECADE OF THE TWENTY-FIRST CENTURY

1 D.A. Miller, *Jane Austen or The Secret of Style* (Princeton: Princeton University Press, 2003), p. 107.

2 Miller (2003), p. 108.

3 Miller (2003), p. 1.

4 Miller (2003), p. 31.

5 Miller (2003), p. 32.

6 Miller (2003), p. 31.

7 Miller (2003), p. 35.

8 Miller (2003), p. 39.

9 Miller (2003), pp. 36–7.

10 Miller (2003), p. 38.

11 Miller (2003), p. 42.

12 Miller (2003), p. 47

13 Miller (2003), pp. 45–6.

14 Miller (2003), p. 46.

15 Miller (2003), p. 46.

16 Miller (2003), p. 47.

17 John Wiltshire, *Jane Austen: Introductions and Interventions* (Basingstoke: Palgrave 2006), p. 49.

18 Wiltshire (2006), pp. 51–2.

19 Wiltshire (2006), p.53.

20 Wiltshire (2006), p. 56.

21 Wiltshire (2006), p. 56.

22 Wiltshire (2006), p. 56.

23 Claire Lamont, 'Jane Austen and the Old', in *The Review of English Studies*, New Series, Vol. 54, No. 217 (Oxford: Oxford University Press, 2003), pp. 661–74, p. 661.

24 Lamont (2003), p. 661.

25 Lamont (2003), p. 674.

26 Lamont (2003), p. 666.

27 Lamont (2003), p. 669.

28 Lamont (2003), p. 669.

29 Lamont (2003), pp. 673–4.

30 Peter Knox-Shaw, *Jane Austen and the Enlightenment* (Cambridge: Cambridge University Press, 2004), p. 5.

31 Knox-Shaw (2004), p. 5.

32 Knox-Shaw (2004), p. 201.

33 Knox-Shaw (2004), p. 201.

34 Knox-Shaw (2004), p. 202.

35 Knox-Shaw (2004), p. 203.

36 Knox-Shaw (2004), p. 203.

37 Knox-Shaw (2004), p. 208.

38 Knox-Shaw (2004), p. 209.

39 Knox-Shaw (2004), pp. 210–11.

40 Knox-Shaw (2004), p. 211.

41 Knox-Shaw (2004), p. 212.

42 Knox-Shaw (2004), p. 212.

43 Knox-Shaw (2004), p. 217.

44 Bruce Stovel and Lynn Weinlos Gregg (eds), *The Talk in Jane Austen* (Edmonton: the University of Alberta Press, 2002), p. xx.

45 Jan Fergus, 'The Power of Women's Language and Laughter', in Bruce Stovel and Lynn Weinlos Gregg (eds), *The Talk in Jane Austen* (Edmonton: University of Alberta Press, 2002), pp. 103–122, p. 101.

46 Fergus (2002), p. 120.

47 Jocelyn Harris, 'Silent Women, Shrews, and Bluestockings: Women and Speaking in Jane Austen', in (Stovel and Gregg, 2002), pp. 3–22, p. 3.

48 Harris (2002), p. 3.

49 Harris (2002), p. 15.

50 Harris (2002), p. 14.

51 Harris (2002), p. 17.

52 Harris (2002), p. 18.

53 Harris (2002), p. 18.

54 Harris (2002), p. 21.

55 Penny Gay, *Jane Austen and the Theatre* (Cambridge: Cambridge University Press, 2002), p. 24.

56 Gay (2002), p. 27.

57 Gay (2002), p. 28.

58 Gay (2002), p. 28.

59 Janet Todd, *The Cambridge Introduction to Jane Austen* (Cambridge: Cambridge University Press, 2006), p. 22.

60 Todd (2006), p. 28.

61 Todd (2006), p. 28.

62 Todd (2006), p. 59.

63 Todd (2006), p. 59.

64 William St Clair, *The Reading Nation in the Romantic Period* (Cambridge: Cambridge University Press, 2004), pp. 277–8.

65 Todd (2006), p. 59.

66 Todd (2006), p. 59.

67 Todd (2006), p. 59.

68 Bharat Tandon, *Jane Austen and the Morality of Conversation* (London: Anthem Press, 2003), pp. 152–3.

69 Tandon (2003), pp. 174–5.

70 Tandon (2003), p. 175.

71 Linda Bree, '*Emma*: Word Games and Secret Histories', in Claudia Johnson and Clara Tuite (eds), *A Companion to Jane Austen* (Malden: Wiley-Blackwell, 2009), pp. 133–141, p. 134.

72 Bree (2009), p. 135.

73 Bree (2009), p. 135.

74 Bree (2009), p. 141.

75 Bree (2009), p. 141.

76 Colin Winborn, *The Literary Economy of Jane Austen and George Crabbe* (Aldershot: Ashgate, 2004), p. 2.

77 Winborn (2004), p. 1.

78 Winborn (2004), p. 1.

79 Winborn (2004), p. 1.

80 Winborn (2004), pp. 67–8.

81 Winborn (2004), p. 68.

82 Winborn (2004), p. 68.

83 Winborn (2004), p. 69.

84 Winborn (2004), p. 69.

85 Winborn (2004), p. 80.

86 Winborn (2004), p. 80.

87 William Deresiewicz, *Jane Austen and the Romantic Poets* (New York: Columbia University Press, 2004), p. 2.

88 Deresiewicz (2004), p. 4.

89 Deresiewicz (2004), p. 7.

90 Deresiewicz (2004), p. 7.

91 Deresiewicz (2004), p. 8.

92 Deresiewicz (2004), p. 86.

93 Deresiewicz (2004), p. 87.

94 Deresiewicz (2004), p. 89.

95 Deresiewicz (2004), p. 90.

96 Deresiewicz (2004), p. 90.

97 Deresiewicz (2004), p. 95.

98 Deresiewicz (2004), p. 97.

99 Anthony Mandal, *Jane Austen and the Popular Novel: The Determined Author* (Basingstoke: Palgrave, 2007), p. 3.

100 Mandal (2007), p. 5.

101 Mandal (2007), p. 135.

102 Mandal (2007), p. 135.

103 Mandal (2007), p. 141.

104 Mandal (2007), p. 142.

105 Mandal (2007), p. 148.

106 Mandal (2007), pp. 153–4.

107 Mandal (2007), p. 157.

108 Mandal (2007), p. 161.

109 Mandal (2007), p. 167.

110 Kathryn Sutherland, *Jane Austen's Textual Lives: From Aeschylus to Bollywood* (Oxford: Oxford University Press, 2005), p. 59.

111 Sutherland (2005), p. 63.

112 Sutherland (2005), p. 62.

113 Sutherland (2005), p. 274.

114 Sutherland (2005), p. 276.

115 Sutherland (2005), p. 282.

116 Edward Copeland, 'Money', in JanetTodd (ed.), *Jane Austen in Context* (Cambridge: Cambridge University Press, 2005), pp. 317–326, p. 317.

117 Maggie Lane, 'Food', in Todd (2005), pp. 262–268, p. 276.

118 Devoney Looser, '"The Duty of Woman by Woman": Reforming Feminism in *Emma*', in *Emma*, Alistair M. Duckworth (ed.) (New York: Palgrave, 2002), pp. 577–93, pp. 577–8.

119 Looser (2002), p. 579.

120 Looser (2002), p. 579

121 Looser (2002), p. 581.

122 Looser (2002), p. 581.

123 Looser (2002), p. 583.

124 Looser (2002), p. 583.

125 Looser (2002), pp. 584–5.

126 Looser (2002), p. 588.

127 Looser (2002), p. 588.

128 Looser (2002), p. 588.

129 Looser (2002), p. 589.

130 Looser (2002), p. 589.

131 Looser (2002), p. 592.

132 Looser (2002), p. 592.

133 Looser (2002), p. 579.

134 Vivien Jones, 'Feminisms', in: Claudia Johnson and Clara Tuite (eds), *A Companion to Jane Austen* (Malden: Wiley-Blackwell, 2009), pp. 282–91, p. 282.

135 Jones (2009), p. 283.

136 Jones (2009), p. 283.

137 Jones (2009), p. 284.

138 Jones (2009), p. 285.

139 Jones (2009), p. 288.

140 Jones (2009), p. 288.

141 Jones (2009), p. 291.

142 Jones (2009), p. 291.

143 Pat Rogers, 'Introduction' to *Pride and Prejudice*, Pat Rogers (ed.) (Cambridge: Cambridge University Press, 2006), pp. xxii–lxxviii, p. xxxv.

144 Rogers (2006), p. lxxv.

145 Rogers (2006), p. lxxv.

146 Rogers (2006), p. lxxvii.

147 Rogers (2006), p. lxxviii.

148 Gabrielle White, *Jane Austen in the Context of Abolition: 'A Fling at the Slave Trade'* (Basingstoke: Palgrave, 2006), p. 3.

149 White (2006), p. 146.

7 FILM AND TELEVISION ADAPTATIONS

1 Kathryn Sutherland, *Jane Austen's Textual Lives: From Aeschylus to Bollywood* (Oxford: Oxford University Press, 2005), pp. 341–5.

2 Linda Troost and Sayre Greenfield (eds), *Jane Austen in Hollywood* (Lexington: University Press of Kentucky, 1998), pp. 4–8.

3 Linda Troost and Sayre Greenfield, 'Filming Highbury: Reducing the Community in *Emma* to the Screen', in Fiona Stafford (ed.), *Jane Austen's Emma: A Casebook* (Oxford: Oxford University Press, 2007), pp. 239–47, pp. 245–6.

4 Sue Parrill, *Jane Austen on Film and Television; A Critical Study of the Adaptations* (Jefferson: McFarland, 2002), pp. 62–5.

5 John Wiltshire, *Recreating Jane Austen* (Cambridge: Cambridge University Press, 2001), p. 7.

6 Wiltshire (2001), pp. 53–7.

CONCLUSION

1 Fiona Stafford, 'Jane Austen', in *Literature of the Romantic Period: A Bibliographical Guide*, Michael O'Neill (ed.) (Oxford: Clarendon Press, 1998), pp. 246–68, p. 261.

2 *The Daily Telegraph*, 5 August 2008.

3 *The Critical Review,* March 1813, pp. 318–24.

4 Walter Scott in *The Quarterly Review*, October 1815, pp. 188–201.

5 Richard Simpson, 'A Memoir of Jane Austen', *North British Review* 52 (1870), pp. 129–52; cited from reprint in *The Critical Heritage*, vol. 1, pp. 241–65, p. 250.

Bibliography

CONTENTS

KEY EDITIONS OF *SENSE AND SENSIBILITY*, *PRIDE AND PREJUDICE*, *EMMA*

This list draws on David Gilson's *A Bibliography of Jane Austen* (New Castle: Oak Knoll Press, 1997) and on his article on 'Jane Austen's Texts: A Survey of Editions', in: *Review of English Studies*, New Series, vol. 53, No. 209 (2002).

EDITIONS IN AUSTEN'S LIFETIME

Sense and Sensibility (London: Thomas Egerton, 1811)

2nd edition: Egerton, 1813

As Gilson points out, for the second edition, 'the author is believed to have revised the text, since there are some major differences and many minor changes' (Gilson (2002), p. 62).

Pride and Prejudice (London: Thomas Egerton, 1813)

2nd edition: Egerton, 1813

3rd edition: Egerton, 1817

Since Austen had sold the copyrights to this novel outright, it is not likely that she was involved in the second or third edition.

Emma (London: John Murray, 1816)

OTHER IMPORTANT NINETEENTH-CENTURY EDITIONS

Sense and Sensibility (London: Richard Bentley, 1833)

Pride and Prejudice (London: Richard Bentley, 1833)

Emma (London: Richard Bentley, 1833)

Bentley bought the copyrights for all Austen's novels and brought out the first collected edition of her works in 1833. His texts are 'in most cases those of the latest previous editions' (Gilson (2002), p. 67), and he uses the same stereotype plates for further editions until 1870, when he resets them.

Sense and Sensibility (London: Richard Bentley, 1882)

Pride and Prejudice (London: Richard Bentley, 1882)

Emma (London: Richard Bentley, 1882)

This is the Steventon Edition, 'the nineteenth century's first attempt at a luxury edition of the novels' (Gilson (2002), p. 70).

Sense and Sensibility, ed. by Reginald Brimley Johnson (London: J.M. Dent, 1892)

Pride and Prejudice, ed. by Reginald Brimley Johnson (London: J.M. Dent, 1892)

Emma, ed. by Reginald Brimley Johnson (London: J.M. Dent, 1892)

This was again a luxury set of the novels, but, most importantly, it was the first edition of Austen's texts that carried any editorial matter. Including an editor's notes gives the novels a different status.

R.W. CHAPMAN'S 1923 EDITION

Sense and Sensibility, ed. by R.W. Chapman (Oxford: Clarendon Press, 1923)

Pride and Prejudice, ed. by R.W. Chapman (Oxford: Clarendon Press, 1923)

Emma, ed. by R.W. Chapman (Oxford: Clarendon Press, 1923)

This edition is the first ever textual edition of any British novelist. It is also the one that is still regarded as authoritative and on which – with one exception, the Penguin Classics edition of 1995–6 – all modern editions are based, or to which they at least acknowledge their debt.

As Kathryn Sutherland points out, any edited text, with 'critical apparatus, emendations and annotations', can never just represent the text itself but is also necessarily 'a critical engagement with that work' and therefore an interpretation (Sutherland, Review of *Emma* and *Mansfield Park* in the Cambridge University Press edition (*Review of English Studies*, November 2006; vol. 57, pp. 833–8, p. 834). Since we do not have manuscripts for any of Austen's published novels, we necessarily need to interpret the printed texts and decide what is a printer's error, what was inserted by a publisher's reader rather than by Austen herself, etc.

Chapman's texts are the last printed editions of Austen's lifetime with those texts in which she can be thought to have had a hand in the changes – *Sense and Sensibility* and *Mansfield Park*. (The copyright of *Pride and Prejudice* was sold; *Emma* only reached one edition in Austen's lifetime; *Northanger Abbey* and *Persuasion* were published posthumously.)

All reprints of the novels since Chapman have followed his practice – except, as pointed out above, the Penguin Classics Edition of 1995–6, with Claire Lamont as the overall textual advisor.

MODERN EDITIONS

Penguin Classics, Textual Advisor Claire Lamont

Sense and Sensibility, ed. and notes by Ros Ballaster (London: Penguin, 1995, 2nd edn 2003)

Pride and Prejudice, ed. and notes by Vivien Jones (London: Penguin, 1996, 2nd edn 2003)

Emma, ed. and notes by Fiona Stafford (London: Penguin, 1996, 2nd edn 2003)

This edition has very helpful notes and introductions and is available in inexpensive paperback. It is based on the first-edition texts for all novels, intervenes minimally in the text and clearly indicates where it does so.

Cambridge University Press, General Editor Janet Todd

Sense and Sensibility, ed. by Edward Copeland (Cambridge: Cambridge University Press, 2006)

Pride and Prejudice, ed. by Pat Rogers (Cambridge: Cambridge University Press, 2006)

Emma, ed. by Richard Cronin and Dorothy Macmillan (Cambridge: Cambridge University Press, 2005)

This edition is as yet only available in expensive hardback volumes. It is based on the texts on which Chapman bases his edition, and is indebted to him in many respects.

It again has helpful introductions and notes to each of the novels.

Oxford University Press, General Editor James Kinsley

Sense and Sensibility, ed. by James Kinsley, introduction by Margaret Doody, notes by Claire Lamont (Oxford: Oxford University Press, 2008)

Pride and Prejudice, ed. by James Kinsley, introduction and notes by Fiona Stafford (Oxford: Oxford University Press, 2008)

Emma, ed. by James Kinsley, introduction by Adela Pinch (Oxford: Oxford University Press, 2008)

Again, this edition is available cheaply in paperback, and has helpful introductions and notes. The volumes are reprints, with a few changes in the editorial matter, of the 1970–1 Oxford University Press edition. The text is basically that of the Chapman edition, with a very few emendations by Kinsley (made in 1970–1).

EARLY-NINETEENTH-CENTURY CRITICISM

The following reviews of *SS*, *PP* and *E* are known:

SENSE AND SENSIBILITY

The British Critic (May 1812), p. 527.

The Critical Review (Feb 1812), pp. 149–57.

PRIDE AND PREJUDICE

The British Critic (Feb 1813), pp. 189–90.

The Critical Review (Mar 1813), pp. 318–24.

The New Review; or Monthly Analysis of General Literature (April 1813), pp. 393–6.

EMMA

The Augustan Review (May 1816), pp. 484–6.

The British Critic (July 1816), pp. 96–8.

The British Lady's Magazine (Sep 1816), reprinted in Ward, William S., 'Three Hitherto Unnoted Contemporary Reviews of Jane Austen', pp. 476–7.

The Champion (Mar 1816), reprinted in Ward, William S., 'Three Hitherto Unnoted Contemporary Reviews of Jane Austen', pp. 469–74.

The Gentleman's Magazine (Sep 1816), pp. 248–9.

The Literary Panorama (June 1817), col. 418–19.

The Monthly Review (July 1816), p. 320.

The Quarterly Review (by Walter Scott) (Oct 1815), pp. 188–201.

VICTORIAN ARTICLES, 1865–80

Anonymous, 'Jane Austen', *St Paul's Magazine,* 5 (1870), 631–43; cited from reprint in *The Critical Heritage*, vol. 2, pp. 226–40.

Anonymous, 'Life of Jane Austen', *Month,* 12 (1870), 371–2.

Anonymous, 'Miss Austen', *Englishwoman's Domestic Magazine,* 2 (1866), 238–9, 278–82; cited from reprint in *The Critical Heritage*, vol. 2, pp. 200–14.

Anonymous, 'Jane Austen', *Month*, 15 (1871), 305–10.

Chorley, Henry F., 'A Memoir of Jane Austen and The Life of Mary Russell Mitford', *The Quarterly Review*, 128 (1870), 196–218.

Hutton, Richard H., 'The Memoir of Miss Austen', *The Spectator*, 25 (1869), 1533–5; cited from reprint in *The Critical Heritage*, vol. 2, pp. 160–4.

Kebbel, Thomas E., 'Jane Austen', *Fortnightly Review*, 13 (1870), 187–93.

Oliphant, Margaret, 'Miss Austen and Miss Mitford', *Blackwood's Edinburgh Magazine*, 107 (1870), 290–313.

Payn, James, 'A Glimpse at a British Classic', *Chambers Journal*, 47 (1870), 157–60.

Simcox, Edith, 'A Memoir of Jane Austen and Sense and Sensibility', *The Academy*, 1 (1870), 118–19.

Simcox, Edith, 'A Memoir of Jane Austen, 2nd edition', *The Academy* (1 August 1871), 367–8.

Simpson, Richard, 'A Memoir of Jane Austen', *North British Review*, 52 (1870), 129–52; cited from reprint in *The Critical Heritage*, vol. 1, pp. 241–65.

Stephen, Leslie, 'Humour', *Cornhill Magazine*, 33 (1876), 318–26; cited from reprint in *The Critical Heritage*, vol. 2, pp. 173–5.

Thackeray, Anne Isabella, 'Jane Austen', *Cornhill Magazine*, 34 (1871), 158–74; cited from reprint in *The Critical Heritage*, vol. 2, pp. 164–70.

EARLY TO MID-TWENTIETH-CENTURY CRITICS

Bradbury, Malcolm, 'Jane Austen's *Emma*', reprinted in *Emma: A Selection of Critical Essays*, David Lodge (ed.) (London: Macmillan, 1969).

Bradley, A.C., 'Jane Austen: A Lecture', *Essays and Studies by Members of the English Association*, 2 (1911), 7–36; cited from reprint in *The Critical Heritage*, vol. 2, pp. 233–9.

Chapman, R.W. (ed.), *The Novels of Jane Austen*, 5 vols (Clarendon Press: Oxford, 1923).

Cecil, David, *Jane Austen* (1935), cited from reprint in *The Critical Heritage*, vol. 2, pp. 119–21.

Farrer, Reginald, 'Jane Austen', *The Quarterly Review*, 228 (1917), 1–30; cited from reprint in *The Critical Heritage*, vol. 2, pp. 245–72.

Forster, E.M., Review of Chapman's edition in *Nation and Athenaeum* (5 January 1924); cited from reprint in *The Critical Heritage*, vol. 2, pp. 279–80.

Garrod, H.W., 'Jane Austen: A Depreciation', in *Essays by Divers Hands, Being Transactions of the Royal Society of Literature*, NS 8 (1928), pp. 21–40.

Harding, D.W., 'Regulated Hatred: An Aspect of the Work of Jane Austen', *Scrutiny*, 8 (1940), pp. 346–62.

James, Henry, *The Lesson of Balzac* (Boston and New York: Houghton & Mifflin, 1905), cited from reprint in *The Critical Heritage*, vol. 2, pp. 229–31.

Kipling, Rudyard, *The Janeites*, in *Story-Teller, MacLean's* and *Hearst's International*, May 1924; cited from http://www.telelib.com/words/authors/K/KiplingRudyard/prose/DebtsandCredits/janeites.html [last accessed 14 August 2009].

Lascelles, Mary, *Jane Austen and her Art* (Oxford: Clarendon Press, 1939).

Leavis, F.R., *The Great Tradition* (Garden City, NY: Doubleday and Co., 1954).

Leavis, Q.D., 'A Critical Theory of Jane Austen's Writings', *Scrutiny*, 10 (1941–2), pp. 1–64; 12 (1944–5), pp. 65–80.

Moler, Kenneth, 'Sense and Sensibility and its Sources', *Review of English Studies*, 17 (1966), pp. 413–19.

Mudrick, Marvin, *Jane Austen: Irony as Defense and Discovery* (Princeton: Princeton University Press, 1952). Quotations on *PP* taken from reprint: 'Irony as Discrimination: *Pride and Prejudice*', in *Jane Austen, A Collection of Critical Essays*, Ian Watt (ed.) (London: Prentice Hall 1963), pp. 76–97. Quotations on *Emma* taken from reprint: 'Irony as form: Emma', in *Jane Austen: Emma*, David Lodge (ed.) (London: Macmillan, 1969), pp. 104–29.

Saintsbury, George, Preface to *Pride and Prejudice* (London: George Allen, 1894); cited from reprint in *The Critical Heritage*, vol. 2, pp. 214–18.

Schorer, Mark, 'The Humiliation of Emma Woodhouse', in *Jane Austen: A Collection of Critical Essays*, Ian Watt (ed.) (London: Prentice Hall, 1963).

Trilling, Lionel, *The Opposing Self* (New York: Viking Press, 1955).

Trilling, Lionel, 'Emma and the Legend of Jane Austen' (1957), reprinted in Lodge (1969), pp. 148–69.

Twain, Mark, comments collected in *The Critical Heritage*, vol. 2 (1987), pp. 232–3.

Woolf, Virginia, 'Jane Austen at Sixty', in *Athenaeum* (15 December 1923); cited from reprint in *The Critical Heritage*, vol. 2, pp. 281–3.

Wright, Andrew, *Jane Austen's Novels: A Study in Structure* (London: Chatto & Windus, 1953).

MID-TWENTIETH TO
EARLY-TWENTY-FIRST-CENTURY CRITICS

INTRODUCTIONS CITED TO VARIOUS EDITIONS OF
SENSE AND SENSIBILITY, PRIDE AND PREJUDICE, EMMA

Armstrong, Isobel, Introduction to Pride and Prejudice (Oxford: Oxford University Press, 1990), pp. vii–xxvi.

Ballaster, Ros, Introduction to Sense and Sensibility (Penguin, 1995), xi–xxxi (quoted from 2003 Penguin edition).

Blythe, Ronald, Introduction to Emma (Penguin 1966), pp. 7–32.

Bradbrook, Frank, Introduction to Pride and Prejudice (Oxford: Oxford University Press, 1970), pp. vii–xvi.

Castle, Terry, Introduction to Emma (Oxford: Oxford University Press, 1995), pp. viii–xxviii.

Doody, Margaret Anne, Introduction to Sense and Sensibility (Oxford: Oxford University Press, 1990), pp. vii–xxxix.

Jones, Vivien, Introduction to Pride and Prejudice (Penguin 1996; 2003), pp. xi– xxxvi.

Lamont, Claire, Introduction to Sense and Sensibility (Oxford: Oxford University Press, 1970), pp. vii–xxi.

Lodge, David, Introduction to Emma (Oxford: Oxford University Press, 1971), pp. vii–xvi.

Rogers, Pat, 'Introduction' to Pride and Prejudice, Pat Rogers (ed.) (Cambridge: Cambridge University Press, 2006), pp. xxii–lxxviii.

Stafford, Fiona, Introduction to Emma (Penguin, 1996), pp. vii–xxii.

Tanner, Tony, Introduction to Sense and Sensibility (Penguin, 1969), pp. 355–83 (cited from Appendix to 2003 Penguin Edition).

Tanner, Tony, Introduction to Pride and Prejudice (Penguin, 1972), pp. 368–408 (cited from Appendix to 2003 Penguin Edition).

OTHER MID-TWENTIETH TO EARLY-TWENTY-FIRST-CENTURY CRITICS

Bree, Linda, '*Emma*: Word Games and Secret Histories', in Claudia Johnson and Clara Tuite (eds) *A Companion to Jane Austen* (Malden: Wiley-Blackwell, 2009), pp. 133–41.

Butler, Marilyn, *Jane Austen and the War of Ideas* (Oxford: Clarendon Press, 1975).

Copeland, Edward, *Women Writing about Money: Women's Fiction in England 1790–1820* (Cambridge: Cambridge University Press, 1995).

Copeland, Edward, 'Money', in Janet Todd (ed.) *Jane Austen in Context* (Cambridge: Cambridge University Press, 2005), pp. 317–26.

Deresiewicz, William, *Jane Austen and the Romantic Poets* (New York: Columbia University Press, 2004).

Fergus, Jan, *Jane Austen: A Literary Life* (Basingstoke: Macmillan, 1991).

Fergus, Jan, 'The Power of Women's Language and Laughter', in Bruce Stovel and Lynn Weinlos Gregg (eds) *The Talk in Jane Austen* (Edmonton: the University of Alberta Press, 2002), pp. 103–22.

Gay, Penny, *Jane Austen and the Theatre* (Cambridge: Cambridge University Press, 2002).

Gilbert, Sandra M. and Gubar, Susan, *The Madwoman in the Attic: the Woman Writer and the Nineteenth-century Literary Imagination* (New Haven: Yale University Press, 1979).

Hardy, Barbara, *A Reading of Jane Austen* (London: Owen, 1975).

Harris, Jocelyn, 'Silent Women, Shrews, and Bluestockings: Women and Speaking in Jane Austen', in Bruce Stovel and Lynn Weinlos Gregg (eds) *The Talk in Jane Austen* (Edmonton: The University of Alberta Press, 2002), pp. 3–22.

Johnson, Claudia L., *Jane Austen: Women, Politics and the Novel* (Chicago: University of Chicago Press, 1988).

Johnson, Claudia, and Tuite, Clara (eds) *A Companion to Jane Austen* (Malden: Wiley-Blackwell, 2009).

Jones, Vivien, 'Feminisms', in: Claudia Johnson and Clara Tuite (eds) *A Companion to Jane Austen* (Malden: Wiley-Blackwell, 2009), pp. 282–91.

Kelly, Gary, 'Jane Austen, Romantic Feminism, and Civil Society', in Devoney Looser (ed.) *Jane Austen and Discourses of Feminism* (Basingstoke: Palgrave, 1995), pp. 19–34.

Kelly, Gary, 'Jane Austen's Imagined Communities: Talk, Narration, and Founding the Modern State', in Bruce Stovel and Lynn Weinlos Gregg (eds) *The Talk in Jane Austen* (Edmonton: the University of Alberta Press, 2002), pp. 123–40.

Kirkham, Margaret, *Jane Austen, Feminism and Fiction* (Brighton: Harvester, 1983).

Knox-Shaw, Peter, *Jane Austen and the Enlightenment* (Cambridge: Cambridge University Press, 2004).

Lamont, Claire, 'Jane Austen and the Old', in *The Review of English Studies*, New Series, Vol. 54, No. 217 (Oxford: Oxford University Press, 2003), pp. 661–74.

Lane, Maggie, 'Food', in Janet Todd (ed.), *Jane Austen in Context* (Cambridge: Cambridge University Press, 2005), pp. 262–8.

Leighton, Angela, 'Sense and Silences', in *Sense and Sensibility and Pride and Prejudice: Contemporary Critical Essays*, Robert Clark (ed.) (London: Macmillan, 1994).

Lodge, David (ed.), *Emma: A Selection of Critical Essays* (London: Macmillan, 1969).

Looser, Devoney (ed.), *Jane Austen and Discourses of Feminism* (Basingstoke: Palgrave, 1995).

Looser, Devoney, '"The Duty of Woman by Woman": Reforming Feminism in *Emma*', in *Emma*, Alistair M. Duckworth (ed.) (New York: Palgrave, 2002), pp. 577–93.

MacMaster, Juliet (ed.), *Jane Austen's Achievement* (London: Macmillan, 1976).

Mandal, Anthony, *Jane Austen and the Popular Novel: The Determined Author* (Basingstoke: Palgrave, 2007).

Miles, Robert, *Jane Austen, Writers and their Work* (Tavistock: Northcote House, 2002).

Miles, Rosalind, *Female Writers and the Conquest of the Novel* (London: Routledge & Kegan Paul, 1991).

Miller, D.A., *Jane Austen or The Secret of Style* (Princeton: Princeton University Press, 2003).

Moers, Ellen, *Literary Women* (Garden City, N.Y.: Anchor Press, 1976).

Monaghan, David, *Jane Austen in a Social Context* (London: Macmillan, 1981).

Newton, Judith Lowder, 'Pride and Prejudice', in *Women, Power and Subversion* (London: Methuen, 1981).

Park, You-Me, 'Father's daughters', in You-Me Park and Rajeswari Sunder Rajan (eds), *The Postcolonial Jane Austen* (London: Routledge, 2000), pp. 205–17.

Parrill, Sue, *Jane Austen on Film and Television; A Critical Study of the Adaptations* (Jefferson: McFarland, 2002).

Poovey, Mary, *The Proper Lady and the Woman Writer* (Chicago: Chicago University Press, 1984).

Sales, Roger, *Jane Austen and Representations of Regency England* (London: Routledge, 1994).

Spencer, Jane, *The Rise of the Woman Novelist from Aphra Behn to Jane Austen* (New York: Blackwell, 1986).

Stafford, Fiona (ed.), *Jane Austen's Emma: A Casebook* (Oxford: Oxford University Press, 2007).

Stovel, Bruce, and Gregg, Lynn Weinlos (eds), *The Talk in Jane Austen* (Edmonton: the University of Alberta Press, 2002).

Sutherland, Kathryn, *Jane Austen's Textual Lives: From Aeschylus to Bollywood* (Oxford: Oxford University Press, 2005).

Tandon, Bharat, *Jane Austen and the Morality of Conversation* (London: Anthem Press, 2003).

Tanner, Tony, *Jane Austen* (Basingstoke: Macmillan, 1986).

Todd, Janet (ed.), *Jane Austen in Context* (Cambridge: Cambridge University Press, 2005).

Todd, Janet, *The Cambridge Introduction to Jane Austen* (Cambridge: Cambridge University Press, 2006).

Troost, Linda and Greenfield, Sayre (eds), *Jane Austen in Hollywood* (Lexington: University Press of Kentucky, 1998).

Troost, Linda and Sayre Greenfield, 'Filming Highbury: Reducing the Community in *Emma* to the Screen', in Fiona Stafford (ed.), *Jane Austen's Emma: A Casebook* (Oxford: Oxford University Press, 2007), pp. 239–47.

Waldron, Mary, *Jane Austen and the Fiction of her Time* (Cambridge: Cambridge University Press, 1999).

White, Gabrielle, *Jane Austen in the Context of Abolition: 'A Fling at the Slave Trade'* (Basingstoke: Palgrave, 2006).

Wiltshire, John, *Recreating Jane Austen* (Cambridge: Cambridge University Press, 2001).

Wiltshire, John, *Jane Austen: Introductions and Interventions* (Basingstoke: Palgrave, 2006).

Winborn, Colin, *The Literary Economy of Jane Austen and George Crabbe* (Aldershot: Ashgate, 2004).

GENERAL SELECT BIBLIOGRAPHY

Altick, Richard D., *The English Common Reader, A Social History of the Mass Reading Public 1800–1900* (Chicago: University of Chicago Press, 1957).

Austen-Leigh, James Edward, *A Memoir of Jane Austen*, Kathryn Sutherland (ed.) (Oxford: Oxford University Press, 2002).

Bautz, Annika, *The Reception of Jane Austen and Walter Scott* (London: Continuum, 2007).

Cady, Joseph and Watt, Ian, 'Jane Austen's Critics', in *Jane Austen; Critical Assessments*, Ian Littlewood (ed.) (Mountfield: Helm Information, 1998), pp. 231–45.

Clark, Robert (ed.), *Sense and Sensibility and Pride and Prejudice: Contemporary Critical Essays* (London: Macmillan, 1994).

Fish, Stanley, 'Interpreting the Variorum', in *Reader-Response Criticism: From Formalism to Post-Structuralism*, Jane Tompkins (ed.) (Baltimore; London: John Hopkins University Press, 1988), pp. 164–84.

Garside, Peter, 'The English Novel in the Romantic Era: Consolidation and Dispersal', in *The English Novel 1770–1829: A Bibliographical Survey of Prose Fiction Published in the British Isles,* Peter Garside, James Raven and Rainer Schöwerling (eds), 2 vols (Oxford: Oxford University Press, 2000), II, pp. 15–103.

Gilson, David, *A Bibliography of Jane Austen* (New Castle: Oak Knoll Press, 1997).

Hayden, John O., *The Romantic Reviewers; 1802–1824*, (London: Routledge & Kegan Paul, 1969).

Jauss, Hans Robert, *Toward an Aesthetic of Reception;* translated from German by Timothy Bahti; introduction by Paul de Man (Brighton: Harvester Press, 1982).

Johnson, Claudia, 'The Divine Miss Jane: Jane Austen, Janeites, and the Discipline of Novel Studies', in Deidre Lynch (ed.) *Janeites: Austen's Disciples and Devotees* (Princeton: Princeton University Press, 2000), pp. 25–44.

Le Faye, Deidre (ed.), *Jane Austen's Letters* (Oxford: Oxford University Press, 1995).

Littlewood, Ian (ed.), *Jane Austen: critical assessments* (Mountfield: Helm Information, 1998).

Lycett, Andrew, *Rudyard Kipling* (London: Weidenfeld & Nicolson, 1999).

Lynch, Deidre, 'Sharing with our Neighbours', in Deidre Lynch (ed.) *Janeites: Austen's Disciples and Devotees* (Princeton: Princeton University Press, 2000), pp. 3–24.

Macdonald, Gina and Macdonald, Andrew (eds), *Jane Austen on Screen* (Cambridge: Cambridge University Press, 2003).

Scott, Walter, 'On the Present State of Periodical Criticism', in *Sir Walter Scott's Edinburgh Annual Register*, Kenneth Curry (ed.) (Tennessee: University of Tennessee Press, 1977), pp. 132–70.

Shattock, Joanne, *Politics and Reviewers: The Edinburgh and the Quarterly in the early Victorian Age* (London and Leicester: Leicester University Press, 1989).

St Clair, William, *The Reading Nation in the Romantic Period* (Cambridge: Cambridge University Press, 2004).

Southam, Brian (ed.), *Jane Austen: The Critical Heritage,* 2 vols (London: Routledge and Kegan Paul, 1968 and 1987).

Stafford, Fiona, 'Jane Austen', in *Literature of the Romantic Period: A Bibliographical Guide*, Michael O'Neill (ed.) (Oxford: Clarendon Press, 1998), pp. 246–68.

Sutherland, Kathryn, Review of *Emma* and *Mansfield Park* in the Cambridge University Press edition, in *Review of English Studies* (Oxford: Oxford University Press, Nov. 2006; vol. 57, pp. 833–8).

Todd, Janet, *The Cambridge Introduction to Jane Austen* (Cambridge: Cambridge University Press, 2006).

Tomalin, Claire, *Jane Austen: A Life* (London: Viking, 1997).

Trott, Nicola, 'Critical Responses, 1830–1970', in Janet Todd (ed.), *Jane Austen in Context* (Cambridge: Cambridge University Press, 2005), pp. 92–100.

Voigts-Virchow, Eckart (ed.), *Janespotting and Beyond: British Heritage Retrovisions Since the Mid-1990s* (Tübingen: Narr, 2004).

FILMOGRAPHY OF *SENSE AND SENSIBILITY*, *PRIDE AND PREJUDICE* AND *EMMA*

1940 *Pride and Prejudice*
MGM, 114 min, black and white
Directed by: Robert Z. Leonard
Screenplay by: Aldous Huxley and Jane Murfin
Produced by: Hunt Stromberg
Principal Actors:
Greer Garson – Elizabeth Bennet
Laurence Olivier – Fitzwilliam Darcy

1948 *Emma*
BBC, 105 min, black and white
Directed and produced by: Michael Barry
Screenplay by: Judy Campbell
Principal Actors:
Judy Campbell – Emma Woodhouse
Ralph Michael – Mr. George Knightley

1949 *Pride and Prejudice*
Philco Television Playhouse, 60 min, black and white
Directed and produced by: Fred Coe
Screenplay by: Samuel Taylor
Principal Actors:
Madge Evans – Elizabeth Bennet
John Baragrey – Fitzwilliam Darcy

1950 *Sense and Sensibility*
Philco Television Playhouse, 60 min, black and white
Directed by: Delbert Mann
Screenplay by: H.R. Hays
Produced by: Fred Coe
Principal Actors:
Madge Evans – Elinor Dashwood
Cloris Leachman – Marianne Dashwood

1952 *Pride and Prejudice*
BBC, six parts, 180 min, black and white
Directed and produced by: Campbell Logan
Screenplay by: Cedric Wallis

Principal Actors:
Daphne Slater – Elizabeth Bennet
Peter Cushing – Fitzwilliam Darcy

1954 *Emma*
NBC Kraft Television Theatre, 60 min, black and white
Dramatised by: Martine Bartlett and Peter Donat
Principal Actors:
Felicia Montealegre – Emma Woodhouse
Peter Cookson – Mr Knightley

1958 *Pride and Prejudice*
BBC, six parts, 180 min, black and white
Directed and produced by: Barbara Burnham
Screenplay by: Cedric Wallis
Principal Actors:
Jane Downs – Elizabeth Bennet
Alan Badel – Fitzwilliam Darcy

1960 *Emma*
BBC, six parts, 180 min, black and white
Directed and produced by: Campbell Logan
Screenplay by: Vincent Tilsley
Principal Actors:
Diana Fairfax – Emma Woodhouse
Paul Daneman – Mr Knightley

1960 *Emma*
CBS Camera Three, 1 hour
Directed by: John Desmond
Produced by: John McGiffert
Screenplay by: Clair Roskam
Actor:
Nancy Wickwire – Emma Woodhouse

1967 *Pride and Prejudice*
BBC, six parts, 180 min, black and white
Directed by: Joan Craft
Screenplay by: Nemone Lethbridge
Produced by: Campbell Logan
Principal Actors:
Celia Bannerman – Elizabeth Bennet
Lewis Fiander – Fitzwilliam Darcy

1971 *Sense and Sensibility*
BBC, four parts, 200 min
Directed by: David Giles
Screenplay by: Denis Constanduros
Produced by: Martin Lisemore
Principal Actors:
Joanna David – Elinor Dashwood
Ciaran Madden – Marianne Dashwood

1972 *Emma*
BBC, six parts, 240 min, colour

Directed by: John Glenister
Screenplay by: Denis Constanduros
Produced by: Martin Lisemore
Principal Actors:
Doran Godwin – Emma Woodhouse
John Carson – Mr Knightley

1979 *Pride and Prejudice*
BBC, five parts, 226 min, colour
Directed by: Cyril Coke
Screenplay by: Fay Weldon
Produced by: Jonathan Powell
Principal Actors:
Elizabeth Garvie – Elizabeth Bennet
David Rintoul – Fitzwilliam Darcy

1981 *Sense and Sensibility*
BBC, seven parts, 174 min, colour
Directed by: Rodney Bennett
Screenplay: Alexander Baron and Denis Constanduros
Produced by: Barry Letts
Principal Actors:
Irene Richards – Elinor Dashwood.
Tracey Childs – Marianne Dashwood

1995 *Sense and Sensibility*
Columbia/Mirage, 135 min, colour
Directed by: Ang Lee
Screenplay by: Emma Thompson
Produced by: Lindsay Doran
Principal Actors:
Emma Thompson – Elinor Dashwood
Kate Winslet – Marianne Dashwood

1995 *Pride and Prejudice*
BBC, six parts, 300 min, colour
Directed by: Simon Langton
Screenplay by: Andrew Davies
Produced by: Sue Birtwistle
Principal Actors:
Jennifer Ehle – Elizabeth Bennet
Colin Firth – Fitzwilliam Darcy

1995 *Clueless (Emma)*
Paramount, 113 min, colour
Directed by: Amy Heckerling
Screenplay by: Amy Heckerling
Produced by: Robert Lawrence and Scott Rudin
Principal Actors:
Alicia Silverstone – Cher Horowitz
Paul Rudd – Josh

1996 *Emma*
Columbia/Miramax, 120 min, colour

Directed by: Douglas McGrath
Screenplay by: Douglas McGrath
Produced by: Patrick Cassavetti and Steven Haft
Principal Actors:
Gwyneth Paltrow – Emma Woodhouse
Jeremy Northam – Mr Knightley

1996 *Emma*
Meridian–ITV, 107 min, colour
Directed by: Diarmuid Lawrence
Screenplay by: Andrew Davies
Produced by: Sue Birtwistle
Principal Actors:
Kate Beckinsale – Emma Woodhouse
Mark Strong – Mr Knightley

2001 *Bridget Jones's Diary (Pride and Prejudice)*

Universal–Miramax, 97 mins, colour
Directed by: Sharon Maguire
Screenplay by: Helen Fielding, Andrew Davies, Richard Curtis
Produced by: Tom Bevan, Jonathan Cavendish, Eric Fellner
Principal Actors:
Renee Zellweger – Bridget Jones
Colin Firth – Mark Darcy

2003 *Pride and Prejudice: A Latter Day Comedy*
Excel Entertainment Group, 104 min, colour
Directed by: Andrew Black
Screenplay by: Anne K. Black (Jane Austen credited)
Principal Actors:
Kam Heskin – Elizabeth Bennet
Orlando Seale – Darcy

2004 *Bride and Prejudice*
Bride Productions, 111 min (English version), 122 min (Hindi version), colour
Directed by: Gurinder Chadha
Screenplay by: Paul Mayeda Berges and Gurinder Chadha (Jane Austen credited)
Music by: Anu Malik
Principal Actors:
Aishwarya Rai – Lalita Bakshi Martin Henderson – Will Darcy
2005 *Pride and Prejudice*
Working Title Films, 2005, 129 min, colour
Directed by: Joe Wright
Screenplay by: Deborah Moggach. Additional Dialogue by Emma Thompson
Produced by: Debra Hayward
Principal Actors:
Keira Knightley – Elizabeth Bennet
Matthew Macfadyen – Fitzwilliam Darcy

2008 *Sense and Sensibility*
BBC, three parts, 180 min, colour
Directed by: John Alexander

Screenplay by: Andrew Davies
Produced by: Vanessa De Sousa, Anne Pivcevic
Principal Actors:
Hattie Morahan – Elinor Dashwood
Charity Wakefield – Marianne Dashwood

Index

amusement, 8, 10–14, 16, 20, 35, 58, 99, 100
Armstrong, Isobel, 86, 90, 93–4
artistic, novel and novelist as, 3, 4, 19, 28–9, 31–2, 3–7, 46–7, 49, 51–2, 121–2, 135–6
Austen-Leigh, J. E., *Memoir,* 3, 22, 24, 28–9, 32, 38, 40, 42, 59, 125–6, 136

Bradley, A.C., 3, 47–8, 52, 136
British Critic, The, 2, 6, 9, 11–14, 16–17, 21
Burney, Frances, 35, 52, 82, 121
Butler, Marilyn, 4, 5, 70, 76–9, 82–4, 86, 88, 90, 94, 102, 138
Byron, Lord George Gordon, 2, 17, 106, 111–13

Castle, Terry, 64–6, 138
Chapman, R. W., 3, 50–2, 116, 137, 152–3
Coleridge, S. T., 111–12
Critical Review, The, 2, 6, 9, 11–12, 14, 16–17, 135

Davies, Andrew, 124, 128, 130–1
Deresiewicz, W., 111–13
Dickens, Charles, 31

Egerton, Thomas, 1–2, 113, 151

Farrer, R., 3, 49, 52, 136–7
Feminism, 4, 62, 66, 69, 70–1, 75–6, 118–21, 127, 129
Fielding, Henry, 7, 80, 97

Garrod, H. W., 44, 136
Gender, 4, 9, 12, 22, 26, 44, 62, 66, 69–70, 75, 82, 89–90, 94, 96, 118, 120–1, 133–9
Gilbert, S., 66–9, 138
Godwin, W., 8, 76, 107
Goethe, J. W. Von, 85
Gubar, S., 66–9, 138

Harding, D.W., 4, 55–60, 137
Harris, Jocelyn, 104

Humour, 20–1, 2–7, 31–5, 37, 39–40, 42, 51
Hutton, R. H., 3, 24–5, 136

Instruction, 8, 10–11, 15, 20, 31, 85, 131
Irony, 24–6, 28, 35–8, 55, 57, 61, 71, 89, 104, 132, 136–7

Jacobin novels, 76–8, 87–8, 91
James, Henry, 3, 46–7, 52, 59, 81, 136
Janeites, 3–4, 42–6, 52, 59, 61, 136–7
Johnson, Claudia, 44–5, 59, 90–4, 103, 120
Johnson, Samuel, 47–8, 52, 70, 86, 103, 121–2
Jones, V., 90, 120–1

Kirkham, Margaret, 69–70
Knox-Shaw, Peter, 5, 102–3, 138

Lamont, Claire, 87, 100–2, 116, 152
Lascelles, Mary, 4, 52–4, 137
Leavis, F.R., 4, 59–60, 137
Looser, D., 76, 118–20, 129

Malthus, T., 111
Mandal, A., 113–15
Memoir, see Austen-Leigh
Miller, David, 4, 96–100, 107, 138
moral, morality, 4, 8–15, 18–22, 24, 27–9, 31, 33–6, 45, 54, 57–60, 70, 74, 77, 79–80, 83–6, 90–3, 107–9, 120–1, 135, 137
Mudrick, M., 4, 55, 57–61, 137
Murray, John, 2, 17, 113

Oliphant, Margaret, 3, 26, 40

Quarterly Review, The, 6, 17, 49

Radcliffe, Ann, 37, 82
realism, 8, 10–15, 18–19, 21, 29–31, 33, 35, 47, 54, 80, 89, 91, 114, 132, 135
Richardson, Samuel, 7, 52, 70, 80
Rousseau, Jean-Jacques, 85, 111,

165

Saintsbury, George, 3, 43–5, 136
Sales, Roger, 82–3
Scott, Sir Walter, 1–2, 6–7, 17–19, 21, 25,
    31–3, 36, 38–9, 42, 50, 70, 101, 106,
    111–12, 114, 135
Shakespeare, William, 14, 15, 33, 36–8, 43,
    48–9, 80–2, 105, 135–6
Shelley, Mary, 70
Simpson, Richard, 3, 31, 36–8, 136
Southam, Brian, 22, 47, 59
Stafford, Fiona, 52, 134
St Clair, William, 63, 107
Stephen, Leslie, 3, 31, 40, 42, 59
style, 4, 8, 11–12, 14, 18, 20–1, 37, 54, 62,
    70, 96–9, 107, 138
Sutherland, Kathryn, 5, 115–17, 124–5,
    128, 138, 152

Tanner, Tony, 80–1, 87–9, 138
Thackeray, Anne Isabella, 3, 22–4,
    26, 136
Thackeray, William M., 25, 31, 35, 42, 97
timeless, timelessness, 60, 63, 76, 79–81,
    90, 137
Todd, Janet, 106–7, 117, 121, 152
Trilling, Lionel, 4, 60–1, 137
Troost, Linda, 127–30, 139
Trott, Nicola, 47, 54

Waldron, Mary, 83–6
Wollstonecraft, Mary, 7, 63, 70, 82, 87–8,
    102–3, 107, 120
Woolf, Virginia, 3, 50–2
Wordsworth, William, 106, 111–13
Wright, Andrew, 54–5